IVAN ILLICH
IN CONVERSATION

Also by David Cayley

Northrop Frye in Conversation

IVAN ILLICH
IN CONVERSATION

David Cayley

Anansi

First published in 1992 by
House of Anansi Press Limited
1800 Steeles Avenue West
Concord, Ontario
L4K 2P3

Canadian Cataloguing in Publication Data

Illich, Ivan, 1926–
Ivan Illich in conversation

ISBN 0-88784-524-X

1. Illich, Ivan, 1926– . —Interviews.   2. Education —
Philosophy.   3. Social Problems.   4. Medicine —
Philosophy.   I. Cayley, David.   II. Title.

LB885.I5A5 1992   370'.1   C92-093286-X

CBC logo used by permission

Cover design: Brant Cowie/ArtPlus Limited
Typesetting: Tony Gordon Ltd.
Printed and bound in Canada

House of Anansi Press gratefully acknowledges the support of
the Canada Council, Ontario Arts Council and Ontario
Publishing Centre in the development of writing and
publishing in Canada.

Contents

Preface

In 1968, in a folder of conference materials distributed by the Canadian University Service Overseas (cuso) to its "returned volunteers," I discovered a paper by Ivan Illich. Illich then directed the Center for Intercultural Documentation (cidoc), in Cuernavaca, Mexico, whose avowed purpose was to subvert the contemporary crusade for international development and discourage the sending of volunteers to what were then called developing countries. The paper recorded a talk he had given earlier that year in Chicago to a group of young American volunteers in which he told them, in so many words, to stay home. My superiors at cuso may have felt that as Canadians we were not included in this injunction, but I took it seriously nonetheless.

At the time I had just returned from a Chinese village in northern Borneo where for two years I had served as a volunteer teacher. A juvenile infatuation with the mystic East had as much to do with my being there as a concern for international development, but the experience had still left me perplexed and unsettled. The village of Kwong Hwa where I lived had recently seen its school converted from Chinese- to English-language instruction. The CUSO volunteer was there to help in the integration of the village school into the Malaysian school system. This made me an unwelcome presence to that part of the community which did not see the abandonment of the Chinese curriculum as progress and disposed me to raise questions about the sense in which my being there constituted development. Illich's writings were the precipitant around which my questions coalesced.

In 1969, I visited Illich in Cuernavaca, and the next year, along with a group of friends, was able to bring him to Canada for what proved to be the last of the great "international teach-ins" at the University of Toronto. His talk focussed on the emerging question of the environment. He argued that unless the degradation of nature was met by a fundamental change in the orientation of modern societies, environmentalism would only end up spawning a new set of tutelary institutions staffed by a new set of experts in the surveillance and management of daily life. The consequences he predicted now surround a citizenry that has learned to accept that social policy should be based on expert calculations of how far nature can be safely pushed.

After this, I lost touch with Illich, although I continued to be an avid reader of his books. Then, in 1987, I learned that he would be in Toronto for a conference on orality and literacy. The conference brought together scholars in the lineage of Milman Parry, Harold Innis, Marshall McLuhan, Walter Ong, and Eric Havelock, who was present, to discuss the consequences of speech and writing as modes of knowledge. Illich had just completed a book with Barry Sanders called *ABC: The Alphabetization of the Popular Mind*.[1] I covered the conference for CBC Radio's *Ideas*, where I work, and eventually produced a three-hour series called "Literacy: The Medium and the Message."[2]

To assist me in preparing these programs, the conference organizers had obliged the invited speakers to do a recorded interview with me at some point during their stay. I accosted Illich in the lobby of the Windsor Arms Hotel before the conference started. He said that the interview I requested was against his inclination and that he would do it only in deference to his hosts. I recorded the conversation in his room and returned to the temporary studio I had set up in the basement of Emmanuel College, where the conference was to take place. I had checked the tape recorder before beginning the interview and monitored the recording throughout; but, when I put the tape on again, I discovered that it had nothing on it.

Later in the day I approached Illich and made my discomfiture known to him. He hinted that he had hexed the recording and then turned away to greet an old friend. This suggestion, which his magus-like appearance and reputation made at least plausible, left me even more disconcerted. However, I had a job to do, and I doggedly courted Illich until he finally agreed to record a second interview. Our conversation warmed during this second encounter, and, in the course of a discussion of the fate of his ideas on education, I mentioned to him that my three youngest children had never been to school. I then proposed that he allow me to prepare a major radio series based on his ideas, a scheme that I was already incubating when I learned that he was coming to Toronto. He said that he had refused all interviews for more than fifteen years but that, if I wished, I could write to his colleague Wolfgang Sachs about my idea.

The following day I had a chance to introduce Illich to my children, who had come to Emmanuel College to meet me following the conference. I then made my proposal to Wolfgang Sachs as instructed. Several months later I received a reply from Illich. It appeared to have been typed with one hand on the wrong keys of the typewriter, but I was able to make out the unaccountable fact that he had agreed. (He said he had been moved to do so by the feeling he sensed between my children and me.) Later we spoke on the phone, and he told me that he would make himself "obedient" to me. He was as good as his word, but what an interesting and refractory obedience it turned out to be.

I arrived in State College, Pennsylvania, where Illich teaches for part of the year at the Pennsylvania State University, in September of 1988. At the time Illich's household was taken over by what he and his colleagues called a "living-room consultation," a gathering of friends from all over to discuss the theme "After Development, What?" (These discussions eventually resulted in the publication of *The Development Dictionary*,[3] an attempt to mark the end of the development era with an anatomy of its key concepts.) From the midst of this gathering, in which I was made welcome and free to participate, Illich and I retired at least once a day to record our interview.

My intention was to survey Illich's thought, and, to this end, I had carefully reread all of his published works. I quickly learned that this was going to strain Illich's promised obedience. He wanted to talk about what was on his mind at the moment, rather than be taken step by step through books he had written ten or twenty years before. I was reluctant to forsake my plan and the structure it promised to give to the programs I would eventually have to produce. This tension became one of the constituents of our conversation.

The fact that I was recording the conversation was also a source of tension. "For a quarter of a century," Illich told an audience in January of 1990, "I have tried to avoid using a microphone . . . I refuse to be made into a loudspeaker . . . I believe that speaking creates a place [and] place is something precious that has been to a large degree obliterated by the homogeneous space generated by speedy locomotion, standardized planning, screens, and loudspeakers." Illich told me that he was willing to participate in this doubtful ritual only out of a spontaneous feeling of friendship for me, and his behavior bore him out. He did what I asked but never listened to the five programs that were broadcast in the winter of 1989 under the title "Part Moon, Part Travelling Salesman: Conversations with Ivan Illich."[4]

After the broadcast Illich's close friend Lee Hoinacki, with whom I had already struck up an affectionate acquaintance in State College, asked if he could listen to the raw tapes out of which I had made the programs. Hoinacki has been associated with Illich for more than thirty years, since he was first sent as a Dominican priest serving Puerto Rican parishioners in New York to the Spanish language institute Illich had established in Puerto Rico. He subsequently worked with Illich at cidoc and has since edited many of his books and articles. After listening to the tapes, he concluded that they constituted a useful supplement to Illich's published works and, with my permission, he transcribed them with a view to publication. Illich reiterated his lack of interest in the work but gave Hoinacki and me a free hand to do as we saw fit with it. It is largely due to Lee Hoinacki that the present book exists. I would like to dedicate this book to him in gratitude for his generous friendship; for his work in transcribing, editing, and footnoting the interview; for his confidence in the project; and for his graciousness in returning the work to my hands when I decided that I wanted to publish it myself. I would also like to thank Jutta Mason for her help in preparing the manuscript.

I have re-edited the manuscript that Hoinacki created. In his *Bourgeois Gentilhomme*, Molière pokes fun at M. Jourdain's astonished discovery that he has been speaking prose all his life; but, in fact, as Northrop Frye liked to point out, few of us consistently speak prose. Speech sprawls and hesitates, leaps to life and then lapses into gestures the tape recorder never hears. Recognizing this, I have tried to prune the interview in a way that reveals its shape without obscuring its origins, discovering precise questions in tentative circumlocutions, turning piled-up phrases into sentences and eliminating dead-ends. Even so, the result is far from linear or purely expository, and the logic is often of the associational speaking-of-this, what-about-that variety. This I have taken for a virtue and left alone.

As a writer, Illich carefully considers his effects; as a speaker he is mercurial, spontaneous and often surprising. Faced with my sometimes clumsy but always determined efforts to arrive at a comprehensive picture of his thought, he found himself sometimes exasperated and sometimes elated, sometimes constrained and sometimes surprised by what he discovered in this constraint. At one point he attacks the staginess of the whole procedure, while at the same time calling it good because it is something he and I have chosen to do together. All this is expressed without inhibition, and I have not tried to censor it.

In places the interview rambles. A question about his first language in a section intended to produce a biographical sketch results in a digression on the recent origins of the ideas of *Homo monolinguis*, one-languaged man. These, and similar digressions, I have also preserved, because, it seemed to me, that in this case at least the order in which things actually happened was more significant than any order I could have imposed retrospectively. Like a river that is shaped by its landscape even as it shapes that landscape, the interview follows a meandering course through the eight days of my visit to State College. It reflects Illich's refractory response as much as my continuously revised intentions. Nothing ends quite where I originally expected, and the interview expresses the beginning of an unexpected friendship as much as my desire to make a coherent exposition of Illich's thought.

What I offer here is vulnerable in a way that the tidier, more intensively edited radio programs that I made for *Ideas* were not. But it is also more revealing than a retouched portrait would have been. Illich is a man who has managed to outrun his reputation by refusing to become a captive of the positions he has explored and staked out. I came ready to interrogate these positions, only to discover that he had moved on to new ones. Once in the interview my exasperation also shows; but, through Illich, I came to see that real surprise is impossible without what Zen Buddhism calls a beginner's mind. A beginner's mind cannot be feigned or deployed as a Socratic technique that allows you to arrive "dialectically" at where you knew you were going all along. It must arise from a genuine curiosity and a genuine disregard for one's own positions. Illich has this ability, and it has seemed to me worth preserving even where it gives the conversation a darting, digressive, and unfinished quality.

The book is divided into ten chapters, each representing a session together. They usually begin from my intention to discuss one of Illich's books, and they often end simply where he called a halt as a result of some other obligation. The final chapter, on "life," was recorded in Bremen in February of 1992, three and a half years later than the rest of the interview. An edited version was broadcast on *Ideas* on April 30, 1992.[5] We had seen a good deal of each other in the intervening years and the tone between us is probably quite noticeably different. I have begun with an essay in which I try to sketch the shape of Illich's intellectual career and digest the material that is covered, sometimes allusively, in the interview. I hope this will provide a context within which the interview can be read.

Introduction

In 1938, when he was twelve years old, Ivan Illich walked through the vineyards on the outskirts of Vienna and smelled the fetid wind that, in a few days, would bring Hitler's troops into Austria and change his world forever. He knew then, he told me, that he would never give children to his grandfather's house. This house had stood on its island in the Adriatic off the coast of Dalmatia since the Middle Ages. It had seen rulers come and go, and empires rise and fall, but daily life had scarcely changed in the intervening centuries.

The very same olive-wood rafters supported the roof of my grandfather's house. Water was still gathered from the same stone slabs on the roof. The

wine was pressed in the same vats, the fish caught
from the same kind of boat . . . For the people who
lived off the main routes, history still flowed slowly,
imperceptibly. Most of the environment was still in
the commons. People lived in houses they had built;
moved on streets that had been trampled by the feet
of their animals; were autonomous in the procure-
ment and disposal of their water; could depend on
their own voices.[6]

All this changed in 1926, the year of Illich's birth.
The same ship that brought the infant to be blessed
by his grandfather carried the first loudspeaker ever
heard on the island. "Up to that day," Illich has
written, "all men and women had spoken with more
or less equally powerful voices . . . Henceforth access to the microphone would determine whose
voice [would] be magnified. Silence now ceased to
be in the commons; it became a resource for which
loudspeakers compete."[7] By 1938 Illich already
knew in his bones that the world into which he had
been born was vanishing. Soon he would become a
wanderer through the uncanny landscapes generated by the loudspeaker's many progeny. But he did
not lose his tap-root into the soil of old Europe or his
family's ancient affiliation with the Roman Church.
He took this fading world within himself where it
would nourish a stance so radically traditional that
for a few years in the late 1960s and early 1970s
excited North American audiences thought it avant-
garde.
    Illich has often drawn attention to how traditional
his views are and to how novel such views can seem

in the context of contemporary cultural amnesia. As early as 1959 he introduced an essay called "The Vanishing Clergyman" by saying that he was not writing "anything theologically new, daring, or controversial." "Only a spelling-out of social consequences," he went on, "can make a thesis as orthodox as mine sufficiently controversial to be discussed."[8] In these pages, he remarks that today "it's very difficult to speak about . . . things which seem to have been obvious and unquestioned during a thousand years of Western tradition." "I often have the impression," he says, "that the more traditionally I speak, the more radically alien I become."[9]

I do not make this point at the outset because I want to suggest that Illich is not a man of his time. In fact, the intelligence and sensitivity of his response to the world around him make him, if anything, more a man of his time than many of his more sheltered contemporaries. But what has made Illich so penetrating and so total a critic are his roots in an older soil. He says here, for example, that "it's good to be very consciously a remainder of the past, one who still survives from another time."[10] On other occasions I have heard him invest history with the crown traditionally worn by theology as "the queen of the sciences." For Illich, history is the privileged road to "that Archimedean point outside of the present" by which the limitations of the present can be known.[11]

One often finds Illich's writings classified in libraries and bookstores as sociology or social criticism, but he is in no sense a sociologist. Even the name of historian, insofar as it evokes the assumptions of a modern positivist science, cannot grasp what he does. Illich is an anomaly among modern scholars because he insists that the habits of the heart are as crucial to scholarship as the habits of the head. He calls the cultivation of the organs of inner sense which root in the heart by its traditional name, *ascesis*, and says that it is the indispensable complement to critical habits of mind. "For a full millennium," Illich has written, "the Church cultivated a balanced tradition of study and reflection . . . The habits of the heart and the cultivation of its virtues are peripherals to the pursuit of higher learning today . . . I want to argue for the possibility of a new complementarity between critical and ascetical learning. I want to reclaim for ascetical theory, method, and discipline a status equal to that the University now assigns to critical and technical disciplines."[12] *Ascesis* prepares the ground for insight. Without it, insight becomes predatory, self-aggrandizing, one-sided, and, ultimately, heartless. Insight grounded in *ascesis*, that mental/spiritual grasp which the Middle Ages called *intellectus*, is the primary mode of Illich's writing. Illich draws on modern social sciences and scrupulously observes their academic conventions; but, in the end, what he practises is closer to cultural "second sight" than to sociology.

Illich's close friend and collaborator Lee Hoinacki originally transcribed the interview that follows in the belief that a portrait of Illich in conversation might lead to greater understanding of his written works. In a draft introduction he wrote before I took over editing the book, Hoinacki quoted the Spanish philosopher Miguel de Unamuno's comment, in *The Tragic Sense of Life*, that the inner biography of a thinker is that "which can mean most to us." Hoinacki has offered courses in Illich's work at several universities and knows how persistently this work has been misunderstood. I share his confidence that some attention to the biographical dimension in Illich's work can help to clarify it. In calling this dimension biographical, I do not mean in any sense to refer to private life but to the unique and fateful signature each one of us bears. Just as the style of a familiar composer is unmistakable even in an unfamiliar piece, an author has his characteristic voice, and no voice in our time has been more distinct than Illich's. But, as the assumptions that support his stance wash out of public discussion, there is a possibility that this stance will remain attractively exotic without any longer being understood. Under these circumstances a biographical examination can yield a sense of the wholeness and consistency of Illich's work, as well as a revelation of its deep roots. Illich has always written with precise purpose and limited aim; different audiences and different occasions have evoked very different responses. He has published no *summa*. A patchwork interview will hardly substitute for one, but it may help to place his work in the context of that inner biography which Unamuno says can mean most to us.

Ivan Illich arrived in New York at the beginning of the 1950s as a refugee from Church politics. Apt in every way for a career as a prince of the Church, he instead asked Cardinal Spellman to assign him to a parish in uptown Manhattan with a growing population of Puerto Rican immigrants. In this way, and not for the last time, he wriggled out of a destiny designed for him by others. The Puerto Rican migration to New York was then in full spate, and the older immigrant populations, the Irish, the Italians, and the Jews, were reacting to the new arrivals with the same prejudice that they had formerly experienced. Illich was scandalized and was soon campaigning to have his parishioners recognized as full members of New York's Roman Catholic community. His efforts culminated in 1956 in a huge outdoor fiesta. Thirty thousand people flocked to the campus of Fordham University, where Cardinal Spellman said mass for the feast day of San Juan, the patron saint of Puerto Rico, and the new community manifested itself with a confidence that Illich had helped to engender.

In the same year Illich was transferred to Puerto Rico as vice-rector of the Catholic University at Ponce. There he started an institute to train American priests and religious involved with Puerto Ricans in the United States. Its primary purpose was to teach Spanish, and to teach it with a certain awe at what learning a new language entails. "Properly conducted language learning," Illich later wrote in the essay "The Eloquence of Silence," "is one of the few occasions in which an adult can go through a deep experience of poverty, of weakness and of dependence on the good will of another."[13] Lee Hoinacki first met Illich as a student at the institute and was deeply impressed by how Illich himself expressed a brisk and worldly competence within an aura of eloquent silence.[14]

It was also in Puerto Rico that Illich came into contact with the first of the great secular bureaucracies whose pretensions he would make a career of puncturing, the school system. He sat on the board that governed the island's entire educational establishment and was soon engaged in a full-scale effort to understand what schools *do*. He came to the conclusion that compulsory education in Puerto Rico constituted "structured injustice."[15] By "putting into parentheses their claim to educate," he was able to see that schools focussed aspiration on a mirage. In Puerto Rico, at the time Illich began studying the question in the late 1950s, children were already required by law to have more schooling than the state could afford to give them. The worst aspect of this for Illich was that people also learned to blame themselves for failing to achieve the impossible. "Schooling," he concluded, "served . . . to compound the native poverty of half the children with a new interiorized sense of guilt for not having made it."

Over the next fifteen years, Illich refined his analysis of schooling and extended its scope. In the late 1960s he published "The Futility of Schooling in Latin America"[16] and then, in 1971, his book *Deschooling Society*.[17] Early on in his research in Puerto Rico he had noticed how schools thwart the very objective at which they ostensibly aim, equality of opportunity, by monopolizing education and pricing it out of reach of the majority. In *Deschooling Society* he identified schooling as the fundamental ritual of a consumer society. *Schole*, the Greek word from which ours derives, means leisure, and true learning, according to Illich, can only be the leisured pursuit of free people. The claim that a liberal society can be built on a compulsory and coercive ritual is therefore paradoxical. By designing and packaging knowledge, schools generate the belief that knowledge must be acquired in graded and certified sequences. And this monopoly of schools over the very definition of education, Illich argued, not only inhibits alternatives but also leads to life-long dependence on other service monopolies.

By describing schooling as a ritual, and calling for its disestablishment, Illich recognized an analogy between schools and Western society's original *alma mater*, the Church. (The Church as the prototype of all subsequent service bureaucracies, and sacramental theology as the source of our unique confidence in technique, continue to be major themes of Illich's reflection.)[18] "The school system today," he wrote, "performs the threefold function common to powerful churches throughout history. It is simultaneously the repository of the society's myth, the institutionalization of that myth's contradictions, and the locus of the ritual which reproduces and veils the disparities between myth and reality."[19] Schools, in other words, foster a belief in unending progress, manifest the impossibility of that goal, and then explain that our failure to achieve it is our own fault.

In calling for the disestablishment of education, Illich did not speak against the feasibility of schooling as such, but against making participation in this ritual a precondition for other forms of social participation. Refusing a job to an unschooled person who is otherwise competent to do it, he said, should be as unconstitutional as discriminating against that person on any other grounds. Disestablishment of churches had a salutary effect on Christianity, he concluded; perhaps it would have an equally beneficial effect on education.

Deschooling Society ended with the essay "The Rebirth of Epimethean Man," in which Illich retold the Greek myth of the brothers Prometheus and Epimetheus. Prometheus, whose name means foresight, stole fire from the gods and gave it to the people on earth. By doing so, "Prometheus turned facts into problems, called necessity into question and defied fate."[20] His brother Epimetheus, whose name means hindsight, was given the reputation of a dullard by Hesiod and later Greek writers. Epimetheus went against the advice of his brother and married Pandora, who had let all life's ills out of her box and trapped only Hope when she closed the lid.[21] Prometheus, according to the myth, invoked Nemesis by usurping the prerogative of the gods. "Classical man," wrote Illich, "was aware that he could defy fate-nature-environment, but only at his own risk . . . Contemporary man goes further: he attempts to create a world in his own image, to build a totally man-made environment, and then discovers that he can do so only on the condition of constantly remaking himself to fit it." He therefore proposed that we should emulate Epimetheus, who embraced the foolish Pandora and her one remaining gift of Hope. "Hope, in its strong sense, means [a] trusting faith in the goodness of nature, while expectation, as I will use it here, means reliance on results which are planned and controlled by man. Hope centres desire on a person from whom we await a gift. Expectation looks forward to satisfaction from a predictable process which will produce what we have the right to claim. The Promethean ethos has now eclipsed hope." In the case of schooling, Illich claimed that we are now gripped by "pedagogical hubris," which seeks to replace the perpetual but unpredictable possibility of learning with a certified process based on the pretension that "Man can do what God cannot, namely, manipulate others for their own salvation."[22]

The scope of the argument in *Deschooling Society* extended far beyond the question of schools as such. In fact, Illich made no objection to the existence of schools so long as they were recognized as privileged enclaves and did not monopolize public choice. His book was founded on a vision of freedom from envy, from addictive dependence, and from what he then called "the institutionalization of values."[23] What began as an analysis of the specific effects of schooling in Puerto Rico became a critique of the whole range of ideas, practices, and institutions implicated in the term *development*. This was carried on at what became the Center for Intercultural Documentation, or CIDOC, in Cuernavaca, Mexico, which Illich established in 1961, the year after he left Puerto Rico. In the same year, U.S. president John Kennedy unveiled his Alliance for Progress, an ambitious development assistance program for Latin America, and Pope John Paul XXIII called on the North American Church to send fully ten percent of its strength to Latin America as missionaries. The Peace Corps was created and, in Canada, the Canadian University Service Overseas (CUSO). Barbara Ward launched CBC Radio's annual Massey Lectures with *The Rich Nations and the Poor Nations*. Development became the desideratum of progressive politics and the moral polestar of international relations. The center in Cuernavaca was set up to contradict this entire crusade.

In retrospect Illich's critique of development can be seen as clairvoyant; at the time it deeply offended the conventional wisdom. Illich described development as "a war on subsistence" and argued that it would disrupt the existing adaptations of peoples to their circumstances without furnishing any real alternative. "Rich nations," he wrote in 1968, "now benevolently impose a straitjacket of traffic jams, hospital confinements and classrooms on the poor nations and by international agreement call this 'development.'"[24] According to Illich, this way of designing development was not only inherently unfeasible — "there is not enough money in the world for development to succeed along these lines"[25] — it also disabled people's capacity to imagine possible alternatives and generated "underdevelopment as a form of consciousness" which occurs with "the translation of thirst into the need for a Coke."[26] The result, he predicted, would be a condition of "modernized poverty" that would shatter the dignity of subsistence without softening its asperity and replace the tolerable burden of necessity with the intolerable prick of reified needs.

Illich pursued his campaign against development

with particular vigor in the Roman Catholic Church, where he already had an audience and a shared tradition of anti-economic thought to which he could appeal. Although he had always insisted on his theological conservatism and behaved as the "humble and obedient son" he called himself in an open letter to Pope Paul in September of 1970, [27] Illich had never spared the vanity of the Church as a worldly institution. In 1959, in his essay "The Vanishing Clergyman," he called on the Church to embrace secularization, dismantle its bureaucracy, forgo political power, and become once again the celebrant of religious mysteries.[28] The idea that the Church can bear having power because it is too humble and self-critical to abuse it, he said in another early essay, is a "fatal and complacent delusion."[29] In 1960 he was ordered out of Puerto Rico by Bishop James McManus when he denounced the intervention of the Catholic hierarchy in Puerto Rican politics on the issue of birth control.[30]

CIDOC, with its open opposition to the Church's missionary effort in Latin America, was equally controversial. Illich offended both the Catholic left who wanted to throw the Church's weight into political revolution — Jesuit activist Dan Berrigan acused him of "intellectual violence aimed at our religious left"[31] — and the Catholic right in Mexico who censured the Bishop of Cuernavaca for associating with "that strange, devious and slippery personage, crawling with indefinable nationalities who is called, or claims to be called, Ivan Illich."[32] Despite his reticence about some of the events of those years — in these pages he speaks in passing of having been "shot at and beaten up with chains" but then deflects my desire to know more[33] — it is clear that he had enemies on both the political and the ecclesiastical right.

Since 1956, when he had assumed an official position at the university in Ponce, Illich had "refused to preside over a Christian congregation"[34] and tried to make it clear that, on political subjects, he did not speak as a churchman, but the distinction seemed lost on Rome. Shortly after his superior, and loyal defender, Cardinal Spellman died in 1967, he was summoned to the Congregation for the Doctrine of the Faith. There he was confronted with an anonymous and tendentious questionnaire, full of rumor and innuendo. It inquired about everything from his relations with Octavio Paz to his views on limbo. Since he was being asked, in effect, whether he had stopped beating his wife, Illich refused to answer. He returned to Cuernavaca and said nothing about what had happened in Rome. Six months later Rome put an interdict on CIDOC and forbade its bishops and religious superiors to send their subjects there. Illich wrote to Spellman's successor, Terence Cooke, of his "irrevocable decision to resign entirely from Church service, to suspend the exercise of priestly functions, and to renounce totally all titles, offices, benefits and privileges which are due to me as a cleric."[35]

The ban was revoked in 1969, and CIDOC continued under Illich's leadership until 1976, when he and his staff voluntarily closed it down. Between 1966 and 1976 it added to its language school an excellent library, an ambitious publishing program, and a series of research seminars that attracted thinkers interested in alternatives. CIDOC was one of the epicenters of the intellectual ferment of the late 1960s and early 1970s. Intergenerational resentments, an oppressive legend, and twenty-twenty hindsight have all tended to obscure the character of this time, but Illich remembers "a real sense of renewal" and people who "sought this renewal through giving themselves totally to the possibility of making a new society, right now!"[36] This atmosphere is tangible in Illich's writings of the time. Although many of his essays evoke a frightening vision of dazed and disabled populations, cut off from nourishing contact with nature and other persons by packaged goods and services, they also make a vivid appeal to the possibility of political change. "The mood of 1971," Illich wrote at the end of *Deschooling Society*, "is propitious for a major change of direction in search of a hopeful future."[37]

Illich's pivotal book of this period was *Tools for Conviviality*, published in 1973 and intended as "an epilogue to the industrial age."[38] In this essay, he outlined a philosophy of technology and a constitution of limits for modern societies. This was the time when the Club of Rome was also pursuing the idea of limits to growth and the fledgling environmental movement was discussing how to restrain the industrial system. Illich made it clear that he was speaking in a different sense and tried to introduce a vital and, in the event, prescient distinction into the discussion. He said that managing the growth of tools would only stabilize the industrial age "at the highest endurable level of output."[39] Even retrofitting industrial societies with clean technologies would fail as long it took only the physical dimension of the problem into acount. In order to bring technology into harmony with social life, Illich claimed, it would be necessary to understand much more precisely both the nature of tools and their multidimensional interaction with nature and society.

Illich chose the word *tools* because he found it both more homely and more pointed than the conventional and abstract *technology*, but he used the term in a sense in which a hammer, a highway, or a health-care system could all equally be described as tools. He argued that tools go through two watersheds, a first at which they become productive and a second at which they become counterproductive and turn from means into ends in themselves. Up to a certain speed and density automobiles may expand mobility, but beyond this threshold society becomes their prisoner. Broad-scale improvements in sanitation may improve public health, while high-tech medicine generates social costs that far outweigh its benefits. Drawing on the work of Leopold Kohr, who pioneered a philosophy of social size,[40] Illich claimed that "to each social environment there corresponds a set of natural scales . . . In each of these dimensions," he went on, "tools that require time periods or space or energies much beyond the order of corresponding natural scales are dysfunctional."[41]

Tools foster conviviality to the extent to which they can be easily used, by anybody, as often or as seldom as desired for the accomplishment of a purpose chosen by the user. The use of such tools by one person does not restrain another from using them equally. They do not require previous certification of the user. Their existence does not impose any obligation to use them. They allow the user to express his meaning in action.[42]   .   `

Illich tried to direct attention away from the Marxist preoccupation with the control of production and towards its structure. In this sense he belongs to the school of Kohr and E.F. Schumacher, who tried to make the scale of technology an independent issue, and to the school of Harold Adams Innis and Marshall McLuhan, who highlighted the symbolic fallout of technology.[43] Illich suggested that charting policy options on a left-right political spectrum would yield only a choice of tyrannies unless they were also graphed on an institutional spectrum running from conviviality to radical monopoly. Convivial tools foster "autonomous and creative intercourse among persons" and "individual freedom realized in personal inter-dependence";[44] radical monopolies force us to use them by generating environments in which we cannot live without using them. Libraries, telephone exchanges, bicycles, and all-purpose roads are obvious utilities that do not dictate how we shall use them; high-speed transportation compels our allegiance by adjusting time and space to its own dimensions. "Highly capitalized tools," said Illich, "require highly capitalized men."[45]

Tools for Conviviality presents a vision of a chastened modernity in which austerity is seen as the condition of enjoyment. Illich quotes Aquinas, who defines austerity in the *Summa Theologica* as "a virtue which does not exclude all enjoyments, but only those which are distracting from or destructive of personal relatedness." Illich sees the choice of austerity, or self-limitation, as the only alternative to intensified surveillance and management by technocratic elites; and, in this sense, the book has a disturbingly apocalyptic undertow. In fact Illich explicitly predicts a "gruesome apocalypse" if society does not master its tools. "The balance among stability, change and tradition has been upset," he says, and "society has lost both its roots in shared memories and its bearings for innovation . . . An unlimited rate of change makes lawful community meaningless . . . engineered obsolescence can break all bridges to a normative past."[46]

Twenty years after it was written, when children grow up among the phantasmal threats of global warming and ozone depletion, *Tools for Conviviality* reminds its readers of a road not taken. What Illich prophesied has happened. The Rio de Janeiro "Earth Summit" of 1992 is not about finding a way of life that is simple in means and rich in ends; it is about the equitable division of pollution optimums under the aegis of global monitoring. Simple survival has become the most commonly expressed motive for political action in defense of the environment. Illich suggested that the degradation of nature is rooted in "a corruption in man's self-image"[47] and that, therefore, "the only solution to the environmental crisis is the shared insight of people that they could be happier if they could *work* together and *care* for each other."[48] Today, the idea that conservation might be intrinsic to the dignity of human nature and not just a requirement for survival is absent from discussions that focus on clean-up, careful consumption, and control. Impossible ideas of responsibility for the planet are enjoined on people, but it is only rarely mentioned that the same tools that damage nature also injure social relations. Rapid transportation, according to Illich, puts society into a speed coma long before its by-products begin to alter the atmosphere, and this insight can show us much better reasons for restricting the compass of technique than the maddening desideratum to "manage planet earth."

Illich followed *Tools for Conviviality* with two further explorations of "paradoxical counterproductivity." *Energy and Equity* (1974) pursued the question into the domain of transportation and traffic. It argued that high energy consumption inevitably overpowers and degrades social relations and proposed the bicycle as the epitome of conviviality. Bicycles incorporate sophisticated materials and engineering while operating at nontraumatic speeds and leaving civic space safe, quiet, and clean. One person who uses a bicycle does not constrain others from doing the same; the more people who use cars, the less useful cars become. *Medical Nemesis* (1975), which was republished in 1976 in an expanded form as *Limits to Medicine*, proposed that medicalization of health beyond a certain intensity increases suffering by reducing the capacity to suffer and destroying "the community setting in which suffering can become a dignified performance."[49] Published at a time when medical power was already under sustained popular assault, *Limits to Medicine* was arguably Illich's most influential book and, along with *Deschooling Society*, the one most often cited by readers for whom Illich is a name from the past.

During the period of his career that ended with the closing of CIDOC in 1976, Illich was concerned with hedging and demystifying the power of "dominant professions." He argued that old liberal professions, like law or medicine, had concentrated privilege without making their services mandatory. Dominant professions were protection rackets, legal monopolies licensed to serve the needs they had imputed to their clients. Grave-diggers, he wrote, "did not become members of a profession by calling themselves morticians, by obtaining college credentials, by raising their incomes, or by getting rid of the odor attached to their trade by electing one of themselves president of the Lions Club. Morticians formed a profession, a dominant and disabling one, when they acquired the muscle to have the police stop your burial if you are not embalmed and boxed by them." In the era of dominant professions, needs become "the off-print of a professional pattern" and ignorance of one's needs "the unforgivable anti-social act."[50]

Illich's work helped to inspire emergent citizens' movements with the confidence to challenge professional expertise. "In the sixties," he wrote in 1977, "lay opposition to legislation based upon expert opinion still sounded like anti-scientific bigotry. Today lay confidence in public policies based upon the expert's opinion is tenuous indeed. Thousands now reach their own judgments and, at great cost, engage in citizen action without any professional tutorship; they gain the scientific information they need through personal, independent effort."[51] But even as he observed this heartening development, Illich also observed a countertendency for people to internalize the categories of professional dominance and, in effect, administer care to themselves.

Ten years after *Medical Nemesis* was published, the venerable British medical journal *The Lancet* asked Illich to commemorate the anniversary by reflecting on the changes he had seen in the intervening years. Illich responded with an article in which he said that he would no longer claim, as he did in the first sentence of *Medical Nemesis*, that "the medical establishment has become a major threat to health." The major threat today, he wrote, is the "pathogenic pursuit" of health itself.[52] In *Medical Nemesis* Illich several times used the term *self-care* to denote an alternative to professional care; ten years later he winced to see that, in practice, self-care had come to mean not people's ability "to suffer their own reality"[53] or "bear their uniqueness"[54] but a condition of total self-administered patienthood. He was not dissatisfied with his text, he said, insofar as it described the ways in which medicine had reshaped the experience of pain, disease, disability, and death. "But I am distressed," he said, "that I was blind to a much more profound symbolic iatrogenic [i.e., physician-caused] effect — the iatrogenesis of the body itself. I overlooked the degree to which, at mid-century, the experience of our bodies *and* our selves had become the result of medical concepts and cares." Failing to see this, he went on, he had also missed the contemporary transformation of the medically objectified body-as-machine into "a body percept congruent with a post-professional, high-tech life-style,"[55] the body-as-system.

Illich's revision of what he had written in *Medical Nemesis* was only part of a broadening and deepening of his thought that had begun even before that book was published. In 1971, on the eve of the publication of *Deschooling Society*, he had become aware that, if his critique was understood as pertaining to schools *per se*, it could be used to bolster the efforts of reformers intent on "the transformation of all society into one huge classroom." In response he began to pose the myth of education itself, and not just schooling, as the problem, noting that "the re-formed classroom, the free classroom and the world-wide classroom represent three stages in a proposed escalation of education in which each step threatens more subtle and more pervasive social control than the one it replaces."[56]

By the early seventeenth century a new consensus began to arise: the idea that man was born incompetent for society and remained so unless he was provided with "education." Education came to mean the inverse of vital competence. It came to mean a process rather than the plain knowledge of the facts and the ability to use tools which shape a man's concrete life. Education came to mean an intangible commodity that had to be produced for the benefit of all, and imparted to them in the manner in which the visible Church formerly imparted invisible grace. Justification in the sight of society became the first necessity for a man born in original stupidity, analogous to original sin.[57]

Identifying an embracing myth of education did not represent a change of direction so much as a change of emphasis for Illich. He had identified schooling as "a mythopoetic ritual" from the very outset. But what he did come to see was how easily his own proposals for reform could be used to consolidate rather than dispel this myth: how "home-schooling" or "self-care" might become total concepts, signifying a much more insidious institutionalization of the myths of education and health than schools or hospitals, and dissolving the boundary between individuals and systems in a way precisely opposite to the autonomous expression of personal meaning that Illich had hoped to foster. Recognizing this, he began to seek the source of those "certainties" which can turn even deschooling into education. What endows the idea of education with the tremendous inertial power it obviously possesses? Under what conditions can an idea so alien to other times and places even arise?

These were the questions that would occupy the second, less celebrated half of Illich's career as a thinker and writer. He immediately identified scarcity as one of the key assumptions he wanted to examine. Education, for example, he defined as "learning under the assumption of scarcity." Books may be plentiful and the world endlessly informative; but, by being husbanded in specialized institutions, education is kept in short supply. Human beings may be — indeed quite obviously are — innately social, but almost no one questions the plausibility of the claim that schools are necessary for "socialization." Scarcity is the prototypical certainty: a condition we constantly reproduce by our fervent belief in it. It is the founding assumption of modern economics, which classically defined itself as the study of the allocation of scarce resources to competing uses, and the necessary condition for a world seen as being composed of resources in the first place.

It was Karl Polanyi who made Illich aware how recent, and how anomalous historically, a market society based on scarcity really is.[58] Illich began to oppose a sphere of traditional subsistence in which culture still shapes and limits economic life to a sphere of scarcity in which economic values predominate. He first spoke of the gestures through which non-modern peoples represent their sense of the good as "vernacular values," and then abandoned the term *values* altogether when he realized that it cast the shadow of economic choice on acts whose essence was, precisely, not choice but unforced attunement to a given environment. Traditional societies, Illich came to see, take stringent precautions against the corrupting effects of exchange relations — they will not allow the unquestionably good to be reduced to monetarized values.[59] Modern societies speak of values, and thereby imply that ways of life become worthy or unworthy according to our choice of whether or not to invest in them.

In 1981, under the title of *Shadow Work*, Illich published five essays, which he presented as drafts "for my major study on the history of scarcity." This book has never appeared as such, but much of Illich's work in the 1980s, as well as the work of colleagues whom he inspired, can be considered as comprising the chapters of such a study. In *Shadow Work* Illich wrote for the first time explicitly as a historian. In order to distinguish *Homo economicus* "from all other human beings," he said, "I choose the study of history as the privileged road."[60] The book was founded on a key distinction between economic society and vernacular life. It was written at a time when economists had just discovered "the informal economy" and were beginning to forge concepts and classifiers by which they could analyze it. It was becoming increasingly clear that in most of the world there would never be as many formal jobs as there were people. The reinterpretation of culturally determined activities as self-help within an informal economy opened a new frontier for development economists. Illich called it "the last frontier of arrogance."

> I consider the indiscriminate propagation of self-help to be morally unacceptable . . . self-help is the opposite of autonomous or vernacular life. The self-help the new economists preach divides the subject of social policy (be it a person or entity) into two halves: one that stands in a professionally defined need, and the other who is professionaly licenced to provide it. Under the policies that are thus labelled as self-help, the apartheid of production and con-

sumption, characteristic of industrial economics, is projected into the subject himself. Each one is turned into a production unit for internal consumption, and the utility derived from this masturbation is then added to a newfangled GNP. Unless we clarify the distinction between this self-help and what I shall call *vernacular life*, the shadow economy will become the main growth sector during the current stagflation, the "informal" sector will become the main colony which sustains a last flurry of growth. And, unless the apostles of new life styles, of decentralization and alternative technology and conscientization and liberation make this distinction explicit and practical, they will only add some color, sweetener and the taste of stagnant ideals to an irresistibly spreading shadow economy.[61]

Illich defined shadow work as the unpaid labor necessary to sustain a commodity-intensive society based on jobs. Getting to one's job, shopping, and similar activities required to make commodities serviceable are forms of shadow work. Illich adopted the term in preference, say, to the Marxian concept of reproduction because he wanted to emphasize the shadow cast by a monetarized, commodity-intensive way of life. He stated clearly that he was not trying to make an idol of "traditional subsistence . . . structured by immemorial cultural transmission," which he said would be "sentimental and destructive."[62] Rather, he was trying to introduce critical distinctions into discussions of public policy. To the right-left axis on which political choices are usually charted, he suggested adding a y-axis representing the choice of hard or soft technologies and a z-axis running from commodity-intensity to subsistence. This type of dimensional analysis, he said, would have the advantage of starting from the undeniable reality that most people will never have jobs. It would draw limits to markets, foster "the right to useful unemployment,"[63] and protect subsistence activities, or activities undertaken for their own sake, from the infection by economic assumptions that results when monetarized values are attached to things done from necessity or love. A passage in a more recent essay illustrates Illich's distinction and the danger of not heeding it:

Notwithstanding the high levels of modernization in Japan, most parents with children over 35 count on the blessing of old age within the household. Economists can calculate how much is saved by domestic care in comparison with what a bed and upkeep in an old people's home would cost. However, the language of economics is unfit to express either the boon or the burden experienced daily in the four-generation household by its members . . . The consequences of utility choices made by an economic actor under the assumption of scarcity are something quite different from the immediacy of loving this person.

The needs discourse uproots grandmother from the household of which she had so far been a part . . . When she is then turned into a subject within the needs discourse, a new person, a *senex economicus* comes into being. This new person is a stranger who by somebody's choice is hospitalized in her own bed. The household henceforth is experienced as a center of care. Grandmother from now on receives what she needs as an old woman. She no longer simply receives her due, irrespective of any claim based on an economically definable need.

During the early eighties, the needs discourse disembedded millions of elderly Japanese from the context of experience which up to then had defined both their status and the household. Even the current Japanese economy is unprepared to meet the needs which were created by this reinterpretation of age within an economic rather than a cultural context. Last year a high-level Japanese mission journeyed to Mexico. It came to negotiate an agreement which would allow Japanese enterprises to open one million beds for the disposal of aging Japanese in a tropical climate, and offered in exchange an industrial development package. The elderly, formerly experienced as a boon and a burden, were turned into a disvalue for the economy.[64]

Illich's effort to add nuance to economic analysis and mark definite limits to its application was motivated by his observation that "the public discussion on the limits to growth" was then entering a third stage. The first stage had focussed on physical limits, the second on limits to institutional services, "the third is focussing on the commons."[65] In this third stage there had begun to be wide recognition that development destroys the usefulness of the environment. Whether it is logging that ruins the subsistence of a forest people, or high-density traffic that deprives urban people of a streetscape which formerly provided a convivial setting for social life, the pattern is the same: a public good becomes a private resource and a formerly useful place is rendered inhospitable. "Up to now," Illich says, "economic development has always meant that people, instead of doing something, are enabled to buy it ... Economic development has also meant that after a time people *must* buy the commodity because the conditions under which they could get along without it had disappeared from their physical, social or cultural environment."[66] Being deprived of the commons without access to the commodities that replaced it is the bad bargain that Illich called "modernized poverty." *Shadow Work* was an attempt to conserve what was left and remove emergent post-industrial forms of subsistence from the petrifying shadow of scarcity.[67]

One of the ways Illich tried to distinguish the sphere of subsistence from the sphere of scarcity was by developing a contrast between vernacular speech and taught mother tongue. Illich had always been interested in words and had chosen them with a fine sense of their tangibility and taste. In *Tools for Conviviality* he had spoken of the importance of "the critical use of ordinary language," and his own writings demonstrate how plain words can yield fresh sense in careful hands. In his essays on language in *Shadow Work* he describes the modernization of the West as the gradual colonization and domestication of vernacular speech by standard forms. In premodern Europe, and even yet in much of the world, there is no such thing as a mother tongue, let alone a perceived need to teach it to people. "The poor in

non-industrial countries all over the world are poly-
glot. My friend the goldsmith in Timbuktu speaks
Songhay at home, listens to Bambara on the radio,
devotedly and with some understanding says his
prayers five times a day in Arabic, gets along in two
trade languages on the Souk, converses in passable
French that he picked up in the army — and none of
these languages was formally taught to him. He did
not set out to learn these tongues: each is one style
in which he remembers a peculiar set of experiences
that fits into the frame of that language."[68]

Out of this vibrant matrix there gradually precip-
itated official languages, which can be guarded in
the national academies of old nations and manufactured in the language institutes of new ones. Illich
finds one of the epochs in this history in the work of
the Spanish grammarian Antonio Nebrija, who, in
the same year that Columbus sailed west, approached Queen Isabella with his proposal to create
a language from the many speech forms he encountered among the people of Spain.[69] Grammar had
previously been thought applicable to dead languages but in no way pertinent to living ones.
Nebrija advised the queen that the language he
intended to engineer by stabilizing the "loose and
unruly" speech of her people would be invaluable
as a tool of popular edification and administrative
control. She demurred on the ground that her sov-
ereignty did not extend to the speech of her subjects
who were already perfectly in command of their
own tongues, but it was Nebrija with his "declaration of war against subsistence" who had the future
in his bones. Today it is a certainty that children

should be taught the proper forms of everyday speech, and teachers should be paid to deliver this commodity. Elements of home-grown speech recur, like weeds growing through the cracks in pavement, in the mouths of poets and dropouts, but speech that is designed, packaged, and administered predominates.

The year after *Shadow Work* appeared, Illich published *Gender*, another study of the European vernacular. His curiosity piqued by his encounter with the reflections of feminist scholars on the history of women's work, he had begun himself to delve into the history of how work had been perceived and made a surprising discovery. Wherever he looked in the past, he could find no trace of work as such, but only men's work or women's work. A demanding line, he noticed, ran through the tool kit of every non-modern society, "separating tools men may grasp from tools women can grasp."[70] The same line separated customs and living spaces. The idea of a human being who is prior to all socially assigned "roles" and only accidentally sexed, he concluded, must be uniquely modern. All previous societies were constituted of two asymmetrical but complementary domains. It followed that the transition from traditional to modern society, which Karl Polanyi had described in terms of the disembedding of market relations from the soil of culture and custom,[71] could also be described anthropologically as "the transition from the aegis of gender to the regime of sex."[72]

So long as men and women were considered to be of different kinds, the abstract categories of modern political economy could gain no purchase. In modern society money is a universal solvent. It "confounds and exchanges all things," Marx says, and this implies a world of one substance in which all things are ideally interconvertible. Gender is the sign of a heterogeneous world in which the fact that men and women cannot be interchanged blocks the emergence of any universal category. "Vernacular speech, gender and subsistence," Illich says, "are characteristic of a morphological closure of community life on the asumption implicit and often ritually expressed that a community, like a body, cannot outgrow its size. Taught mother-tongue, sex and a lifestyle based on the consumption of commodities all rest on the assumption of an open universe in which scarcity underlies all correlations between needs and means."[73]

Gender, unlike sex, is a social rather than a biological construct. Gendered domains vary by society — what only men may do in one place, only women may do in another — but what is constant is the exclusion of competition, or invidious comparison, by the principle of complementarity. Gender contradicts the contemporary idea that men and women share a human identity that is prior to all differences beween them. It belongs to a worldview in which an irreducible experience of otherness is fundamental to being alive. Wherever I stand, there is something that remains out of reach, something that "I can know about only through its reflection in the opposite gender's words, looks and actions."[74] There is something I can never do, something I can never know, an interdependence I can never overcome, a gulf that only metaphor can represent and only imagination can bridge. Gender, in Illich's account, represents an epistemological, as well as a social, style, a way of knowing that finds an impassable limit in the dualistic character of reality itself. In an age in which the earth is comprehended at a glance, and the possibility of a "planetary culture" is no longer considered a contradiction in terms, it is at least sobering to remember a way of knowing in which otherness was constitutive of the being of things.

Illich, despite what his critics claimed, does not fantasize in his book about a return to the past. He does offer a disciplined and documented account of what gender was, as a way of standing outside the present and seeing it with a vision sharpened by the knowledge of a profoundly different past. He does contradict any effort to construct "a central perspective" based on the normatively human within the social sciences by insisting that "only non-scientific research that uses analogy, metaphor and poetry can reach for gendered reality."[75] And he does suggest that we cherish what he calls "the rests of gender," a phrase by which he suggests not just what remains, but also what refreshes us in our lives as modern economic neuters.

Gender was explicitly not a book about patriarchy. The division of society into complementary domains can occur in circumstances where men predominate, where women predominate, or where power is balanced. "In this essay," Illich says, "I have not tried to explain why society places the man on top and the handicap on women." What he did assert was that sexism could occur only under genderless conditions. The claim of discrimination on the basis of sex supposes that a presumed equality between the sexes has been violated. Where men and women are incommensurable beings no such claim can exist. Once it does, Illich says, the majority of women will be worse off than before because they will be exposed to unlimited competition with men. "Under the reign of gender, men and women collectively depend on each other; their mutual dependence sets limits to struggle, exploitation and defeat. Vernacular culture is a truce between genders, and sometimes a cruel one . . . In contrast to this truce, the regime of scarcity imposes continued war and ever new kinds of defeat on each woman. While under the reign of gender women might be subordinate, under *any* economic regime they are *only* the second sex." Sexism and patriarchy, in other words, are separate questions, but confusion between them will persist so long as feminist historians attempt "to reconstruct the past . . . with concepts mined in utopia."[76]

Gender constituted a powerful critique of feminism. It claimed that feminist scholarship was engaged in a fruitless and deceptive attempt to comprehend an utterly foreign past within the ideological categories of the present — "putting on the hand-me-down Marxoid categories discarded by social historians," was Illich's tart phrase. It also claimed that the goal of feminism's legislative program, equality, was a will-of-the-wisp. "The struggle to create economic equality between genderless humans of two different sexes," Illich wrote, "resembles the efforts made to square the circle with a ruler and straight edge."[77] The harder this struggle was pressed, Illich argued, the more paradoxical would be its results.

Because of the particular ways in which they are injured by the genderless assumptions of a purely economic society, he said, women would have been uniquely placed to undertake "a radical questioning of the categories of economics, of sociology and of anthropology."[78] By opting instead for legally engineered equality within these categories, feminists have committed themselves to creating a liberal utopia of frictionless universal competition. According to Illich, the results of this final spasm of Western revolutionary zeal, now increasingly structured as part of "development" under the banner of "global feminism," will be the same as the results of previous development crusades: greater privileges for a few, and greater degradation for the majority. This majority will find itself confined in what Illich's colleague Barbara Duden calls a "double ghetto," removed from the protection of gender with the promise of equality still undelivered. "The era of scarcity could come to be," Illich said, "only on the assumption that 'man' is individual, possessive, and, in the matter of material survival, genderless."[79] It follows that reflection on gender, and careful attention to the seeds of possibility that lie hidden in its traces, might have led to a fundamental challenge to this assumption. Instead, numbers of people now seem to have arrived at the notion that economic society is a perverse by-product of testosterone, which generates as a corollary the idea of woman as man with a difference, *Homo economicus* with a moral halo.

Gender took Illich into new territory, but his thesis remained entirely consistent with his previous writings. He had based himself from the outset on the assumption that development was a doomed enterprise, jobs for all a destructive utopia, and the monopoly of commodities over satisfaction a prescription for envy and frustration. With *Gender* he hoped to show that, insofar as sexism is the inevitable by-product of an industrial mode of production, "the fight against sexism converges with efforts to reduce environmental destruction and endeavours to challenge the radical monopoly of goods and services over needs." Contraction of the economy and recovery of the commons, he said, were the common conditions for the success of all three movements. Illich claimed no clairvoyance about the shape of a new commons and, typically, refused on principle "to allow the shadow of the future to fall on the concepts with which I try to grasp what is and has been." But he did hold out hope that "a contemporary art of living can be recovered" and concluded that "the hope for such a life rests upon the rejection of sentimentality and on openness to surprise."[80]

Gender was easily the most vilified of Illich's books. Review after review dismissed him as a romantic or a reactionary or both; and the tone of these reviews suggested, to me at least, that even if Illich's text had been more tactful and less astringent than it was, it would have made little difference. Seven such commentaries were published in the spring of

1983 in the journal *Feminist Issues*.[81] Illich had used the text of Gender as the basis for a series of lectures he gave in Berkeley in 1982, and these seven critiques were responses recorded at a symposium held after the lectures had finished. What is most striking about them is not that the feminist scholars who spoke disagreed with Illich but the extent to which they misrepresented his argument. He was accused of dressing ideology up as science when he had said explicitly that he was taking a non-scientific stance; he was accused of portraying gender as part of the natural order, as if he were a closet sociobiologist, when his whole argument depended on the recognition that gender was a vanishing and highly variable cultural construct; and he was accused of wanting to return to the past when he had tried to make clear that he viewed his text as a contribution to current discussion on the limits to growth. Robin Lakoff even claimed that "all the salient features of modern propaganda, as exemplified in classics of the genre, like *Mein Kampf*, are to be found in *Gender*." Of the seven critics only one, anthropologist Nancy Scheper-Hughes, challenged Illich's evidence. The rest offered only *ad hominem* (*ad feminam*?) arguments and relied on ideological prejudice for their conclusion that Illich must be wrong.

I mention *Feminist Issues* because I was shocked by the extent to which his critics misrepresented Illich and by the indication that feminist dogmatics may now block even discussion of the question Illich wanted to raise. I also believe, on the basis of several conversations with people who told me they disagreed with *Gender* without having read it, that the *Feminist Issues* critique has been influential. For years I have looked in vain for references to Illich's book in other works to which its argument would have been germane. It is sad, I think, that a book which might have been a source of renewed friendship and respect between men and women became instead a source of controversy and then, after virtually introducing the now pervasive term *gender* into public discussion, itself slipped from sight.

There is a thread that still connects *Gender* to Illich's books of the 1970s. His subsequent works display a new dimension, which is revealed in his remark to me that "in the mid-1980s there has been a change in the mental space in which many people live." "The subject of my writing," he said, "has been the perception of sense in the way we live; and, in this respect, we are . . . passing over a watershed. I had not expected, in my lifetime, to observe this passage."[82] This change can be expressed, in shorthand, as the transition from a textual to a cybernetic image of the self. Illich became increasingly aware of it as he shifted his focus from the question of what tools do to a society, which he had pursued in *Tools for Conviviality*, to the question of what tools say to people about who they are — technology's symbolic fallout, as McLuhan called it. He concluded that the computer had now replaced the book as "the root metaphor of the age."[83]

In *ABC: The Alphabetization of the Popular Mind*, Illich and his co-author, Barry Sanders, tried to gain perspective on the catastrophic change they sensed

around them by exploring two comparable historical watersheds: the transition from epic orality to
literacy in ancient Greece, and the appearance of a
recognizable ancestor of the modern book in
twelfth-century Europe. Such scholars as Milman
Parry and Eric Havelock had reflected on the mo-
mentous changes in consciousness that occurred
when the technique of alphabetic literacy created
visible words out of the irretrievable river of speech,
and an entirely new kind of thought became possible.[84] Illich's original research focussed on the
twelfth century, where he studied changes in the
appearance of the medieval book. In the manu-
scripts of the early Middle Ages, words were unsep-
arated. In order to tease the words out of a
continuous line of letters, it was necessary to read
aloud, and numerous accounts agree that the monks
and Church fathers buzzed and mumbled as they
read. Reading was a laborious activity by which the
reader physically embodied the words he first tasted
on his tongue — "Let the reader seek for savour, not
science," said a Cistercian monk of the time.[85] According to Dom Jean Leclercq, "Doctors of ancient
times used to recommend reading to their patients
as a physical exercise on an equal level with walking,
running or ball-playing."[86]

Words were occasionally separated as early as the
eighth century; but, in the twelfth century, the practice became general and converged with a host of
other changes. Chapters were given titles and sub-
titles; quotations were marked; paragraphs, marginal glosses, tables of contents, and alphabetical
indices were all added. Books could now be con-

sulted for reference as well as for reading. Libraries with books set out on shelves came into existence, and monasteries began to catalogue their holdings.

Illich believes that these changes, taken together, amounted to a revolution. The old book was an overwhelmingly physical object that incorporated the reader into *its* order, leading the reader on a pilgrimage through its lines. Hugh of St. Victor calls it a vineyard in which he walks, tasting the words as he goes. With the transformed book of the twelfth century, a new reality, which Illich calls the visible text, appeared, hovering above the actual page. The book became "the mirror of a mind," capable of reflecting an entirely new kind of order and authority. This visible text, says Illich, was something much more than just a new tool for the production of knowledge. It was also a new kind of metaphor, a new way of defining the social and psychological space in which people lived. Illich called this new space "literate mind" or "lay literacy," and he argued that it changed the world long before most people could read.

Oral society knows no "self" — "Thinking itself takes wing; inseparable from speech, it is never there, always gone."[87] The stability and narrative consistency with which we endow the self is a reflection of textual literacy. Very few people could read and write at the end of the twelfth century, and their number increased only slowly; but, in Illich's view, even illiterates soon acquired a new textual image of the self. Changes that McLuhan had ascribed to the printing press Illich found, in embryonic form, two centuries earlier. Oaths became writs, and

honor became conscience. The Church institutionalized confession by which people produced for a
priest the inner inscription of their thoughts and
deeds. Authors appeared who were creators and no
longer just conservators of culture. Regardless of
who possessed the skills of the scribe, the im-
plications of textual literacy penetrated everywhere.

The significance of this idea of "lay literacy" for
Illich is in the light it throws on the appearance of a
new kind of mind today. To describe it, Illich has
borrowed Morris Berman's term "the cybernetic
dream,"[88] sometimes transposing it to the cybernetic nightmare. A person today who speaks about
getting something out of his "system" locates himself within this new state whether or not he has any
aptitude for computers. In calling the computer the
"root metaphor" of this new age, Illich does not
suppose that the computer has in any simple sense
caused it, and his concept of lay literacy emphasizes
this point. Ferdinand de Saussure had supposed
that language was a system of signs, Alan Turing
dreamed of a "universal machine," Norbert Weiner
coined the term *cybernetics*, and Erwin Schrödinger
guessed that even the human genetic stuff is a binary
information code long before the existence of even
the room-sized Univac became public knowledge in
the 1950s.[89] If we take Illich's term *watershed* in its
second sense, in which it represents a whole drain-
age basin and not just the height of land that defines
its boundary, then it is clear, at least in retrospect,
that during the course of the twentieth century
many tributaries have flowed into the stream that
Illich realized in the mid-1980s was now in irresist-

ible flood. He himself recalls the sense of outrage he felt in 1964 when "for the first time in my life I became aware that I was being addressed not as a person but as a transmitter."[90] But, at some point, a change in quantity becomes a change in quality; and, by the time we spoke in 1988, Illich was very much preoccupied by the abstract and disembodied character of the new systems discourse, which was increasingly becoming the source of self-definition in the age of post-textual literacy.

In the Vineyard of the Text, a book now in press, further refines Illich's approach to the current watershed between text and system as root metaphors by examining in detail the reading of Hugh of St. Victor, who stood at the very cusp of change in the twelfth century. "For decades now," Illich says at the beginning of the book, "a very special affection has tied me to Hugh of St. Victor, to whom I feel as grateful as I am to the very best of my still living teachers." Illich first wrote about Hugh in *Shadow Work* in a wonderful essay called "Research by People," where he made the claim that Hugh was the "first and last" person in Europe "to have an alternative philosophy of technology."[91] Illich was then trying to define the new dimension of citizen activity he saw opening up amongst people who were doing a type of science that was "critical and public but definitely not Research and Development."[92] He spoke of a type of science that was aimed at creating beauty and comfort for those who do it without sponsorship, access to prestigious journals, or the hope of distribution through supermarkets. His search for precedents led him to Hugh, the abbot

of a community of Augustinian canons on the outskirts of twelfth-century Paris. Hugh created a place
for what Illich called "critical technology" within
philosophy. He saw technology as a remedy for the
bodily weakness that is the heritage of Adam and
Eve's fall, and this modest view of technology as a
remedial activity allowed him to set clear limits to
its application. In Illich's eyes, Hugh was the first to
isolate technology as a subject and the last to insist
that it was properly part of philosophy. (The place
of village technology in Gandhi's "constructive program" for India is a close modern analogue.) Within
a generation of Hugh's death, his thoughtful attempt to navigate between fatalistic resignation and
an ethos of domination and control had been
eclipsed. Philosophy and technology took separate
roads. Monasteries became centers of uncritical enthusiasm for new techniques, while, at the same
time, what Hugh had called "mechanical science"
was being excluded from the new academic curriculum.

In the Vineyard of the Text shows Hugh to have been
an equally brilliant anomaly in the history of reading. Today, like Hegel's owl of Minerva which flies
only at twilight, Illich confronts what George Steiner
calls "bookish text" in the poignant light of its disappearance as the dominant way of knowing the
world. "Only now," says Illich, "with nature conceived as encoded information, can the history of
'The Readability of the World' be made into an issue
for study."[93] Hugh too stood at the brink of a new
age and, in some ways, already belonged to it. St.
Victor was a new type of monastery established for

the edification of an expanding urban population; and, in his writings, Hugh codifies the practice of monkish reading in order to make it accessible to his townsmen. Hugh was aware and capable of the new practice of silent reading, but what he teaches is still the *lectio divina* in which "the reader's order is not imposed on the story but the story puts the reader into its order." For Hugh the page is still a soil — the material substrate for a journey into nature and God. There, in his pilgrimage towards the light, the reader encounters "creatures who wait to give birth to their meaning." Reading is an "ontologically remedial technique" that removes the darkness from the eyes of fallen man and restores his capacity to perceive the light that shines from all things. In practising it, we seek not ourselves, but another, who is ultimately Christ.

Hugh was the last for whom *lectio divina* was the only worthwhile kind of reading. With the emergence of what Illich calls the visible text, the book shrank from cosmic to individual proportions. Bookish text became "the materialization of abstraction." It still made the book its "port and anchorage" but, at the same time, floated above it. Nature ceased to be the object to be read and became the object to be described. Exegesis and hermeneutics became operations on the text, rather than on the world. The new proto-modern individual no longer belonged to the book — the book belonged to him as the visible object of his thought.

Studying the transition from sacred to scholarly reading enables Illich to clarify certain features of the present. It enables him to see that the type of reading in which he engages as a modern "man of letters" has a historical beginning and might therefore have a historical end. Moreover, he knows that the kinship he feels with Hugh extends across the watershed that divides them. This allows him to recognize "that the bookish classical reading of the last 450 years is only one among several ways of using alphabetic techniques." What he wants his readers to see, I think, is that all techniques induce corresponding mental states. Knowing how Hugh read can provide perspective on the era of bookish reading. "A new ascetism of reading" is still possible but can no longer be presented as something natural. It must now be conscious choice in the face of alternatives and in the light of "the historical fragility of bookish text."

Illich does not present "the two mind-sets [which] confront each other"[94] in our world as an either/or. He does not wish to turn literacy into "an anti-cybernetic ideology," and he warns against this fruitless fundamentalism. Typically, he has made it a point to learn a good deal about computers, and he suggests that "for . . . anti-computer fundamentalists a trip through computerland, and some fun with controls, is a necessary ingredient for sanity in this age" and even "a means of exorcism against the paralyzing spell the computer can cast."[95] The cybernetic dream is not induced by the computer as such but occurs only when the "cybernetic metaphor" displaces all others and leaves people without marker or compass in the weightless world of information systems. The point, therefore, is to keep awake and cleave to the watershed where one remains aware of both realities and their profound difference. "The world of cybernetic modelling, of computers as root metaphors for felt perception," Illich says, "is dangerous and significant only as long there as there is still *textual literacy* in the midst of it."[96]

It would be impossible here to give more than a sketch of the new reality that has made Illich so keenly aware of the fragility of his own assumptions. What I think he sees emerging around him is a world that is quite literally sense-less because sense has been washed out of the words people use. Whether people imagine that they live on a planet that they have a responsibility to "save" or think in terms of communication in which they exchange information in response to feedback signals, they adopt terms that cannot grasp embodied existence and that locate them in a realm of impalpable entities and shadowy processes that only an increasingly abstract science can even define. Between the image of the blue earth and the person who treats it as an object of veneration lie the costly, violent, and incomprehensible sciences on whose mediation the image depends. The word *information* can be precisely defined only by the science that reduces it to signal and noise. In ordinary speech it is as inert as a wad of cotton batting which puffs up the speaker's discourse with an obeisance to the expert who actually knows what information is, while at the same time smothering his ability to say what he means. According to Illich, the common-garden vocabulary with which people could once express their joys and sufferings is now so infiltrated by what Nietzsche more than a hundred years ago already recognized as "the madness of general concepts" that its power to denote any sensible reality has grown pale and vitiated. "The day by day experience of a managed existence," Illich says, "leads us all to take a world of fictitious substances for granted." We live among "management-bred phantoms," which convince us that our reach exceeds our grasp, put an ethical gloss on intolerable realities, and "connote self-important enlightenment, social concern and rationality without, however, denoting anything which we could ourselves taste, smell or experience."[97]

The first sustained treatment of the theme of disembodiment in Illich's work was a lecture he gave in Dallas in 1984. It appeared in extended form a year later as *H2O and the Waters of Forgetfulnes*. Some people in Dallas had asked Illich to contribute to a municipal debate on the desirability of creating an artificial lake in the center of the city. He responded with what he called an essay on "the historicity of stuff," which asked whether the "recycled toilet flush" out of which the city of Dallas proposed to make its lake had lost the imaginative resonance that historically had belonged to water and become something better called merely H_2O because it could no longer "mirror the water of dreams."[98] Drawing on Gaston Bachelard's *Water and Dreams*, in which he shows how matter is given form in the deep imagination of a given cultural epoch, Illich explored the ways in which stuff is a social creation. Archetypal waters make the invisible accessible to our senses. The waters of baptism sanctify; the waters of Lethe wash the memories from the feet of the dead and carry them to the pool of Mnemosyne where bards can retrieve them. But, beyond a certain intensity of management, Illich supposed, this connection is cut. He suggested that this was the case with the cleaning solvent which circulates through the homogeneous space of a modern city. "The twentieth century," he concluded, "has transmogrified water into a fluid with which archetypal waters cannot be mixed."[99]

H_2O is a rich and rambling excursion on the mythology of water and the history of urban space. What is germane here is Illich's account of how cultural space, or "space-as-substance," is created. The founding of an ancient city involved an elaborate ritual which culminated in the plowing of a sacred furrow that defined its boundary. In this way space was contained and given the horizon within which it acquired its substance. Within such a discreet space people can dwell and leave their traces. "Preindustrial societies could not have existed in homogeneous space. The distinction between the outside and the inside of the body, of the city, of the circle was for them constitutive of all experience." Modern urban space, by contrast, is homogeneous and indiscreet, an endless worldwide extension of the same, whose proper symbol, according to Illich, is the bulldozer, which from time to time reconfigures this sameness. "Only those who can recognize the nightmare of non-discreet space," he says, "can regain the certainty of their own intimacy and thereby dwell in the presence of one another."[100]

Illich returned to the theme of how boundaries generate vernacular space in what was called the

Hebenshausen Declaration on Soil. This was a short manifesto-like statement Illich produced with Sigmar Groeneveld, Lee Hoinacki, and a group of friends after a meeting on agriculture at Groeneveld's home in the village of Hebenshausen, in Germany. The declaration opposed the local en-cultured reality of soil to the abstractness of "the ecological discourse about planet Earth, global hunger [and] threats to life."[101] Echoing the theme of Alasdair MacIntyre's *After Virtue*,[102] the authors claim that virtue is embodied practice that can only exist where custom has shaped and limited a field for its application. "By virtue," they say, "we mean that shape, order and direction of action informed by tradition, bounded by place, and qualified by choices made within the habitual reach of the actor ... We note that such virtue is traditionally found in labor, craft, dwelling and suffering supported not by an abstract earth, environment, or system, but by the particular soil these very actions have enriched with their traces." The declaration also notes that "soil . . . is remarkably absent from those things clarified by philosophy in our Western tradition" and ends by issuing "a call for a philosophy of soil."

This call picks up a point Illich had made in "Research by People," where he claimed that Hugh of St. Victor's attempt to create a philosophical theology of technology died stillborn when technology was left outside the walls of the new university and philosophy took wing on the long transcendental trajectory that has finally brought it into its contemporary cul-de-sac. In a sense, Illich's whole career can be seen as an effort to revive Hugh's project and re-embed technology in a philosophical and theological matrix. Tools, in Illich's sense, amplify and entrain our senses and so belong to the physical realm of soil and body above which Western philosophy has soared. In his constantly reiterated insistence on limits as the condition of meaning, and suffering as the expression of this experience, he has tried to show that these limits are inherent in embodied existence. Tools can remedy the ills of the body, as agriculture can improve soil, but only to a point. Beyond that point lie dispersion, grandiosity, and, ultimately, nemesis.

In a passage in *Gender* about Raymond Williams's book *Key Words*, Illich comments that "each entry conveys the surprise and passion of an aging man telling us about the inconstancy of a word on which his own integrity has rested."[103] Illich has known the same experience. *Responsibility* was a word that carried considerable weight in his writings until at least the time of *Medical Nemesis*; but, in 1990, in a lecture given in Hannover, Germany, entitled "Health as One's Own Responsibility: No Thank You!," he renounced it. In this talk he argued that the word had now acquired connotations that had made it into the opposite of self-limitation. How could he be responsible, he asked, when health now implies "the smooth integration of my immune system into a socioeconomic world system" and responsibility "an interiorization of global systems into the self, in the manner of a categorical imperative." "In a world which worships an ontology of systems," he went on, "ethical responsibility is reduced to a legitimizing formality."

I can imagine no complex of controls capable of saving us from the flood of poisons, radiations, goods and services which sicken humans and animals more than ever before. There is no way out of this world. I live in a manufactured reality ever further removed from creation. And I know today what that signifies, what horror threatens each of us. A few decades ago, I did not yet know it. At that time, it seemed possible that I could share responsibility for the re-making of this manufactured world. Today, I finally know what powerlessness is. "Responsibility" is now an illusion. In such a world, "being healthy" is reduced to a combination of techniques, protection of the environment, and adaptation to the consequences of techniques, all three of which are, inevitably, privileges.

As an alternative to responsibility, Illich proposed renunciation. "We no longer have a word for courageous, disciplined, self-critical renunciation accomplished in community — but that is what I am talking about. I will call it *askesis*." He specified that he did not mean mortification but rather an "*epistemological askesis*," a purge of those corrupting concepts that give "fictitious substances" the semblance of a sensible existence.

Illich did not hide the fact that he was imposing a painful proscription, but he argued that only by refraining from those modes of speech and action that disguise their own powerlessness can people recover a sense of the surprising power of this moment, this place, this person. Responsibility for health is what he calls a rain dance: a way of warding off evil that at the same time domesticates it by making it appear to be in the dancer's power. Evil, for Illich, is not manageable; and such things as nuclear weapons, genetic manipulation, and the chemical transformation of earth and atmosphere by industrial poisons are evils, not problems. "We can suffer such evil," he says. "We can be broken by it, but we cannot make sense of it, cannot direct it."

At the end of "Health as One's Own Responsibility: No Thank You!" Illich takes up the question of "life" that occupies the last chapter of this book. Life, in Illich's view, is the master concept of what he calls "a new stage of religiosity,"[104] the *primum mobile* in the empyrean of fictitious substances. Two years before, he had shocked a convocation of Lutheran bishops by pronouncing a solemn curse on the use of this word as substantive. Life is used as a substantive when people speak of life on earth, or the appearance of a new life at conception. Doctors who claim responsibility for the lives of their patients, and bioethicists who asses the quality of those lives, speak in the same sense. In this radically new discourse, Illich says, life loses its anchorage in persons and becomes the ultimate resource.

Illich believes that this usage can be explained only as a corruption of Christianity. In the gospel of John, Jesus says to Martha, "I am Life." Through the Incarnation this life becomes a person and, in consequence, transforms the meaning of personal existence forever. "This one Life is the substance of Martha's faith and ours," Illich says. "We hope to receive this Life as a gift, and we hope to share it. We know this Life was given to us on the Cross, and that we cannot seek it except on the *via crucis*. To be merely alive does not yet mean having this Life. This Life is gratuitous, beyond and above having been born and living. But, as Augustine and Luther constantly stress, it is a gift without which being alive would be as dust."[105] It is Illich's impression that the faithful experience of Life incarnate in Christ deeply shaped the Western worldview. Only in the space vacated by this tradition is the reification of biological being as "life" even thinkable.

Life, according to Illich, is now the linchpin of a new religiosity. Evidence is not hard to find. New synthetic "spiritualities" abound, and their common feature seems to be that they enable people to worship their own reflections. Illich speaks of "a cosmos in the hands of man."[106] Life appears in such discourses as an object venerated and manipulated in one paradoxical gesture. Judaeo-Christian religion put a peculiar emphasis on creatureliness and stressed the difference and the distance of the creature from God. This stress is reflected in Illich's emphasis on dissymmetric complementarity, the mutually constitutive difference between here and there, self and other, man and woman. Life is the sign of a monistic and homogeneous process that dissolves this difference. When British scientist James Lovelock attached the name of the ancient goddess Gaia to his hypothesis that the earth constitutes a single cybernetic system, he reflected this style of thought.[107] "The revelation that one human person, Jesus, is also God" has undergone a profound inversion.[108] The life that was God's gift of himself has become a shadowy substance out of which new hypothetical gods are now conjured.

Illich told his audience in Hannover that life was a blasphemy, but then specified that he wanted to be understood "as a historian, not as a theologian." Three years earlier he had drawn the same distinction for an audience at the McCormack Theological Seminary in Chicago. "In the Roman Catholic Church's more recent tradition," he said, "you imply teaching authority which derives from the hierarchy when you claim to speak as a theologian. But I will not do this." The distinction might at first seem coy, but I believe it is critical to the understanding of Illich's work. Illich is a Christian, but he has not attempted to claim authority for his views on that basis. Nor has he argued from concealed Christian premises. When he says life is a blasphemy, he means by blasphemy what my dictionary calls "the act of claiming the attributes of God," and he believes that, historically speaking, that is precisely what substantive life is: the perversion of a peculiarly Christian idea that would make no sense outside this context. You do not have to be a Christian to accept this idea that the modern West, with its vast architecture of institutions that care about people's needs, is a perverse extension of the Church's attempt to institutionalize the Gospel. Illich summarizes this insight in the Latin adage *corruptio optimi quae est pessima* — the corruption of the best is the worst, or, in other words, the depth to which we have fallen is the measure of the height to which we were called. He lives his faith in the face of a tragic recognition of "the mysterious darkness which envelops our world, the demonic night paradoxically resulting from the world's equally mysterious vocation to glory."

Lee Hoinacki once said to me that he thinks Illich is "doing theology in a new way."[109] Illich says simply that he speaks as a historian. I see him as an iconoclast, in the literal sense, who has tried to clear a space for living by demolishing idols rather than dictating how people should live. His friend John McKnight calls this engaging in proscription, rather than prescription.[110] Believing as he does in "the extraordinary creativity of people and their ability to live in the midst of what frustrates bureaucrats, planners and observers," Illich restricts himself to a criticism of the ideas and practices that inhibit and distort this creativity.

As a thinker, Illich is impossible to classify in conventional categories. He is a man of neither the left nor the right, as little a romantic as he is a conservative, no more an anti-modernist than he is a post-modernist. He might be called an anarchist, but only insofar as he believes the refusal of power to be the heart of the Christian Gospel, not because he subscribes to the political tenets of anarchism. The most that can be said, I think, is that he shows how revolutionary a faith Christianity is. The first millennium of Christianity, to which Illich often refers, understood the action of the Holy Spirit as both charismatic and conservative. It built and destroyed, ordained authorities and undermined them, revealed ways and showed their shortcomings. Illich's career, with its turnings, revisions, and sudden ruptures, shows his attentiveness to this spirit. He has been both a celebrated intellectual and an anonymous pilgrim; loved the Church as the shield of a glorious tradition and spoken against its worldliness and timidity; accepted academic honors and sloughed them off; established public positions and then revised them. His thought is consistent — perhaps more consistent than he sometimes allows — but he has always tried to follow it further, valuing the journey more than the arrival. He has never submitted to his own reputation or made himself responsible for the expectations it engendered in others. And, as much as he has spoken, he has always continued to listen.

A friend, after she read *Gender*, put down the book, looked at me quizzically, and asked in a tone of genuine astonishment, "How does he know these things?" I probably attempted some answer, but then she answered herself: "He's like a bird, who cocks his eye this way and that, taking everything in." The image has stayed with me. I can remember Illich himself recalling how as a boy he often sat under the table at his grandparents' house in Vienna, absorbing the conversation. A vivid curiosity, and an intuitive feel for what is really going on, are certainly part of Illich's genius. He is also a keen satirist and a writer whose nice sense of both the heft and etymology of his words mixes Anglo-Saxon pith with Latinate ornamentation. But beyond this, there is a penetrating power of thought that modern English can only call insight. He has fostered this power by ascetic practice and allowed it to take root in his heart, but it is, ultimately, a gift, and one he has shared generously.

At the end of our interview, Illich said that he had
set aside his misgivings about being interviewed out
of "foolish trust, full-hearted trust." This is the
attitude of a friend who has never lost his capacity
for surprise or the courage to put instinct above
ideology and play a hunch. Its foundation is what
he calls obedience.

Obedience in the biblical sense means unobstructed
listening, unconditional readiness to hear, untram-
meled disposition to be surprised by the Other's
word. The pagan looks at the manifestation of his
gods, the Jew is open to God's voice: Moses only saw
his behind, like "a whisper that vanishes." ... When
I submit my heart, my mind, my body, I come to be
below the other. When I listen unconditionally, respectfully, courageously with the readiness to take
in the other as a radical surprise, I do something else.
I bow, bend over towards the total otherness of
someone. But I renounce searching for bridges between the other and me, recognizing the gulf that
separates us. Leaning into this chasm makes me
aware of the depth of my loneliness, and able to bear
it in the light of the substantial likeness between the
other and myself. All that reaches me is the other in
his word, which I accept on faith. But, by the
strength of this word I now can trust myself to walk
on the surface without being engulfed by institutional power. You certainly remember how Peter
just walked out on the waves of the Lake of
Genesareth on the Word of his Lord. As soon as he
doubted, he began to go under.[111]

Illich takes the possibility of going under seri-ously. He does not feign horror at the contemporary world. He is genuinely horrified, and his sadness is sometimes deep and uncomfortable. He believes that there are evils in our world that can burn out hearts, and, like the Gorgons' glare, turn us to stone; and he is convinced that the power of these evils waxes with the fantasy that we can be insured against them. But he also knows there is a light in the world that the darkness cannot comprehend. In obedient friendship, we can let this inextinguishable light shine into each other's lives. Embarrassed as I am by the technique of the interviewer, who wears sincerity as a disguise and walks the knife edge between spontaneity and calculation, I still believe that that light shines in these pages.

I
The Myth of Education

DAVID CAYLEY: What was the origin of *Deschooling Society*? Did you begin as a conventional believer in schooling?

IVAN ILLICH: No, I considered that school met the needs of others. I had been brought up without much schooling. At the age of six, when my normal languages were French and Italian and German, my mother wanted to put me in a school in Vienna, a very good school where they already gave tests to children. They found that I was a retarded child. That was a great advantage for me because for two years I could sit in my grandmother's library and read her novels and look up all the interesting things that might intrigue a nasty boy of seven in the dictionaries. Yes, I went to school, but only by bits.

For instance, suddenly at eight it was decided that I had to learn Serbo-Croatian to be ready for a test and possibly to go into a school in Yugoslavia, where my father had some kind of official position. So I learned the language from a professor who taught at the diplomatic academy, Ivanovich, who taught me very interesting stuff about the iterative mode and the reiterative mode in Serbo-Croatian. I never really learned to speak the language, but eventually was ready to go to school.

I never took school seriously. Practically everything I learned occurred outside of school. But I also never made an issue of schooling. So when in 1956 I suddenly found myself the vice-rector of the Catholic University in Ponce, Puerto Rico, and, a year later, a member of the government's Board of All Education, the Consejo Superior de Ensenanza, governing everything from the universities to grade schools, I couldn't but ask myself, What is this stuff about education? I had never really reflected on it. It took me about ten years. You met up with me when for ten years I had been trying to puzzle out what the whole thing meant.

CAYLEY: And why did you conclude that it didn't make sense?

ILLICH: I first concluded that it was structured injustice to compel people to go to school and only then began to reflect whether it made any sense. On that road, the meeting with Everett Reimer was important for me. A good fifteen years older than I, Everett at that time — 1956 — was chairman of the Human Resources Planning Commission. I met him soon after I arrived at a meeting of top administrators on how to organize planning to design education. Bottles are designed. Packages for bras are designed. How to design education and how universities should collaborate in making design into a subject were the issues on that day.

Most of my life is really the result of meeting the right person at the right moment and being befriended by him. This was the case with Everett. But I was confused by his title — planning — a word I had never used before. I looked it up in dictionaries and didn't find it. It appeared for the first time in dictionaries *after* World War II. Human resources was another issue. How do you make human beings — these Puerto Rican *jibaritos* with whom I was dealing — human resources?

I remember on my next trip to New York going to Princeton to see Jacques Maritain, the philosopher, who was then living there. We had met up in Rome in a seminar and he had become a dear friend and advisor. His imaginative Thomism meant a lot to me. He was then an old man with a face, as Ann Freemantle once said, cut from a stained glass window in Chartres.[112] I had seen him occasionally in the United States because when he had his heart attack, I was honored to substitute for him in a seminar he directed of the *de ente et essentia* of St. Thomas. In 1957, I was now sitting there with him again. He had a teacup in his hand and was shaking when I talked to him about the question which bothered me, that in all his philosophy I didn't find any access to the concept of planning. He asked me if this was an English word for accounting, and I told him no . . . if it was for engineering, and I said no . . .

and then at a certain moment he said to me, "Ah! Je comprends, mon cher ami, maintenant je comprends." Now I finally understand. "C'est une nouvelle espèce du péché de présomption." Planning is a new variety of the sin of pride.

It was along this kind of circuitous road that I came to understand what this educational system of Puerto Rico was doing. First, thanks to years of conversation with Everett, I read my way into the pragmatists and empiricists of the English tradition of thinkers and philosophers. Second, I asked myself, what do schools do when I put into parentheses their claim to educate? Perhaps only in that way will I find out what they do. They then had a machine which was called a computer. It had nothing to do with what you see around now, but it could already gobble up so-called data and organize them. So I was in a position to ask for data. When I looked at the printouts they gave me, it was quite evident that after ten years of intensive development (another one of these words!) of the school system in the country, which at that moment was, together with Israel, the showcase for development all over the world, schooling in Puerto Rico was so arranged that half the students — that half which came from the poorer families — had a one-in-three chance of finishing five years of elementary education, the amount which was compulsory.

Most of the discussion around me was about immediately making many more years of education compulsory. Nobody faced the fact that schooling served, at least in Puerto Rico, to compound the native poverty of half of the children with a new interiorized sense of guilt for not having made it. I therefore came to the conclusion that schools inevitably are a system to produce dropouts, and to produce more dropouts than successes. Because the school is open for sixteen years, eighteen years, nineteen years of schooling and never closes the door on anybody, it will always produce a few successes and a majority of failures. In the minds of the people who financed and engineered them, schools were established to increase equality. I discovered that they really acted as a lottery system in which those who didn't make it didn't just lose what they had paid in but were also stigmatized as inferior for the rest of their lives.

CAYLEY: That was what impressed me when I taught in the school system of Sarawak in East Malaysia. At that time there were no more than a handful of people who were going on to university in Moscow or at the University of British Columbia. And yet the whole country was entering the primary grades, and aspirations were being focussed at least at the level of graduation from high school. So it only took a nudge from you for me to recognize that this extraordinarily steep pyramid constituted a kind of rationale for failure.

ILLICH: Don't you think that by now you have to be a little bit benighted, silly, or high with some dreams about your society not to know these things? Then it was really a surprise for people. Today I can't surprise anybody with the evidence — which has remained the same. I think the idea that schooling leads to an education went out during the 1970s, but in the 1960s and especially in the 1950s you were really treated like a skunk, like a criminal, when you questioned this. Things have changed.

CAYLEY: But they've changed in such an odd way. In the early 1970s, when your views on schooling had a brief vogue, everyone seemed to agree with you. But fifteen years later . . .

ILLICH: Nothing has changed.

CAYLEY: Well, something presumably has changed, but it hasn't changed in the direction of deschooling.

ILLICH: But the deschooling I meant was the *disestablishment* of schools. I never wanted to do away with schools. I simply said, We live under the American constitution — I spoke to Americans — and in the American constitution you have developed the concept of the disestablishment of churches. You disestablish by not paying public monies. I called for a disestablishment of schools in that sense. I suggested that instead of financing schools, you should go a little bit further than you went with religion and have schools pay taxes so that schooling would become a luxury object and be recognized as such. In that way discrimination because of lack of schooling would be at least legally discontinued in the same way that discrimination because of race or sex has been made illegal.

CAYLEY: In asking for disestablishment and by using the language that was used historically to separate church and state, you imply that schooling has in effect become a new form of compulsory religion.

ILLICH: Perhaps I have to explain how I got to my analysis of schooling. I told you what led me into it practically: I was responsible for making or presiding over very serious decisions and the creation of legislation touching the education of Puerto Rico. So I had to reflect, What am I doing? And it seemed to me quite clear that I was acting within a context that seemed ridiculously similar to a religious one. So I began to speak *intuitively* about the disestablishment of schooling. Later on I made much more of a point of this, because I actually treated the school system as a continuation of the Christian church system in Western culture.

When I studied theology, my preferred subject was ecclesiology, which is the scientific study of that particular community which the Church conceives as its ideal, and has since the fourth century. It is the first attempt to study a social phenomenon which is not the state, nor the law, as such. Ecclesiology, therefore, can be taken, in a funny but very real way, as the predecessor of sociology but with a tradition about twenty times as long as sociology since Durkheim. Now I was very much interested in the traditions and the disputes about this phenomenon, which really exists only in Western culture, of a community which claims to be as all-embracing, as catholic, as the state — or what civil law governs — and yet claims to be independent from it.

I was interested in this phenomenon from a very special point of view. Within ecclesiology there is a special branch — which very few people know about — called liturgy. Now liturgy can be the study of how people sing in church, but it can also be studied as an intellectual discipline which again has a history going back to the Greek and Roman Church fathers. In the later second and third centuries, this branch of intellectual analysis was concerned with the way in which rituals create that community which then calls itself church and is studied by ecclesiology.

When, therefore, under the influence of Everett Reimer, I began to engage in a phenomenology of schooling, I first asked myself, What am I studying? Quite definitely, I was not studying what other people told me this was, namely, the most practical arrangement for imparting education, or for creating equality, because I saw that most of the people were stupefied by this procedure, were actually told that they couldn't learn on their own and became disabled and crippled. Secondly, I had the evidence that it promoted a new kind of self-inflicted injustice. So I said to myself, Let me define as schooling the compulsory attendance in groups of no more than fifty and no less than fifteen, of age-specific cohorts of young people around one person called a teacher, who has more schooling than they. And then I asked myself, What kind of a liturgy is used there to generate the belief that this is a social enterprise that has some kind of autonomy from the law?

CAYLEY: And?

ILLICH: I came to the conclusion that this was a myth-making, a mythopoetic ritual. Gluckman, who was my hero at that time, says that rituals are forms of behavior that make those who participate in them blind to the discrepancy which exists between the purpose for which you perform the rain dance, and the actual social consequences the rain dance has.[113] If the rain dance doesn't work, you can blame yourself for having danced it wrongly.

Schooling, I increasingly came to see, is the ritual of a society committed to progress and development. It creates certain myths which are a requirement for a consumer society. For instance, it makes you believe that learning can be sliced up into pieces and quantified, or that learning is something for which you need a process within which you acquire it. And in this process you are the consumer and somebody else the organizer, and you collaborate in producing the thing which you consume and interiorize.

I therefore came to analyze schooling as a myth-making ritual, a ritual creating a myth on which contemporary society then builds itself. For instance, this builds a society which believes in knowledge and in the packaging of knowledge, which believes in the obsolescence of knowledge and in the necessity of adding knowledge to knowledge, which believes in knowledge as a value — not as the good, but as a value[114] — and which conceives of it therefore in commercial terms. This is all basic for being a modern man and living in the absurdities of the modern world.

CAYLEY: These were your observations of schools in the 1960s. Would this have been true of schools a hundred years before, or was this a new phenomenon?

ILLICH: It would be easier for me to go a little bit further back. Recently, I supervised somebody doing an interesting thesis on about 120 pietists in Germany who wrote diaries in the later seventeenth century. Now this person observed that these pietists who wrote the diaries were very simple people, and began to study how many months they had attended a village school — which was certainly before the little red schoolhouse. It turned out that with three exceptions, these 120 had learned all they got from school in less then eleven months of attendance. They didn't go to school to get an education. They went to school to learn how to hold the pen. I can talk in the same way about the Middle Ages. The idea that you go to school to get an education develops very slowly. I always said it begins with Comenius, who says that everybody must be taught everything perfectly so that he doesn't pick it up badly outside of school.[115]

The idea that competence in the world derives from being instructed about it, taught about it, is an idea which from the seventeenth century on slowly takes over. In fact, the social effects of schooling which I spoke about became possible in Puerto Rico only with the idea of universal compulsory schooling. I've nothing against schools! I'm against *compulsory* schooling. I'm not in the same way against schools. I know that schools always compound native privilege with new privilege. But only when they become compulsory can they compound lack of native privilege with added self-inflicted discrimination. Schools that are freely accessible allow the organization of certain specific learning tasks which a person might propose to himself. Schools, when they are compulsory — as we see at this moment in the United States — create a dazed population, a "learned" population, a mentally pretentious population, such as we have never seen before. The last fifty years of intensive improvement of schooling —

here, or in Germany, or in France — have created television consumers.

We live in a strange society in which people believe that they act on empirical evidence. But the empirical evidence, in relation to schooling, is quite obvious and not only with respect to justice. Since that excellent book by Ivar Berg, *The Great Training Robbery*, which was given to me by Paul Goodman, many similar studies have been done. Berg shows you that there is absolutely no connection between the subjects people have learned in school and the effectiveness of those people in jobs requiring preparation in those subjects. There is a very close connection between how much money has been spent on a person's schooling and the total life-long income which he'll get on the job, but no provable relationship between the competence he is supposed to have acquired in school and his effectiveness on the job.

CAYLEY: So schooling is a form of capital investment in which the return is proportional to the investment, regardless of competence.

ILLICH: Yes. Nobody doubts that. It's capital investment, but it's also social control, it's grading, it's the creation of a class society consisting of sixteen levels of fewer and fewer dropouts. But these are things that *then* interested me. I somehow have the impression that, even though not much has changed in the general commitment of our society to schooling, there are thousands of people around who see clearly, with truly wise and cynical eyes, what the institution does. Today, I would be interested in completely different questions.

CAYLEY: When you wrote about this, in 1970, you suggested that things would have to change, and when they did, they would change quickly.

ILLICH: I was wrong. At least in the time frame, I was wrong. I did not believe that so many people could be so tolerant of nonsense. Now that I'm back in the United States after twenty-five years and again have to do with student populations, I sometimes am so sad in the evening that I have difficulty falling asleep. The college and university systems at least have become like television. There's a bit of this and a bit of that and some compulsory program with its components connected in a way that only a planner could understand. It creates students who have gotten utterly used to the fact that what they learn they must be taught, and nothing they are taught must really be taken seriously. I did not believe that people could remain as morally tolerant as they have of the further growth of the school system.

The first person who told me I was wrong and would be proven wrong was Wolfgang Sachs.[116] He was a student of mine. In Germany, I met with him and a small group of other students, then in their mid-twenties, who criticized the articles collected in *Deschooling Society*. They claimed that by making so much of the unwanted side effects of compulsory schooling, I had become blind to the fact that the educational function was already emigrating from the schools and that, increasingly, other forms of compulsory learning would be instituted in modern society. It would become compulsory, not by law, but by other tricks like making people believe that they are learning something from TV or compelling people to attend in-service training, or getting people to pay huge amounts of money in order to be taught how to prepare better for intercourse, how to be more sensitive, how to know more about the vitamins which they need, how to play games, and so on.

They made me understand that my criticism of schooling in *Deschooling Society* might have helped people like yourself to reflect but that I was barking up the wrong tree and that I should ask myself, How can we better understand the fact that societies get addicted — as to a drug — to education? Then, during the 1970s, most of my thinking and reflection — to put it very simply — centered on the question, How should I distinguish the acquisition of education from the fact that people have always known many things, have had many competencies and, therefore, have learned something? So I then came to define education as learning under the assumption of scarcity, learning under the assumption that the means for acquiring something called knowledge are scarce.

At this point my reflections were no longer rabble-rousing and nobody on campus discussed them. I tried to bring the question into the educational research associations and failed completely. For example, I was honored to give a major talk at the twenty-fifth anniversary of the founding of the International Association for Educational Research. There were thousands of people there and I begged them, "Listen! What we really need is a study of the constitution of the *idea* of education, of learning under the assumption of scarcity." Years later, I see only a little ripple of response here and there.

You asked me to say how I came to what I am doing at this moment. That was the second period of deschooling, the awareness — through Sachs and his team — that the issue was not primarily schooling but being hooked on education, and therefore the analysis of the unwanted side effects of all forms of adult education. Then came the third step, the recognition that education had to be understood as learning under the assumption of scarcity. From there I was led to my project since the mid-1970s of writing a history of the perception of scarcity.

I asked the question, Which are the conditions under which the very idea of education can arise? You can't have the modern idea of education if you don't believe there is knowledge — knowledge which can be packaged, knowledge which can be defined, knowledge which constitutes a value which can be appropriated. I therefore became concerned with the mental frame or space within which the concepts by which we construct the notion of education can take shape.

CAYLEY: You remark in *Limits to Medicine* that, if your critique of medicine is taken as an attack on doctors, the result will be analogous to what has already happened in the matter of schooling. Were you saying that because your attack was understood to be on schools, this actually helped the school to reconsolidate itself as a sort of universal school-room?

ILLICH: Correct.

CAYLEY: And this is what you feel you didn't see at the time you published *Deschooling Society*.

ILLICH: I did not see it when I wrote the article called "The Futility of Schooling in Latin America," which *The Saturday Review* published. Three years later, six articles of mine were put together in that book, *Deschooling Society*. The book was nine months at Harper's, because it takes nine months for a good book to go through its gestation period. During the last month, the prepublication month, I suddenly realized the unwanted side effects the publication of my book could have. So I went to the editor of *Saturday Review*, Norman Cousins, a friend of my neighbor and friend Erich Fromm,[117] and said, "Norman, would you kindly allow me to publish an article during the next month?" "Yes," he answered, "but only if you write it in such a way that we can make it the lead article."

So I wrote an article in which I basically said that nothing would be worse than to believe that I consider schools the only technique for creating and establishing and anchoring in souls the myth of education. There are many other ways by which we can make the world into a universal classroom. And Cousins was so kind as to allow me to publish what I consider the main criticism of my book.

CAYLEY: There have been many criticisms of *Deschooling*. I remember one by Herb Gintis, in the *Harvard Educational Review*, which I think typified a Marxist critique of your work.[118] It was similar to what Vicente Navarro later did for *Limits to Medicine*.[119] Gintis says that you have made schooling a matter of addiction, or an initiation into the myth of unending consumption, but you have overlooked its central role in the productive system. You have overlooked the way it is a mirror of the productive system. You have made people responsible for their own deschooling when in fact they are behaving rationally and appropriately within the system as a whole, and therefore you're giving them a counsel of despair. Because, he says, unless they can transform the system it's impossible for them to deschool, since the school is intrinsic to the system. That's a very rough paraphrase.

ILLICH: I never answered Gintis. But I did answer Navarro, when he told me the same thing about health, and I did so in a footnote for the next edition of my book. I said: "Mr. Navarro accuses my proposals on medicine of denying the poor a right to iatrogenic damage. He wants to distribute iatrogenic damage equally." With Mr. Gintis I would say, "You are worried because the poorer part of Americans" — at that time, the blacks and Puerto Ricans in the ghettos — "don't get enough schooling to know what's good for them and so remain independent. Poor people drop out of school before they can fall into your hands and be told that you know what's good for them." But I had literally hundreds of critics. John Ohliger collected three volumes of citations of these criticisms and discussions.[120] And in all that stuff there was no attention to the only two chapters I wanted to have discussed, "The Ritualization of Progress" and "The Rebirth of Epimethean Man."

CAYLEY: In your book *Gender*, you say that you could not have written either that book or *Deschooling Society* without the work of Philippe Ariès.[121]

ILLICH: Ariès is the only person I quote in *Deschooling Society*. It is through Ariès that I was introduced to the historicity of the perception of "the child." I probably fell for Ariès because I had always disliked it when the children of my friends would take the attitude "I'm a child and you must pay attention to me." Since I was fifteen, I had refused to notice or to enter into any kind of intercourse with such a person. Some of my friends, better friends, family friends, have considered me all my life a brute. But an interesting thing has happened a number of times. When these kids had difficulties with their parents, they suddenly appeared on my doorstep — at age fourteen or fifteen. In two cases, they came to another continent, seeking refuge.

My intuition is that one of the most *evil* things our modern society does is produce children in this specifically modern sense. As a young man, I decided that I wouldn't do that. That was the reason I decided at age twelve not to marry.

Later on, I rejected the idea of childhood altogether and particularly the little suffering child of the nineteenth century. Ariès made me understand that the child in this sense is a modern construct. And then Ariès helped me very much in writing *Medical Nemesis*, with his excellent articles on death.

I had not yet published *Medical Nemesis*, and was in Paris once, for a day and a half, and met Valentina Borremans there.[122] I asked her, "Whom do you want to see?" And she said, "Well, if we have only one lunch and one dinner, Sartre and Ariès." "Who first?" "Ariès." So I picked up the telephone and called. "Monsieur Ariès? . . . Ivan Illich." Complete silence. Then a very cold, "Yes?" So I said to him: "I have a great desire to meet you and I have a special occasion. There's a lady I think you would like who wants to make your acquaintance." "All right, let's meet." So we met in a little restaurant. I was just lucky and chose the right restaurant where I knew you could get a one-liter bottle of Cahors. We had three of these bottles.

When we came to the end of dinner, I said to him — after three liters of Cahors — "When will you finally publish these articles in book form?" He says, "Well, in seventeen years." I said, "Ariès, how old are you?" He told me his age. I said, "You don't believe in death!" So that very same day we went from le petit Zinc to the publisher le Seuil, and he arranged for the publishing of his big book on death.

Later on, in 1982, he was my successor in the chair at the Institute of Advanced Studies in Berlin. In 1983 his wife died of cancer and I went to stay with him during the days when he had to come back alone to the apartment.

CAYLEY: You said that at twelve you concluded that you would never have children.

ILLICH: I remember it exactly. I walked through the vineyards outside of Vienna. I knew that within days Hitler would be occupying Austria, and I said to myself that, under these circumstances, certain things will happen which will make it impossible for me to give children to these towers down on the island in Dalmatia where my grandfathers and great-grandfathers made children.

CAYLEY: Then you weren't saying simply that the modern institution of childhood — which produces these yammering children — was so unpleasant that you didn't want to have anything to do with it.

ILLICH: No, I meant that on my non-Jewish side, I was trained to say that a son is given to the house, and I saw that this would not be possible for me.

CAYLEY: So this was a feeling about the fate of Europe, and the world, and not just about the institution of childhood?

ILLICH: Yes, but it was from Ariès that I learned to see the reason why it is extraordinary, why it is surprising that we still call ourselves human and still consider ourselves descendants of history. You know, until last year, I never thought of it. Then I had to explain to somebody what an exponential curve means — that the area subtending the last doubling period is equal to all the previous doubling periods. Later I was sitting in the market in Mexico on the Day of the Dead — it's a feast in Mexico when they make these pyramids of sugar skulls and everyone gives his boss a sugar skull with his name written on it. You can tell the boss anything, you can tell him off, and he knows he can't be angry with you. Anyway, there were these skulls and many colored flowers and people milling by, and I began to see the dead also walking through the market in my fantasy. And I asked myself, Why are there so few? There must be many more. Then I realized that in the period in which I have lived — since 1926 — more people have been born and have died than in the whole of previous history taken together. And suddenly I had a keen sense which was not statistical, but experiential, of how unique the period is in which I live and speak.

CAYLEY: To stay with childhood for a moment — does identifying it as a specifically modern idea invalidate it? Is it not also in some sense an advance?

ILLICH: It's just that with all advances, the greater they are, the more they are an extreme form of privilege. We are sitting here and having this conversation together because I was, at one glance, so impressed by the feeling between you and your children, whom you have kept out of school. Now for them, the fact that you have abandoned the idea of childhood in order to take these kids who live in a world of childhood fully seriously as kids is an extraordinary advantage. But this is not a model. This is something to be emulated, not imitated. It's the spark of uniqueness that must be cherished.

II
A Question of Witness

CAYLEY: Where did you grow up?

ILLICH: Because I supposedly created difficulties for my mother, threatening her with my arrival, she was taken to the best doctors, who at that moment sat in Vienna, Austria. My father was not then living in central Europe. So I was born in Vienna. Then, at the age of three months, I was exported, with my nurse, to Dalmatia to be shown to my grandfather and to be baptized, there, in Split, on Vidovdan, the Day of Great Liberation, the first of December. Then I grew up, spending a part of the year in Dalmatia, a part with the other grandparent in Vienna, and a part of the year in France or wherever my parents were. Then, during the later 1930s, my place of ordinary residence was at the house of Grandfather in Vienna — where I got stuck as a half-Aryan with dip-lomatic protection, which being the son of my father afforded — to shelter my Jewish grandfather, until he died a natural death there in his own house in 1941. At that time, I ceased to be a half-Aryan and became a half-Jew, according to the law. We had to more or less go underground and slip out of what was then Germany. I spent the rest of my youth, from the age of fifteen, mainly in Italy, in Florence and Rome.

CAYLEY: With your parents?

ILLICH: No. My father was dead by then, and I took care of my mother and two smaller brothers, who are twins. They stayed in Florence. From 1951 on, I have been on this side of the ocean. Since I left the old house on the island in Dalmatia, I have never had a place which I called my home. I have always lived in a tent like the one in which you are sitting at this moment.

CAYLEY: The house was on an island?

ILLICH: My father's old home, a house which goes back to Crusader times. And then I was five years in New York, as a parish priest, working with Puerto Ricans on 175th Street. I was in Puerto Rico for five years, officially engaged in educational institutions. I was five years in Cuernavaca, Mexico, renting a big hotel from which we ran this modest political effort, to upset volunteer programs for Latin America, from 1961 to 1966. From 1966 to 1976, I made possi-ble this alternative university in Cuernavaca, the Center for Intercultural Documentation (CIDOC). This center lasted exactly ten years to the day, from April first to April first. It began with a big fools' feast and ended with a dance. So that gives you my where-abouts.

CAYLEY: Your education was in Rome?

ILLICH: It still goes on.

CAYLEY: You said you were fortunate in having only sporadic schooling.

ILLICH: I registered for purely practical reasons in chemistry, and finished in crystallography in Florence.

CAYLEY: What was practical about that?

ILLICH: I got legitimacy by obtaining an ID card, which provided me with a false identity, under the Fascists. It was one little tool which was useful. Later, I seriously studied philosophy and theology at the Gregorian University, in Rome. I also did a doctorate in history in Salzburg. Right after the war, I got stuck in Salzburg. I wanted a residence permit, and my lawyer advised me that the best thing would be to register at the university. So I went there in order to maintain my legitimacy, and then got fascinated with two professors, Professor Albert Auer and Professor Michel Muechlin, who became my great teachers in historical method and in the interpretation of old texts.

CAYLEY: Who were these two men?

ILLICH: Albert Auer, who was not a moralist, but an old Benedictine monk, specialized in the theology of suffering in the twelfth century. He wrote three almost unknown volumes on the subject. And Muechlin's seminar was most important. It's really the only educational course I remember which really gave me something. One semester was on the transformations in the image of the phoenix during the second part of the third century. He was pretty demanding in the interpretation of texts. I'll never forget what I owe him. Professor Auer — I was writing my doctoral thesis on Toynbee with him — used to take me on three-hour walks along the Salzach, and then for a beer and dry bread.

CAYLEY: Was Leopold Kohr there then?[123]

ILLICH: I didn't know him then. He might have been there, I don't know. Leopold Kohr and I met on my first evening at the University of Puerto Rico in Rio Piedras, in front of his little house. He was teaching in Puerto Rico at the time. Because he smiled so nicely, I just sat down next to him and very quickly we shifted from his very perfect broken English and his somewhat funny Spanish into Salzburg dialect, and began to speak about the importance of developing the history of customs, which is the field in which he had enormous influence on me. He's the man who taught Schumacher, you know. I remember a beautiful remark he made when somebody said to him, "But Professor Kohr, what you say here is so much more complex and complete and rounded than the Schumacher articles I'm reading." And he says, "Yes, but, you see, there is a difference between a man like me and a really intelligent man like Schumacher. He put it all in one sentence: small is beautiful."

This is Kohr. You probably mentioned him because you saw that I was honored to give a *Laudatio* for him — a very German activity.[124] I was called in to sing his praises. I think it's good to be able to thank people from whom you've gotten a really crucial idea. I had always been interested in what in the

1920s and 1930s one would have called morphology. I had read D'Arcy Thompson,[125] and I had read Haldane's "On Being the Right Size."[126] Then Kohr came along, and without him saying so much I realized that here was a man who would apply the concept of morphology, as developed by these two people, to social reality. He would say, just as his predecessors recognized, that a *mousy* thing with its thin legs and that big roll-shaped body of a rat or a mouse can exist for physical reasons only in the range of one to ten inches long. It couldn't possibly grow to the size of an elephant. No materials are known out of which legs could be made to remain that thin if they had to move that weight. So also there are societies and aspects of societies which can survive only within certain narrow limits of size. So there is a close relationship between form and size. As crazy as this sounds, Kohr has been most influential in explaining this idea to a few people in the generation after his own. Most people who have read him have done so with the idea that "small is beautiful." Very few people have understood how deep the relationship is between social form and social size.

So I met Kohr in Puerto Rico, and whenever we meet we have the strange beautiful experience of bowing in front of each other. He's very deaf now. Even ten years ago, he had to stick his microphone, connected somehow with his ear, right in your mouth. He somehow felt that the deeper he pushed it in the clearer he could hear you. I remember meeting him once, twelve to fifteen years ago, at a high meeting of European physicians, where I launched the idea of *Medical Nemesis*. How he got

there, I can't tell you. Somebody wanted to interview us, and, seeing that Kohr, because of his deaf-
ness, couldn't give an interview just seated in a bar,
this radio journalist somehow pulled us into a
ladies' toilet, locked the door, and did the interview
there. Kohr, angelic, found that here at last one could
get away from all that terrible noise in the building,
and didn't notice where we were.

CAYLEY: Why did you move to the United States?

ILLICH: I wanted to get away from Rome. I didn't
want to go into the papal bureaucracy, so I thought
of doing a postdoctoral thesis, which they call a
Habilitation in German universities, on alchemy in
the work of Albert the Great. There are some very
good documents at Princeton, and I had an invita-
tion. But then on my first day in New York, literally
the first evening, with some friends of my grandfather, I heard about Puerto Ricans. My hosts, who
lived on East 76th Street, in an old, traditional apartment building, said, "We have to move out, because
all these people are moving in here." And then the
black cook, speaking about her family — old Southern blacks — added, "We have to move out of Har-
lem because these Puerto Ricans are coming in." So
I spent the next two days up in the *barrio* on 112th
Street and 5th Avenue, 112th Street and Park Avenue, beneath the tracks of the New York Central,
where they had their market. Afterwards, I went to
Cardinal Spellman's office and asked for an assign-
ment to a Puerto Rican parish. And that's how I got
stuck in New York!

CAYLEY: Stuck?

ILLICH: Yes, I mean that these were my only five

years of acquaintance with what others might call real life.

CAYLEY: What made you decide to become a priest?

ILLICH: I don't know. I don't know about most of the important decisions in my life.

CAYLEY: You mean that?

ILLICH: Yes, to a point. It was something as unreasonable as sitting down with you to do an interview, after having sworn in the 1970s that I wouldn't do such things anymore.

CAYLEY: It was similarly impulsive?

ILLICH: Depending on which meaning you give to *impulse*. Impulse has had many meanings since the twelfth century. In Spanish, we have that word *ganas* — *porqué me da la gana*. You can't translate it. In German, you can say *Ich habe Lust*. In French, *J'ai envie*. English is chaste. It doesn't allow you to make a decision in your heart, and even less out of a feeling which comes from somewhere below the navel. That's what *ganas* are. I remember when I first learned the word. It was from little Mañe Estades, the daughter of a professor in Puerto Rico. She was four or five then, and I was sitting with her father, a dear friend. Her father says to the little girl, "Mañe, bedtime." Mañe says, "No me da la gana." And I ask him — this learned professor of philosophy — What does that mean, *gana*? And he said, "Ivan, it means different things for a man and a woman. When a woman tells a *caballero* '*no me da la gana*' or, I don't have *ganas*, a *caballero* doesn't ask anything further." Perhaps my study of gender began then.

CAYLEY: In New York, you formed a relationship with Cardinal Spellman, I think.

ILLICH: You're the third man to ask me that question. The other two both claimed they were writing biographies on Spellman. And I'll always give the same answer: For gossip purposes I don't give any information on dead people.

CAYLEY: All right.

ILLICH: But let me say a few things about him. I quickly understood that this was a pious man, very similar to other pious firemen, policemen, and similar second-generation Irish whom I met in Incarnation parish. Pious, with *all* the licence piety of that kind gives a man, forcing him to have a conscience and giving him excuses to justify, in conscience, what he does. He was certainly an unusually shrewd, bright man. He had a fantastic memory, which could also have made him president of the United States — that kind of ward politician's memory which is, I think, one of the important things you need to be a good politician in the United States and not just one of these silly guys who are lifted up. All that I saw in a minute.

CAYLEY: I've heard it said that he had a remarkable loyalty to you.

ILLICH: Oh, yes . . .

CAYLEY: Which some have regarded as improbable.

ILLICH: Yes. To Dorothy Day, too.[127] Let me hide behind Dorothy Day.

CAYLEY: You went as vice-rector to the Catholic University in Puerto Rico.

ILLICH: The rector knew that he was on his way out and got into a mess. I went there because they needed somebody who was neither Puerto Rican nor American. I was camouflage, window dressing.

I fitted them and it fitted me to have a place outside the United States in which I could begin to train personnel for New York — priests and nuns, certainly, but also school teachers, policemen, city planners, social workers, Protestant ministers, even a couple of rabbis to deal with the Puerto Rican immigrants flowing into New York at that moment. It seemed important to me that people in New York would know enough Spanish and would have breathed enough tropical air not to be frightened by these little brown chattering people intruding upon them.

CAYLEY: I take it that you had concluded early on that the Church and other agencies were not dealing with this very well.

ILLICH: I thought it was a scandal. And I was pretty much alone in the beginning. But Joe Fitzpatrick can tell you about this. Joe Fitzpatrick was then the man who ran the social science department at Fordham University. The two of us became very close friends. I think that if anybody wants to know about the history of Puerto Rican immigration in New York, then Fitzpatrick's book is an unusual achievement because it's so simple, so readable, and so thoroughly documented.[128]

CAYLEY: How did the transition from the Catholic University to what became CIDOC take place?

ILLICH: By 1959, I felt that I had done more or less what I wanted to do in Puerto Rico. I had established, at the Catholic University in Ponce, a major summer institute, which in fact ran on for twenty-five years, and I had created a few other very simple institutional bridges for people from Nueva Yorki,

[margin note: Illich's most vehement word, thus far]

which included, in a Puerto Rican view, the *barrio* of Chicago. I felt very much attached to Puerto Rico. It's the only place in the world — because you have asked me where my home is — where I would have said to other people, "Yes, here in Puerto Rico, we . . ." I would never say, "We Puerto Ricans . . ." but "Here in Puerto Rico, we . . ." I would never say that in the United States, or in Göttingen, or in Marburg, or in Mexico, or anywhere else. I would say, "Here, people do this." But in Puerto Rico, I said, "Here, in Puerto Rico, we wouldn't do that."

But the time had come, and a situation presented itself in which I felt that I had to intervene in a political way. The two Irish Catholic bishops, Bishop James Davis, a self-seeking, vain careerist in San Juan, and Bishop James McManus in Ponce, a well-meaning Irish turkey, had gotten themselves into politics by threatening excommunication for anybody who voted for a political party which didn't proscribe the sale of condoms in drugstores. And this was a month before the nomination of a Catholic, John Kennedy, as the presidential candidate of the Democratic Party. It was not that I wanted to support Kennedy. But I felt that it was highly unsound to allow the religious issue to creep back into American politics, just because Puerto Rico was the only place where two American bishops had an absolute Catholic majority as their subjects. At the same time, with the assistance of the papal nuncio responsible for the area, they had also sponsored the creation of a Christian Democratic–like party on the island. So I had to do something, since most people didn't take it seriously and those who did would not intervene. I attracted to myself the full odium of exploding that situation. I knew that I was sacrificing any possibility of doing anything publicly in Puerto Rico for many years without being mixed up with the memories of that political intervention.

CAYLEY: One of the things you were doing in Puerto Rico was running a language school which taught Spanish. What was your own first language?

ILLICH: Most people, throughout history, haven't learned one language to the exclusion of another. You learn to speak differently to a peasant and to a shoemaker. You speak differently to your mother, who comes from Burgundy, and to your father, who comes from Swabia. As a toddler, you speak differently with your nurse. It still happens today in India. You can't ask somebody "What is your language?" unless you grow up among the elite where English is spoken, and children are told, "Don't talk the bad language of your nurse," which might be Marathi. People forget that most of the world is still in the privileged condition of those of us who had the advantage of growing up in that area which before the war was called the Balkans, today Southeastern Europe. We were brought up mentally in the world where the Austro-Hungarian Empire with its seventeen languages bordered directly on the port of Istanbul, the seat of the sultan. My aunt always called it Czarigrad, the place where the emperor sits, the old Russian Slavonic way of referring to it. This was a multi-people, multi-language empire.

The idea of *Homo monolinguis* — one-languaged man — the idea of children having to grow into one system before we confuse them with another mental system, is an idea with which, unfortunately, many people are brought up now. Today, educational tracts, psychological tracts — when I speak of tracts, I mean those with which children are treated, textbooks, developmental psychology books — just take it for granted that man is born monolingual, and that he would be disturbed if he spoke from early childhood in two languages. This idea has crept into science as a certainty, as an assumption, and during the last twenty years it has become militantly dominant. As a historian, I'm trying to upset this idea, claiming that most people in Africa, in Asia, don't learn languages, they learn how to speak, and then they speak differently to their nurse and to their mother. The difference might be dialectal, might be word choice, but might also be — and most of the time was — something which linguists today call two languages from completely different extractions, and man was meant for this.

I noticed there was something happening — it must have been in 1974, at Rutgers University at a party, a faculty party after a talk of mine. A professor who looked very serious, somewhat pompous, older than I, asked me for the privilege of seeing me afterwards for a drink. I then went for this drink with him and he, hemming and hawing, said to me, "This is a very personal question I want to ask you. You know, I am a psychologist but you look quite balanced for a man who has been brought up multilingual." I answered, "Yes . . ."

So, at the first opportunity, I went to the library to look up bibliographies on multilingualism, and found out that there were, of course, many books, giving you citations, quotations, and comments to hundreds of articles on the subject. Most of them dealt with multilingualism either as a problem for the child, the parents, the state, the educator, or as a privilege which is acquired by people who learn a second or a third language under special circumstances and which should be shared with the many. This *completely* overlooks the fact that the whole hypothesis that *Homo monolinguis est*, this whole assumption about human nature might be a very recent invention related to the creation of nation-states.

So, as I always do on these occasions, I called together friends to discuss this question. I wish you could have been at one of the four meetings we've had thus far, starting out in Trento, in northern Italy — Austrians would say, in the southern valleys which the Italians took from us — at the Institute for Italo-Germanic Historical Research, run by a man whom you would like, Paolo Prodi. He's a major, very serious academic historian who kept his four children out of school, saying, "I want them to go somewhere where they can have a master." Therefore, he sent them to the conservatory where you have a master, not teachers. Three of them became musicians, two of them outstanding professional musicians, and on the side one of them also became a physicist.

Anyway, at his institute, we began to have seminars on the history of the construction of one-languaged man, monolingual man. Well, I've given you a circuitous answer through my own experiences. I didn't have a language.

CAYLEY: What can your professor at Rutgers have meant by "balanced"?

ILLICH: It came from the idea that language is a tool and the idea that when we speak we *communicate* with each other. I remember when the concept of communication really hit me for the first time. It was in Chicago, perhaps twenty years ago, at a meeting with social scientists at the University of Chicago. And there was a young man — he's pretty well known by now as one of the American Marxists who has given a new respectability to Marxist analysis; I have to respect what that guy has done in the meantime — but there he sat and said, "Illich, don't kid yourself, I don't read you. You don't communicate with me. I don't get your message." My immediate answer was, "Sir, I have *no* intention of being a transmitter." I thought that he was offending me by identifying me with a radio station. Only later did I realize that he had probably just seen his department renamed from English to the Department of Communications!

I told this story at the University of Freiburg at a seminar with Uwe Pörksen, the man who works on amoeba words.[129] This meeting had a strange composition: fifteen to twenty men of my age, and twenty or thirty students but with the middle range missing. When I told the story, none of the young people could understand what I was saying. They took it for granted that we are transmitting information to each other. But a quarter of the older people, each in his own way, remembered how much he had been struck the first time somebody imputed to him the qualities of a computer or a system.

CAYLEY: Let's go back to the main line of the story you were telling today. Why did you establish CIDOC?

ILLICH: There was one thing I had done in Puerto Rico which I wanted to continue. When you're a top administrator, you have to have something else to do with your left little finger. So I had begun a series of workshops and seminars to reflect on a fashion which was just coming in, namely, the fashion of soliciting volunteers in rich countries and sending them to poor countries. There was the Peace Corps, and then that *ghastly* letter which a Maryknoll priest called John Considine wrote and convinced Pope John XXIII to sign, commanding North American bishops and religious superiors to send one-tenth of their personnel to South America to save South America from communism!

There was some criticism of this, mainly from people who said this was a McCarthyite project, but it was on the point of becoming the great fashion. I wanted to look at what volunteers did — volunteers in development — in a completely different light. I asked myself — not about the average bureaucratic little puppet which most of these missionaries and papal volunteers and Peace Corps people were, people who were just seeking experience, avoiding the draft, or looking for adventure — I asked, What happens when the serious, the good ones, the responsible ones, are sent to Peru, come to a village, and try to live like the people? Four or five wells are dug and after three years, the guy goes home — very few people stayed more than three years in the same place, something like five percent. Everybody remembers Johnny or Catherine with whimsical plea-

sure, but everybody also learns that, for digging
wells, he knew how to do it because he had gone to
Harvard. Therefore, the volunteer becomes a demonstration model for high levels of service consumption when you send him to Latin America. I wanted
to point out the damage, the damage done by
volunteerism, the damage to the person who went
there through the establishment of a sense of supe-
riority, a savior complex, and the damage to the
image in the U.S. of what poor countries are.
Through volunteers this image came to be dependent not only on journalists but on people who
claimed that they could report with much better
knowledge of local situations — in the light of these
people *needing* us!

CAYLEY: So the purpose of CIDOC was subversive,
explicitly subversive, from the very beginning.

ILLICH: I created the place with the institutional
purpose of providing at that moment the most intensive, the best training in spoken Spanish available at *any* price, and in an atmosphere of reflection
so arranged that during a four-month intensive
course using the Foreign Service Institute Manual
for teaching Spanish, people would have to reflect
on the cultural reality of the country to which they
were going, and to look back on the United States
from outside its borders, often for the first time. I set
up the place, as I have run my life, in such a way that
it would be independent of any grants, charging the
institutions which sent people to us for Spanish
studies enough to have some extra income above
expenditures in order to build up the library and to
bring in every year a couple of dozen people of every

social class and orientation from outside Mexico, from south of the border. Our purpose was not to teach the students, but to allow our guests to talk with each other or with me, with the students participating in our conversation if they wished.

My institutional goal was to pick up the most generous men and women from the two dozen volunteer organizations which had sprung up and to offer them a *very* difficult course, creating an atmosphere which said, If you think that you have to learn Spanish, and if you want to learn it well, then see if you can make it at CIDOC. It was simply a filter to get those people who would most certainly learn Spanish and be able to throw out those whom we didn't want. I wanted to get the future leadership, the potential leadership, of the different organizations, have them live with me and my friends and colleagues for four months and, if possible, come to decide to upset their own program. I wanted to point out the unwanted side effects on people caught up in these programs, the potential damage they would do in Latin America, and how crazy the illusion was that better understanding, international understanding would happen because of their reports back to the U.S.

Simultaneously, I engaged — through the people whom I brought to Cuernavaca — in a variety of other organizational jobs. One of these was an international ridiculing campaign for people like yourself — or against people like yourself. We also wanted to encourage people who had the feeling "We really don't need that gringo" by giving them good arguments why. This was then interpreted as anti-Americanism, which it was not, or as communism, which it evidently was not, or as madness, which I leave to the psychiatrists to judge.

CAYLEY: This eventually created a scandal in the American Church.

ILLICH: Because there I was more successful. In the Roman Catholic Church I was more successful than in other institutions in gaining a significant minority for the idea that people should carry on anti-war, anti-Marines, anti-bank, anti-corporate activities *in* the United States, rather than in Latin America. I remember when one of these people, Dan Berrigan,[130] suddenly called up. I wasn't there. Lee Hoinacki, my right-hand man, took the phone call and made the arrangements. Berrigan had to get out of New York right away. Spellman wanted him out. Could he take refuge in Cuernavaca? A week later, I saw the newspaper articles: Spellman's policeman keeping Dan Berrigan locked up in his cellars in Cuernavaca! Dan stayed for a few weeks and I had difficulties convincing him that the likes of him and others weren't needed in South America and that perhaps they should go there as tourists. Well, he went and he had a marvellous trip on which he reported in a somewhat purplish but beautiful way. I'm not saying that he learned it from us, but he became my example of what people should do.

Volunteering was such a magnificent escape valve. People brought radical Christianity or, later, socialism to Latin America, instead of fighting for whatever they wanted in their own political context, where they felt so impotent.

I tried to tell people that if they went, they should

go as cynics. But there were, of course, exceptions. As we sit together and reflect on it, I can remember a dozen or two, out of the two thousand whom I personally observed, who were heroic and whom, in the Middle Ages, I would have recommended for the catalogue of saints. There was, for example, a certain Helen, who went with the Papal Volunteers for a period of three years, into the high Andes, and then applied for another three years. She was accused and persecuted by her own organization and the U.S. government, simply for the example she gave. Along with a Peruvian woman, she attended dying people for six years, sitting up with them when they were beyond being able to speak and all they could seek was somebody who held their hand. Well, she did this, instead of engaging in community organization, as they wanted her to do. Helen has remained to this day one of the pillars to which I hold on.

CAYLEY: I recall an essay in *Celebration of Awareness* called "The Seamy Side of Charity," which made the case you've been outlining here against Church involvement in development. Did that create quite a stir in the Church?

ILLICH: Yes, but it was written and launched for that purpose. There was then an organization, which was *most* attractive to the enlightened people because it presented itself as the new Church going left, after the Council. This organization claimed to take the State Department seriously about international co-operation and tried to push it in an anti-imperialist direction.[131] Poor old, by then slightly benighted, Cardinal Cushing made a speech at their

annual meeting in Boston that year. I knew that
Irishman! So I wrote that pamphlet you refer to and
sent it up with one of my secret weapons, Betsie
Hollants. She was a lady twenty-five years older
than I, originally from Bruges, multilingual — she
had worked at the U.N. — a person of political
engagement, and during those years our Foreign
Secretary. During the war she was in the underground, providing the people who had to hide with
false identities by training them to wear religious
habits in a convent. An extraordinary, powerful
woman. So I sent her to the Boston meeting with
about a thousand copies of the article, which had
just been published in *America* a few days earlier. It
was meant to destroy that well-meaning organization, to delegitimize it by making fun of it. I always
found that if I had to intervene in public controver-
sies, then the one type of planned violence in which
I could engage was to destroy lies through laughter.

CAYLEY: You opposed the left-wing Catholic movement which was emerging at that time. What was
your view of the place of the Church in society?

ILLICH: When I left New York and went to Puerto
Rico, I went there, first, as vice-rector of a *Catholic*
university. But I knew that I couldn't possibly engage in an educational, administrative job there
without considering it primarily as a political activity. So I refused to preside over a Christian community as a priest. For my own purposes, and because
I liked to do it, I bought a little hut for twenty dollars
in a fishing village, Playa Cortada, and I said Sunday
mass for them. It was a little village of poor fisher-
men who earned most of their money working in a

sugarcane factory for a couple of months a year. That was a good experience, but the moment I went to Puerto Rico in 1956 I got out of any kind of official relationship to a bishop for whom I would work in the pastoral care of his people. I didn't want to get mixed up in a conflict between the priestly office of making the other-worldly unity and brotherhood of the liturgy real and my personal stance as a politician. There was no danger of getting the people of Playa Cortada mixed up in my proposal to transfer university budgets back to the primary educational system.

CAYLEY: Why did you suspend your work as a priest altogether?

ILLICH: In 1967 I received formal documents from the Roman Curia, which I knew were cribbed from CIA reports which had been leaked to the Holy See.[132] I said, You have made a scandal out of me. I will never again, in *any* way, engage in *any* action which the Roman Catholic Church considers that of a priest. I refuse *any* privilege and *any* duty within the liturgical system of the Roman Church and, much more, within the administrative, clerical system of that Church. I will just keep my distance. Destiny has brought me into the situation where I cannot do otherwise.

CAYLEY: You're referring to this indictment that was drawn up against you by the Holy Office?

ILLICH: Yes, some silly Roman business, but that is all past. My position, of course, couldn't be understood because people always thought that I was speaking as a churchman. But, since 1960, I had refused to speak as a churchman. If trappings of importance were heaped on me, I said, that's none of my business.

CAYLEY: So what does that say about what you think the role of the Church is?

ILLICH: It's a historical idea, not something ahistorical. Concretely, this has to be an extremely historical issue. Let me tell you a story. During the Second Vatican Council I worked with a man named Suenens, then the cardinal of Malines-Brussels. The Pope had asked him to be the president of a group of four cardinals who moderated the Council. Much earlier, Suenens had known me pretty well through a variety of circumstances, and he asked me to come to Rome as one of the direct advisors of this committee. We met every day during the second and third sessions. One morning, I asked him if we could have a cup of coffee together up at Quattro Fontane, where he was staying at a little Belgian college. I said to him, "I'm leaving now. Yesterday you proved to me that this Council is incapable of facing the issues which count, while trying hard to remain traditional."

The day before, in the aula of St. Peter's, the bishops had accepted the fact that the document which would come out on the Church and the world would say that the Church could not as yet condemn governments for keeping atomic bombs, that is, for keeping tools of genocide . . . for the moment.

It was a wise decision, *world*-wise.

And I gave Suenens a little caricature which somebody had drawn up for me. In that cartoon you see five popes, with their characteristic noses, one behind the other, all pointing with one finger at one of two objects standing there — an already slightly flaccid penis with a condom filled with semen hanging on it, and an atomic rocket, ready for takeoff. In the balloon was written, "*It's* against nature!" I am proud to have been and to be associated with, and to be loyal to, an agency, a *worldly* agency, which still has the courage to say, even today, "It's against nature." The finger might be pointing at the wrong object.

There is my issue. I do not believe that the major churches, as organizations today, can take the stand demanded by the times, on the principles they hold. Just as I'm proud to be an Illich, I'm proud to be a Roman Catholic, even though I am rooted also in the Eastern Church. That island from which I come is one of the very few places where Rome permitted, after the Council of Trent, the Roman mass — which was established at the Council of Trent — to be read in Slavonic, in old Slavonic. I've increasingly been certain, as I've grown older, that it's good to be very consciously a remainder of the past, one who still survives from another time, one through whom roots still go far back, and not necessarily examined roots. I'm aware of the tremendous privilege of coming from certain traditions, and of having been deeply *imbued* by them.

CAYLEY: Today, organizations of bishops do denounce nuclear war. In Canada, they've made what is considered a very important statement on the economy. How do you view these things?

ILLICH: They're very interesting but beside the point. What I need from Catholic bishops is to ask themselves — as Wolfgang Sachs does — How did it happen that this major organization could accept usury? Not the kind of statements they can make today about the limits and proper ethics in the *use* of usury. I'm not saying that we should go back to the Middle Ages, but the Church has taken an anti-economic stance, and not just a stance in favor of a just economics, throughout its history. I wish that I could serve the Roman Catholic Church in thinking through and expressing those things which the Church cannot discuss in an official manner where majorities count. It's not a question of democracy, it's not a question of committee decisions, it's a question of witness.

The Canadian bishops, and the U.S. bishops, have made *very* interesting statements about the economy. They are *certainly* of a higher level of decency and intelligence than this absolutely *crawling* statement by the Pope, *Sollicitudo rei socialis*, where he slaps evangelical sentences on the assumptions of modern development economics and sings with opportunism in the chorus of people who decry the demise of development.[133]

Certainly there is some very intelligent popular education possible in thinking about economic issues. What I would expect to come from the message of the Gospel is the strength to look with a spirit of independence at what the bishops of Canada take for granted, namely, that the economy runs our lives. I'm not asking them to make nice statements about the atomic bomb which are *world*-wise and practically necessary. It seems to me that a *minimum* of decency — not of *Gospel* decency but simple basic decency — demands that one speak an *absolute no*, as Bishop Hunthausen has done so beautifully. *An absolute no.*[134] But Hunthausen is a tolerated outsider, and the American bishops have nothing to say about him except to tell Rome, "You may not touch one of us." All this shows you *not* what's wrong with the way the Church administers its personnel, but what the limits are of an official Church which wants to intervene on the issues of today. This is a time for martyrdom, this is not a time for solemn committee statements. Because of the methods by which their positions are arrived at, they cannot, by definition, take the moral stance which corresponds to the vocation implied in the Gospel.

This is not an attempt to speak *against* the Church. It is an attempt to raise the fundamental issue of what a Church with this tradition represents in the world of today. That is why I try to lead my students to an understanding that most of the key ideas which make the contemporary world into that unique reality which it is have a Christian origin.

CAYLEY: You haven't expressed this quite the way I expected. In an essay you published in the 1960s called "The Vanishing Clergyman" you said that in order to celebrate the mystery of faith, the Church must abstain utterly from using its power as an institution.

ILLICH: Yes, I thought so twenty-five years ago. I thought it had to abstain from using its power even if it meant not doing whatever good its power might accomplish. Today I wonder if this is not an impossible demand to make on a Church built so solidly on the certainties of the modern day and age. This is the reason why, out of a deep respect for the corruption of the best which becomes, in a way, the worst, some of us might have the vocation of testifying to our love of the Church by making ourselves completely powerless outside its context.

III
A Catastrophic Break

CAYLEY: Throughout your career, you've been concerned with what Marshall McLuhan called the fallout from technology. How do you see the question of technology today?

ILLICH: I've answered this question many times over the last twenty-five years. I think, from year to year, I've answered it differently. The most straightforward answer I could give now would be to say that sometime in the next year I want to take two months to write up a commentary on an early twelfth-century manuscript, *De Variis Artibus*, by Theophilus Presbyter, an anonym, who lived on the middle Weser River of what is today West Germany.

CAYLEY: How can you call him anonymous if you've named him?

ILLICH: Because he calls himself Theophilus Presbyter — the God-loving priest — which is obviously
not what his mother called him. If Theophilus is his
real name, then he must have been a Greek monk
who landed there and who wrote, as far as I know,
Western history's first book on tools in general.
There are books in antiquity and the Middle Ages
like *De Arte Metalica* — on metal-working — *De Arte
Bellica* — how to make war — or *De Arte Aedificato-
ria* — how to build — but the idea of perceiving tools
as something you can intellectually separate from
the hands of shoemakers or smiths or journeymen
who use them appears with Theophilus in 1128. At
the same time in Paris, Hugh of St. Victor, a dear
friend of mine, also produces a philosophy of tools
in his *Epitome Dindimi*. This is a discourse he sets up
between Dindymus — a guy whom he invents, a
Brahmin king, the king of all the gymnosophists, the
naked sages — and a pupil. Here also tools are
discussed as tools.

Now why do I want to finish this paper, on which
I've taken notes for the last fifteen years? I first
stumbled across a reference to this guy fifteen years
ago reading Lessing,[135] who had discovered the
manuscript of Theophilus Presbyter two hundred
years before. I want to do this because I have a
suspicion that the concept of the tool and the theological concept of the sacrament are intimately related. In fact, Hugh of St. Victor, the first theoretician
of mechanical science in *De Sciencia Mechanica*, was
also the first one who clearly spelled out the idea of
the seven sacraments. Out of the hundreds and
thousands of carefully formalized blessings and

priestly curses of the devil and such things he picked out seven which, he said, did something totally different from other blessings. Less than a hundred years later, at the Fourth Lateran Council in 1215, it became a dogma of the Church. I believe that there is a relation between the idea of a tool, which does what you want it to do, and a sacrament, which is a sign God allows men to place but which does what God wants to do, more or less independently from the ability, the power, the intention, or even the decency of the priest who administers it. These two concepts are characteristically Western, and it is silly to speak about the perception of the tool as tool in the same way outside of Western history since 1215.

For decades now I've been involved in analyzing what tools do to society. I wrote my first book on the subject, *Tools for Conviviality*, when I was invited to join the deliberations of the Club of Rome. I said, "No, I have something more important to do. You people are concerned with what tool use does to the environment. You are concerned only about material products and their unwanted side effects. I'm obsessed by the idea of what the tools used by the service producers do to society. Let me speak for the moment about schools," I said to them. "Later on I'll handle transportation and medicine." (I then thought also of the law, but I didn't want to do any more than necessary.) What are the inevitable side products of service-generating tools?

People then began to speak about them as systems, but I stayed with my concept of tools. We have spoken already about schooling, which inevitably degrades more people than it privileges. This is an unwanted side effect, like the unwanted side effects of chemical agriculture, which generates more grain in a given five-year period, with a certain number of workers, in a certain area, but also poisons the earth, leeches the soil, and does many other things.

I first wrote on a general theory of tools in a pamphlet, an essay. I wanted to revive the art of pamphleteering on the intellectual level. I didn't want to write social criticism or philosophical reflections. From the beginning, I said I wanted to write a pamphlet which would make people discuss the question. So I wrote *Tools for Conviviality*. I chose the title consciously. The old owner and director of Harper's squinted with his eyes and said, "Mr. Illich, are you acquainted with American slang?" I said, "Yes, I know how and why I choose my words . . ."

CAYLEY: Did he mean that, for most people, convivial means getting tipsy?

ILLICH: That was Silvers, the editor of *The New York Review*, who said, "This is not a correct use of the word. Convivial means only tipsy joviality." But the aristocratic American director of Harper's was of course fully aware that tools — your tools — are between your legs . . .

CAYLEY: Ah. But tell me, while you're interrupted here, why you chose the terms *tools* and *convivial*. At first glance, a hospital or a school is not a tool.

ILLICH: It is an engineered device to achieve a purpose, and I needed a simple word anybody would understand. I thought that most people, if they weren't too prejudiced and made a little bit of effort, would understand smilingly, and say, ah-ha!

Schools lead to schooled society. I remember once when I discussed this in a slum in Chicago at the Urban Training Center, and a little black girl got up and said, "Yeah, yeah, you're right, we're all schooled up." And I answered, "Yeah, we're all schooled up." So after lunch, I see all these kids there with buttons, "SCHOOL YOU!"

For thirty years now I've tried to figure out how to use ordinary language in that slightly obscene way that makes people see something new without them knowing exactly why. I've tried to discover very precise terms that let people say what they want to say. It was with the hope of doing this that, against the advice of all my editors and all my colleagues, I stuck to the word *tools* for a means to an end which people plan and engineer. It is not just a stick picked up in the street. I call a revolver, a gun, or a sword a tool for aggression. I don't call every stone which lies around such a tool. There is a poem I like of Robert Lowell's on this theme.[136] I wish I could recite it for you.

Lowell was several times in Cuernavaca, and I had him meet with Francisco Julião. Julião was a peasant leader from the northeast of Brazil who had to flee during the dictatorship. Julião spoke to Lowell and explained to him that the only violence which does not corrupt you is that which you do without tools. The women who stood in front of the prison did not engage in a violence that demeaned them when they picked up the first stones and sticks they found to storm the prison.

I tried to make it clear that there are things we do not use as tools. My claim is that when we really speak to each other, we do not *use* language, we do not pick from a code, as the professional linguists think that we do. We talk. In *Tools for Conviviality*, I presented a meditation on how tools, when they grow beyond a certain intensity, inevitably turn from means into ends, and frustrate the possibility of the achievement of an end. I tried to establish the concept of counterproductivity, the fact that a given tool — for instance, a transportation system — when it outgrows a certain intensity, inevitably removes more people from the purpose for which this tool was created than it permits to profit from its advantages. Accelerated traffic, for commuter purposes — that is, compulsory traffic — inevitably increases, for the great majority of society, the time they have to spend every day in going from here to there. And only a few people get the privilege of being almost omnipresent in the world.

I analyzed medicine as a tool, coming to the conclusion that once you medicalize expectations and experience beyond a certain point, medicine inevitably generates more misery, more pain, and more disability than it cures and at the same time decreases people's ability to engage in the art of suffering or in the art of dying. I've analyzed counterproductivity from its various angles. That's what I did in *Tools for Conviviality*.

CAYLEY: Was Jacques Ellul an influence?

ILLICH: Certainly, as you suggest, I picked up on Ellul. Jacques Ellul has been, especially then, a very great teacher of mine even though I discovered him only when I was already sitting down to write *Tools for Conviviality*. People sometimes ask me, "What is your difference?" I always say that he is and remains terribly Calvinist, gloomy. I have no expectations from technology, but I believe in the beauty, in the creativity, in the surprising inventiveness of people, and I continue to hope in them. But Ellul's thoughts and mine definitely developed more or less along the same lines. Ellul, by the beginning of the 1980s, had come to see technological society as explicable *only* as a perversion of Christian ideals. This was exactly at the moment when I had begun to realize that conscious engineering — consciousness about means which have the ability to become efficient elements — was the common root of both technology *and* sacramental theology. Sacraments, according to Christian theology before Catholics and Protestants separated, are efficacious signs. They do, inevitably, what they symbolize.

I became increasingly interested in analyzing not what tools *do* but what they *say* to a society and why society accepts what they say as a certainty. If, therefore, I tell you that today I am concerned with a commentary on that twelfth-century text, my main purpose in doing so is to point out that we have come to live in a society where *the* most important effect which our major tool systems have is to shape our view of reality and to generate in us a set of certainties.

CAYLEY: Can you say more of what you mean by certainties?

ILLICH: Yes, that's very easy. Two years after having finished *Tools for Conviviality*, I wanted to develop one dimension of that book somewhat further. So I wrote *Energy and Equity*. Again, a pamphlet. A pamphlet written because of a request from a friend to contribute on any subject I liked to *Le Monde*. I called it, from the beginning, *Énergie et Équité*, and the article began with the statement, "The energy crisis is an illusion." I met the director of this very venerable Parisian paper on the second of May of that year for lunch,[137] after having deposited the manuscript with him the day before on a trip through Paris. The man was very happy. He told me that they would put it on the first page and run it over three days. I agreed with this, and then I said, "You have a great journal — Couldn't you give me some editorial advice?" "Well, you know how to write," he said . . . then, finally, "Monsieur, I have one thing to say. Usually, when we begin a journalistic article, we don't begin it with an expression nobody knows. 'La crise d'énergie,' M. Illich. Q'est-ce que c'est?" What is that, the energy crisis? Well, I said, that word stays there. Seven weeks later, he ran a special issue on the energy crisis! I'm telling you this only as a story to locate for you when this was. This was very far back.

Now, in that book, I analyze what transportation does to a society — inevitably, irremediably — unless you keep it below bicycle speed. If I look back at this book, many years later, I am very much surprised. I really took for granted, for instance, that it is possible to compare a motor and a human being, because there are no motors as energy-efficient as a human being on a bicycle. I based this on White's paper in which he demonstrated that sturgeons are the most energy-efficient locomotion-producing "engines," even more effective than people who walk, but people on a bicycle are even more energy-effective.[138] I really believed then that it made sense to calculate how much energy people consume when they ride on a bicycle. I completely forgot that people don't need more energy inputs or more food whether they ride to school or not.

CAYLEY: I'm not sure what you're saying . . .

ILLICH: I'm saying that if I walk or don't walk, I'm not an energy consumer. As Jean Robert put it last year, "In India, cow shit is not energy. It's culture, it's fuel, it's sacred."[139]

CAYLEY: Oh, I see. You're talking about certainties you once held and now renounce.

ILLICH: Yes. I was one of the first people who underlined the possibility of calculating the energy efficiency of human beings. It was idiotic. Even more idiotic, if I look back at that book, *Energy and Equity*, was the fact that I had not understood that locomotion is a very modern concept. People have walked in all societies, but they had no way of moving through a three-dimensional Cartesian space. It didn't exist. From anthropology we know that most people do not perceive space as three-dimensional. Nor is it possible, until much later, to conceive of walking as moving from one spot described by a Cartesian triplet to another point described by a triplet — establishing a distance over which you move yourself. Conceiving human beings as engaging in locomotion when they walk leads to something quite common in transportation books where one speaks about feet as the instrument for self-locomotion. Well, you immediately see in what a maddening world we live. So my reflection on tech-

nology increasingly moves from a study of what it
does towards what technology necessarily *says*.

The prevalence of wheels says that I am engaging
in locomotion when I walk and that I'm doing the
same thing whether I walk from here to the university with you, reciting poetry, or whether I take a car
and drive there. Thinking of myself as engaging in
locomotion places me in Cartesian space; and, by
placing myself in Cartesian space, I limit my experience, and my sense of reality, to Cartesian space.
That's just one example.

I still stick to the expression — but not to the mood
in which it was used — of Jean-Paul Sartre: I will feel
forever responsible for what has been done to me,
not only by other people but also by the milieu in
which I live. It is my duty *not* to be constrained into
three-dimensional space.

What would happen to me there? I would lose the
interiority of my heart. I have no co-ordinates —
Cartesian co-ordinates — in my heart. But I want it
to grow and become comfortable and accommodat-
ing for other people. As interesting as the reflections
of modern cosmology might be, I understand myself
much better when I accept another model, out of
which my culture came, the model of contingency
in which God holds creation in his hand, as you can
see on any Romanesque or Gothic apse.

CAYLEY: *Tools for Conviviality* is your clearest political statement. It suggests that the political and legal
means to achieve your vision of a society which
respects a whole series of natural scales are actually
at hand. In your subsequent work you have relent-
lessly criticized the entire vocabulary of contempo-

rary politics. Do you see political possibilities arising from your work today?

ILLICH: What do you mean by politics?

CAYLEY: I mean a way of acting that could be conveyed to a majority.

ILLICH: Let me see if I've understood your question. You say that in *Tools for Conviviality* I came as close as I could to establishing some principles for possible political action around 1972. Do I expect to do better today? No. I then believed in the possibility of a true flipping in consciousness, of which I spoke at the end of *Tools for Conviviality*. Today I fear that many of the things which made me believe in this have changed.

At that time, I still used such words as *in society*. I wouldn't use them anymore. But at the same time, the very concepts I then forged for myself are now hard to grasp. Many of the certainties by which people lived in 1973 are *gone*. This generates deep cynicism, confusion, and inner void among people who live in an intensely monetarized society, like the urban United States. But it also creates extraordinary opportunities for a new way of existence which I see emerging in Mexico, and in a dozen other places in the world also, places which I know somewhat and can make a judgement about. People can use the so-called benefits of development for *their* purposes, not for the purposes they were made for. They can cannibalize cars. They can use junk. The educational system in most countries has become so corrupt that they can easily buy certificates and diplomas if they want them for a specific purpose. They don't have to go to school to learn something.

There are other ways to get certificates, and, increasingly, the system accommodates that because it can't afford the schools. Or there are ways to cheat at the exams.

People begin to see that it would be stupid to go to a hospital when you are sick. It's incredible with what speed all the things which Americans call quackery — from homeopaths to osteopaths to herbalists to vegetarian restaurants — have grown up all through Latin America, mainly because they're cheaper. And as we know from sociology, when people have chosen to buy something, they'll defend it as superior to what other people have, no matter if others spent much more than they did, unless they are in a highly monetarized society.

When I wrote *Tools for Conviviality*, I got very deeply disturbed because I foresaw so clearly trends and the convergence of trends which by now are obvious to everybody. But I was lacking in trust in the extraordinary creativity of people and their ability to live in the midst of what frustrates bureaucrats, planners, and observers. Mexico City, for instance, has grown in these fifteen years from a city of four million to a city of twenty million. A city of twenty million should not be governable. But people still come from all over the world to figure out how Mexico City is governed, instead of trying to figure out *how come* a city like that can survive *without* government. A city like that should be paralyzed.

People in Mexico, especially during the last three or four years — just ask Gustavo Esteva[140] — have decided by the hundred thousands not to seek jobs at a distant place, but to somehow eke out a living close to home in order not to waste their time on transportation.

In 1954, the UNESCO, at its regional meeting in South America, complained that the main obstacle to education was the indifference of parents to sending their children to school. Fifteen years later, they had to notice that the demand for schooling exceeded the number of available classrooms by seven times. But today I know from my own experience that there is widespread cynicism, not among old people — grandparents or great-grandparents — but among people who went through school, and who don't see any reason why their children should go through the same experience. People can see what scientists and administrators can't.

CAYLEY: When you wrote *Tools for Conviviality*, you laid out a political program for inverting the structure of tools, as you put it. And now you're saying, I think, that it happened, but not in the way you anticipated.

ILLICH: It happened in a way I had not anticipated. In the last words of that book I said that I knew in which direction things would happen but not what would bring them to that point. At that time I believed in some big, symbolic event, in something similar to the Wall Street crash. Instead of that, it is hundreds of millions of people just using their brains and trusting their senses. We now live in a world in which most of those things that industry and government do are misused by people for their own purposes.

CAYLEY: In *Tools for Conviviality*, you also speculate about what will happen if we don't take command

of our tools, and you issue this rather chilling warning that "engineered obsolescence can break all
bridges to a normative past."[141]

ILLICH: I'm having a very funny experience in talking to you. I said, yes, I will talk to you, I will expose
myself to a conversation between two friends in
which one, namely you, takes the initiative and
other people listen in. I will do it because you asked
me. In the 1960s I trained myself to be interviewed,
and to get out of the interview what I wanted. Then
in the '70s I gave up interviews. I refused to appear
on television, I refused any major radio interview —
with the exception of a technical thing I did — and
also abstained from newspaper interviews. I felt
somehow that it was something I didn't want to do.
I know how to write. I know what I want to write
about. Let people read me. I don't want to reach
anybody else. This is still my attitude. But you think
that you can do something. So I said, let's do it!

Now when you question me I no longer feel offended by your pretence of pulling out of me things
you want to know from me for the benefit of other
people. Fifteen years ago, I was offended by such a
procedure. I felt it was a cultural offence which one
shouldn't submit to. Now I feel fascinated by your
questioning because I see that without submitting to
this particular kind of inquisition, I would have no
need to go back and see what I wrote in *Tools for
Conviviality*. It is quite painful, but you know that
book better than I. I haven't read it for seventeen
years. I remember once or twice having to quote
something from it and looking it up.

There was a time in my life when I was taken up

by campaigns — a campaign against the arrogance of sending American volunteers to South America, a campaign to make people think about the unwanted side effects of development, and the incredible damage done by establishing what they then called demonstration models for high service consumption in the form of volunteers throughout the Third World. There was a time when I was on a campaign trying to make people reflect on what schools do, on what education implies, on the unhealthy results of the medicalization of society, and so on. This campaigning period of my life extended from, let's say, 1962 to 1972. And during that time, at a certain moment I came to feel like a jukebox. Arguments I had made a year or two before on a 33 rpm record were now down to a short one, to a 45 rpm. When I arrived in front of my audience, I told them, "Just push the right combination of buttons, I'll deliver what you called me here to do and then, let's talk. Let's get it over with so we can have our discussion."

Now, as you sit here, after having read my work carefully, and grill me on it, I see that in an examination of what Illich has said and meant, you would pass with flying colors, and I wouldn't get a passing mark! I feel embarrassed and fascinated when I look at an old book. With a very pointed pencil, I succeeded in saying many things quite well. But the context and my way of saying things have changed. So I close the book and put it away. This is the strange experience that I'm having at this moment. You have asked me about a man who has been. It is I, yes, I take full responsibility. I wrote these books as pamphlets for the moment. It's amazing, in a certain way, that they should still be around. It's very lovely. It honors me. But they are dead, written stuff of that time. When I wrote *Tools for Conviviality* I was in the middle of a political struggle in South America, actually being shot at and beaten up with chains because I ridiculed the Peace Corps and the volunteers the Pope sent down there, and because I questioned the desirability of making the professional state of the art of northern countries into the norm of how schools or hospitals or thinking about health should develop in South America. I was in a different situation, and I saw certain things much more clearly than I see them now.

I then spent several years learning Oriental languages, and getting my feet for long periods on roads which I walked in southeast Asian countries. For a short time I had the dream that what I really should do would be to describe the history of Western ideas in an Oriental language that was far enough away from those languages which I know that I would really get some distance. I thought of Chinese, and found out that I'm too old. I ran into a man, Jean Domenach,[142] who told me, "Ivan, if you really want to alienate yourself, really want to look at it from the outside, learn Japanese!" I found out that my brain was already too used up. I couldn't do it. And, even if I could have done it, I probably wouldn't have been able to write the stuff I wanted.

I found that northern India — when I finally got enough into the languages and people — wasn't far enough away, and was already too British to do what I wanted to do, so I moved another step further, into the Middle Ages. I went back to the twelfth century, which I had always loved, to certain authors, like Héloise, like Abelard, like Hugh of St. Victor, all these names whom I have been affectionately acquainted with, and began to teach medieval intellectual history — for almost ten years — in French, and mostly in German. I wanted to figure out what would happen if I described a modern transportation system to a very brilliant and adaptable and sensitive monk of 1135. So I began to play with Latin dialogues in which I explained *de transportatione* and *de educatione* in order to get a certain distance and to become a migrant between two space times or, as Einstein says, spimes, our certainties and that other world of certainties. Always, however, I remained mainly concerned with looking at tools because they existed then as now. I couldn't speak about them in Chinese, even if I knew the language. Needham has shown us why.[143] When he speaks about Chinese technology, it's something other than what we talk about as technology. Just think of his many pages on seminal retention in intercourse as a technique. Astrology is not what we usually think of as technology. A tool is a tool is a tool to a certain degree only.

CAYLEY: You alluded to some incident in which you were attacked with chains?

ILLICH: I take for granted that people know that during the later 1960s and well into the early 1970s, we had — at CIDOC, in Cuernavaca — a lot of violent attempts . . .

CAYLEY: I never heard about it.

ILLICH: Well, that's for historians. Everybody sur-

vived it. I always insisted on discipline with my
collaborators. We have no idea who hates us. We
know who our friends are. Never think about who
might want to do something evil to you. If you go
under, too bad for you. Nobody went under.

CAYLEY: How did you get this idea of learning first
Chinese, then Japanese? You thought that you were
too locked into your own certainties?

ILLICH: Exactly. I know how much help it gives me
to switch from one European language to another
when discussing, for instance, needs. In French it's
besoin, but Spanish doesn't have such a word for it.
I expected that by writing about the history of ideas
in Europe in a very foreign language, I would get
entirely new perspectives, I would look at it from a
different frame. The idea, at the age of forty-seven,
that I could imitate Joseph Needham and say, well,
I can learn a language like Chinese was, of course,
completely wrong. Needham learned it to study
Chinese documents. I wanted to learn it in order to
write in Chinese about Europe. It couldn't be done.
There have been a few times in my life when I've
had projects which I had to give up, following my
grandfather's advice, "Never throw good money
after bad, good time after bad."

The Indian experience surprised me because of
how easy it was to begin to read, to understand, and
to feel somewhat at home there — at home is not
really the word but to know how to move there. But
I discovered that writing about Western ideas in any
of the languages of modern India, or even in an
ancient language, made no sense, because the se-
mantic fields of Indian languages were already pro-

foundly Anglicized. That project failed me, so I went back, humbly and happily, to my own Latin. In my studies, for almost ten years, I kept all my notes in Latin — kitchen Latin, medieval Latin.

I enjoy that particular generation of people born around 1100, whose teachers made them read classics, even though they were barely capable of writing a decent Latin sentence. Each one of them by 1120, 1130, 1140, had developed his own personal, beautiful Latin style, in a language into which he had not been born. This has always fascinated me. So I found it very pleasurable to teach the history of pilgrimage to Santiago, or the iconography and architecture of the middle of the twelfth century, to German students who were well equipped to follow me. And I found this move into a *totally* different world an extremely useful way to gain distance from the present.

CAYLEY: I'd like to return to the question I was asking when you were suddenly struck by the odd situation I had put you in by quoting old texts that are fresher in my mind than in yours. What I was quoting was your prediction that if our society continued on its present track we would in effect cease to be human beings. The way you put it was that we would "break all bridges to a normative past."

ILLICH: This has happened. Today increasingly people occupy a new dimensionless cybernetic space. It finds a cynical, cold expression in those bright people who say we cannot any longer conceptualize what it means to be human. We can only create icons for it, science-fiction icons. The best way to speak about a modern person is to speak about a cybernetic biological organism, a cyborg. Donna Haraway, a very bright historian of science, makes this point clearly in an article about the modern woman as a cyborg.[144]

When I wrote the phrase you quote, the break between the contemporary type of modernity — industrial society at the point of becoming a cybernetic society — and the many pasts which have existed in the world, including our own tradition, was already extremely deep. Sometimes I use the mathematician René Thom's catastrophe theory to illustrate this break. My mathematician colleague, Costas, disapproves because he says you can't use mathematical terms as metaphors, but if I ignore his threat then there has been a catastrophic break between the early nineteenth century and the century in which I live.[145] The mental space in which I live is a different one than that of Goethe or of Schiller. The conceptual and perceptual topology in which I live is noncontinuous with the past. The axioms that spin out the space in which I move are not the same axioms my grandfather still took for granted.

The certainties by which we can talk to each other without ever mentioning them — because they lie, so to speak, beyond the horizon of our attention — are different today than fifty or a hundred years ago. And research on the history of these implicit certainties which tries to pick up the warp and the woof of these percepts will show that these warps, in our perception, run in a new direction. We woof our conversation into a warp that is incomparable to the warp of any other period because it's made, so to speak, of nylon threads.

CAYLEY: I was also asking whether you think that those who didn't jump off the bus in 1970 ended up going over a cliff. When you say — in your essay on Epimetheus[146] — that Man, capital M, the archetype, himself is at stake or at risk, you're not just saying that we are entering another epoch-specific mental space, another mental topology among many possible human topologies.

ILLICH: No.

CAYLEY: You're saying there's a chance that we will leave the human, in any normative sense, behind.

ILLICH: Yes, only in 1988 I wouldn't any longer be able to speak so easily of man. Not because I would say "he" or "she," not at all, it's just that I have become more prudent. I've learned a few things. But what you describe is absolutely true and it is now symbolically being enacted in genetic engineering with the dream of creating people.

I have become increasingly silent in public because I have more and more learned to recognize that even very careful and traditional use of words does not allow me to bespeak the percepts my grandfather knew, because they aren't there anymore. And in a society in which we fantasize — when we speak about genetic engineering — about creating people who look like us but in fact are not descendants of any parents, we go much further than the last generation, who believed that you could have parents without having communities of households.

There is a man called Robert Brungs you might want sometime to interview. He's extraordinary, an outsider even among his own Jesuits.[147] Brungs has a theological argument, which says: I will not accept genetic engineering because I will not accept the existence of people who don't belong to the human family which was redeemed by God through Jesus. That's a very theological argument.

Dirk von Boetticher and I will give a seminar at the University of Chicago in November on the social creation of "life" during the last hundred years, the creation of that substantive something which people believe is there when they say "a life," and on what this does to perception of the human person.[148] Doctors now feel responsible for *a* life, from sperm to worm, or from fertilization to organ harvest, rather than for a suffering person. At the seminar, we will reflect on what happens when "a life" becomes a subject within the state, or *a* life becomes a citizen. We will discuss what it means when medical management no longer deals with persons but with a manageable construct from before birth to after brain death.

This is just one example of a number of — I don't know if I should call them concepts — of *constructs* which are of an epistemologically explosive nature. These are deeply corrupting images that I will not allow to enter into conversation except to exorcise them. When the conversation takes place in front of me, I either ask the people to stop or I leave. I believe that by careful consideration of old texts, I can still bring students out of the world which we take for granted and show them that contemporary English, the English we speak on the street, is no longer able to translate a Latin text of the twelfth century. I try to make them see that they could make such a translation only with an older, now nearly dead English which has at best a marginal existence among us today. This, of course, makes me very unpopular with many creative authors. I do this in order to make these students aware that virtuous behavior today might mean something different than at any previous time in history.

I live with the refusal not only to say certain things but also to use certain words or to permit certain feelings to creep into my heart. I cannot allow myself to meditate on the atomic bomb without going under. Reflection on certain things we take for granted is, in my opinion, acceptance of self-destruction, of burning out your heart. And in addition to these easy-to-speak-about things, which cannot be discussed but only exorcised — such as genetic engineering, such as the atom bomb — there are other things, other realities which, once you accept that there might be intolerable realities, come very close to these destructive devices. Most of what's going on at this moment in so-called bioethics, for example, belongs, in my opinion, to this area of apocalyptic randiness. I don't know how else I should speak about it. One hears the triumphant "I have an even more horrible example to tell you! Let's imagine an even worse situation . . ."

I think Lifton's work on the Nazi doctors is important.[149] This book is not about horrors. It's about the extraordinary ability of these particular Nazi doctors to split between effective experimentation and administration of death-dealing poisons to the prisoners, and kindness and affectionate concern with their daughters and wives. If Daniel Berrigan got Lifton right, he wrote that book with the intent of following it by a second book in which he analyzes the same kind of splitting which goes on among contemporary doctors, highly paid and practising in our hospitals.[150] I hope that Lifton, who is uniquely competent to do it, will finally write this book. I wanted to do it and didn't have the ability.

We cannot be careful enough in refusing to act as splitters or in refusing to live a split life in that sense. And yet, in many circumstances, we cannot avoid acting as economic men of our time, performing certain professions and thus maiming our hearts. I look at this isssue in the perspective of the "has been," the historian, and in that way I avoid the deforming shadow that the future might throw on what I am analyzing.

CAYLEY: When you say that you can't meditate on the atomic bomb without going under, what do you mean? Do we not have to acknowledge and speak about the things which actually exist in our world?

ILLICH: What can you say about *one* atomic bomb in the world except . . . a shout? When I began to teach in Germany, at the time the Pershing missiles were to be stationed there, I made myself available to the young people, mostly high school students, who wanted to organize protests.[151] And I said, we can't protest in any other way but by standing there silently. We have nothing to say on this issue. We want to testify by our horrified silence. In horrified silence, the Turkish immigrant washerwoman and the university professor can make *exactly* the same statement, standing next to each other. As soon as you have to explain, opposition becomes again a graded, an elite affair and becomes superficial. I do not want to take part in a conspiracy of gab about peace but claim the privilege of horrified silence, in front of certain things — if I can make my horror visible. And I *do* understand people who go much further and say, "I can't do anything else but pour gasoline on myself." I *do* understand, but I want to give examples of how you can give testimony to your horrified silence without broaching this — for most people — questionable liturgy.

CAYLEY: Liturgy?

ILLICH: Well, if somebody pours gasoline on himself and puts a match to it, I don't know what else I should call it. And this I do not consider a diabolic liturgy, a black mass, but precisely the contrary, *exactly* the contrary.

CAYLEY: This danger, then, that "we will burn out our hearts" as you've said . . .

ILLICH: Talking about it does burn out hearts. Discussing it, arguing about it, somehow makes genocide an issue of discussion. Can you imagine anybody willing to discuss the possible uses of concentration camps or at least readying concentration camps, extermination camps, in 1943? What would you think of a person who would have been willing to engage in a discussion on principles about keeping concentration camps ready, as a threat? And then we see our major churches saying, Well, we can't really condemn a country that keeps atom bombs ready.

CAYLEY: I was thinking of those who protest but still try to engage their opponents' principles.

ILLICH: I would call to their attention the fact that there are words which do not fit ordinary discourse. Jews have a tradition of not using *his* name, because any sentence in which that name appears wouldn't be a sentence anymore. Wittgenstein and such people say that it is silly to say that after my death I want this shirt to be yours, because after my death I won't want *anything*. Philosophy allows me to clarify, step by step, what it means for a word to have this exceptional epistemic status. I think that genocide and cyborg creation and many other extreme vanities have a similar status as words. Let's come back to this.

IV
A Flame in the Dark

CAYLEY: You spoke a bit the other day about the period after you closed CIDOC, when you tramped the roads of southeast Asia, you said . . .

ILLICH: And afterwards I went back to Marburg in Germany, an old university where Luther and Zwingli had their big dispute in the early sixteenth century, to a little town with a university which contains a good old theology and philosophy library, where I rented a small apartment and taught medieval history. They offered me excellent conditions for this purpose, particularly three hundred students, and, amazingly, most of these could follow my Latin text when I interpreted it. I was surprised to find this at the most venerable *Lutheran* theological faculty when I would no longer find it in any humanistic or even Roman Catholic milieu. In the seminar, held after the lectures, I recruited four or five excellent young men who really wanted to do research on the twelfth century, studying history as I taught them to study history. For example, we interpreted a text by Héloise where she tells Abelard that she *is* married to him because she *obeyed* him in saying yes. This is the first time that any woman — in fact, any man *or* woman — makes marriage depend on a mutual yes. We interpreted texts like that and other texts as well. I tried to get people to understand how immensely distant is the mental world in which the twelfth-century authors moved. I did this in order to pull the students away from their typewriters, and their felt-tipped pens, and the telephone which they have to grab — to give them the sense of a trip between two space times. And then I tried to keep them there for a while, making them aware what strangers they are and how little they can use their own concepts, their own modern German or English or French words to translate these Latin texts. I prepared them to re-enter the modern world with a crucial question about it and, at the time of re-entry, to become aware, for a moment, what a different universe they are entering when they resume the certainties of the world in which they feel at home.

So, I worked on teaching history. Some people said I *used* it, as if it were a drug. I said no, I was cultivating disciplined states of altered awareness, cultivating daydream states, but rooted thoroughly in what has been in the past, recovered by good historical method. I found there an alternative to the fantasy of writing the history of penance, or the history of usury in Europe, by using Japanese or Chinese. I began to write about the contemporary world — about transportation systems, about the machine gun, about a library catalogue — and I tried to talk about these things to people at the beginning of the twelfth century. In this proceeding, with my students, I learned an awful lot.

CAYLEY: You actually tried to talk with your friends in the twelfth century about a machine gun?

ILLICH: It is obviously a literary genre, but *not* what Eco did when he wrote *The Name of the Rose*. I remember when I saw that book in manuscript form on the desk of the man who was editing it, in a room where I was sleeping for two nights. I said to myself, I mustn't give the impression that this trip is real. I must make people aware that this is something analogous to highly disciplined reading. But then I'm not writing historical novels. I love to read them. I admire, for instance, Marguerite Yourcenar.[152] I am delighted with the way she interferes with the historian's job by creating out of her fantasy a romanced, a novelistic past, which is both closer to the late Roman Empire than description from the outside in the cold terms of the historians *and*, at the very same time, consciously and clearly a novel. I'm not trying to do this. I'm trying to develop the fantasy world of two cynics who know that they are not real, talking to each other — let's say Hugh of St. Victor and my student Manfred Werner. They should both be cynics. Hugh is there only in his text, and the exegesis of this text is what counts. I won't let Werner be sloppy. I would then like him to go into the woods and fantasize a conversation with Hugh about cancer, or about the many people overseas who must be helped to survive, a couple of the certainties among which Werner lives today.

CAYLEY: Have you found the source of some of these certainties in this period?

ILLICH: I went into the twelfth century, not into the seventeenth or the early nineteenth, out of laziness and destiny. During the period of my studies — my philosophical studies, my theological studies, my historical studies — I was always fascinated by this particular generation of writers, who wrote between 1120 and 1140. It was serendipity which led me there when, already a man consciously beyond the middle of his life, I returned once more to a question of method: How could I reach that Archimedean point outside of the present which I wanted to look at? I had failed to find it in mathematics, obviously, or in abstract logic, had failed to find it by going into the primitive world of the Aztec — I never sought it seriously there — during my twenty-five years in Mexico. I failed in my project of looking at this world through the eyes of a non-European language. And I was so much at home in the twelfth century. So I'm not claiming any special status for the twelfth century, simply a special preference during my life for some authors like Alain de Lille or Aelred of Rievaulx.

Now the twelfth century is a hinge period. It's a historian who constructs the hinge, that is true, but it can be made very credible as a hinge period. During the twelfth century I can observe the emergence of many of those assumptions which, by going unexamined, have turned into today's certainties. It would, of course, be possible to look at the genealogy of these certainties at a later point or at an earlier point, but my limits obligate me to stay within a couple of generations whom I know well and about whom I can speak with competence.

CAYLEY: What is one such certainty that you can see emerging in those two generations?

ILLICH: I do believe that, within that generation, several enormous certainties begin to emerge. There is, for instance, a new certainty about the body; texts become visible in an entirely new way;[153] and there is also the certainty that society is built around mutual commitment, contract — the marriage bond is born there. It did not exist before. You can pick any one of these you want.

CAYLEY: The body.

ILLICH: Okay. Let me begin by quoting Barbara Duden, with whom I've been working on body history for the last ten years. She has written a book, based on the records of an eighteenth-century doctor who made verbatim transcriptions of the cases of the seventeen hundred women who visited him.[154] Duden attempted to reconstruct the way in which these women perceived their own flesh, how they felt in their bodies, how their sensations were oriented, and what they meant when they said "body." In her introduction to this book Duden says that the first thing she had to learn was that she could not construct a bridge back to those women out of the feelings she had about her flesh as a modern woman. She says that she first had to learn to recognize that her own perceptions of her body were totally epoch-specific, and that these perceptions went through a very significant crisis in the epoch of her grandparents, and again after World War II. Only then could she listen to what these women told the doctor between 1720 and 1740.

With this same mentality, I look at what happens to the body between 1100 and 1180. Let me give you a few examples. A historian must always base himself on the documents he has. In 1100, the crucified Christ — who is one of the most important representations left to us of what people thought about the body — is still very much the Christ of the first millennium. Now the first three hundred years of Christianity knew absolutely no crucifix. I know of only one picture from this period, and it has always been very important for me. It's a graffito, a sketch on the outside of a house which, from the way it is built, might have been either a brothel or a school. From the remains of the building itself, you can't tell. And there you see a man, nailed to a cross, with a donkey's head. Below him there is a man holding up his hands in prayer, and the scribbling, "Anaxemenos adores his God." It pokes fun at a Christian's devotion to a man who died a shameful death on a cross. I always have a picture of it on my desk. This is the only representation of that experience preserved for three hundred years.

But from then to the eleventh century, essentially, he who is on the cross is dressed up as a priest. He is a living person, crowned by the sun, even though his heart is pierced and the blood flows out. You can see that he is fully alive. It's an icon or an ideogram; it is not a *body* which is represented. In the ninth century, the clothes slowly begin to disappear from the body, and he's represented in his nakedness, but still as a live body, with eyes which look at you, even if his heart is opened. By the end of the twelfth century, he's a dead man, his head is inclined, his body tortured. Physical pain is represented as acutely as you can possibly represent it. No wonder that, twenty years later, Francis will go and begin to kiss the wounds of lepers. No wonder that the man of Assisi will feel something new, for which even Christianity had no real word — *compassion* — so strong that the sufferings of Christ will write themselves as stigmata on his hands and feet, and an epidemic of stigmata will appear all over central Europe.

Let me relate another body-related change. You know what relics are?

CAYLEY: Yes.

ILLICH: Bones of saints. Now, I have the impression that running around with old bones sounds disgusting and somewhat ridiculous to people today, to Catholics as much as to anyone else. But this is how Christianity started — celebrating the glorious victory of people who had voluntarily accepted ultimate punishment. Call it crazy! That's what it was!

Now, by the tenth century, there's a major trade in relics all over Europe. A man who has studied this very well claims that about one-third of all value transported across the Alps consisted of relics. Of course, it was a value which was well insured, as one would say today, because if somebody did steal your relics — of course, no one would — but if somebody did steal your relics, you could go to the next cemetery and dig up a few more bones and say that these were really the bones that you were bringing back from the Roman catacombs.

But what was important was that the people themselves smelled the sanctity of a relic, the odor of sanctity. I'm not joking, I have too much evidence of this. You asked me to tell you about a foreign world. The odor of sanctity was so much perceived by everybody that, at the beginning of that century, there was one bishop in Milan who claimed that he didn't feel it, and people asked themselves, Why did God so punish him, or what sin did he commit that he couldn't feel the smell of relics? By the end of that century, an agency, which later on became the Office of the Inquisition, had already been established to identify bones as belonging to a certain saint, by drilling holes through them and plumbing them in the name of the Holy See. The smell of sanctity was no longer perceived. May I go on?

CAYLEY: Yes, this is fascinating. In English one can still speak of the odor of sanctity.

ILLICH: It disappears. I must speak from my sources. I can't tell you what I can't read. And I read mostly about what people were worried about and, therefore, wrote a lot about. For a thousand years, Christians had assembled around a table where bread and wine made their Lord Jesus present. Suddenly, in the middle of that century, it became a major question how the flesh of Christ is *really* present under the appearance of bread and wine. The foundations for religious wars were laid. It didn't happen at any other moment.

There are strange people around the world. A

Professor Lottin some decades ago gathered previously unpublished treatises — all of them from between 1160 and 1190 — concerned with moral and ethical reflection on the first movements of the flesh, *motus primo primi carnis*.[155] This had never been discussed before! I can't find anything about it in antiquity. The flesh which moves, of course, is found between the legs. Erection becomes a point of massive, widespread reflection — why it happens, whether it happened in paradise, whether Adam suffered it, or could produce it as he moved his finger because there was not yet sin and he was completely free. You see what I mean by body history?

CAYLEY: Yes . . .

ILLICH: This connects with other issues such as marriage. Weddings exist in all societies. But the idea that a special relationship comes into existence when a man and a woman say yes to each other, make a bond or contract between themselves, take an oath to each other and thereby establish something which society has to respect — what today is called the marriage bond — this idea does not exist before about 1140 or 1145. And, in terms of our present conversation on the body, it is interesting that, by this marriage bond, they give each other rights to their respective bodies by common consent.

At this very moment also, at the end of that century, there is evidence that the doctor dares to dispute the priest's place at the bed of the dying for the first time. It happens sporadically, but this is the first attempt by the doctor to watch his patient up to the moment of his death. The dead body, and the burial of the corpse, become very important. Important bodies were boiled down! Just think! St. Thomas Aquinas was carefully boiled so that his bones, like chicken bones, could be distributed among his friends, right after his death.

Another example is a papal edict forbidding the dissection of dead bodies for the purpose of burying their various parts in different churches so that they can be present throughout the region. Keen interest in the body emerges in those years. And I know how to read the documents. This helps me to understand how I got the perception of a body which I *have*, which I take for granted.

Now let's reflect on what has happened in the last fifteen years. Fifteen years ago, I published *Medical Nemesis*. The book was written as a pamphlet and was widely commented on. Its argument was summed up in the first line, "The medical establishment has become a major threat to health." It was an ideal opening statement for 1974. If someone asked me today, Is that true? I would say yes, but so what? And I think I would not be alone. Lots of people would say so what? I know how to escape it.

In *Medical Nemesis*, my main argument is that, as a result of the high intensity of medicalization in our society, and of the medical monopoly of both diagnosis and therapy, people learn what they feel through being taught about it by the doctor. There is no question that the relationship of modern society to medicine has gone through two major watersheds in my lifetime. In the period between the early 1930s and the mid-1950s, doctors increasingly constituted the patient apart from his consciousness.

Arney and Bergen have nicely described this in a book on taming the last beast.[156]

CAYLEY: Constituted the patient apart from his consciousness?

ILLICH: They brought the patient to the hospital and, with their newly discovered diagnostic methods, they established a chart. They then treated the chart, they changed its parameters. When the chart was healthy, frequently without looking at the guy — I'm caricaturing, of course — they told him to put on his shoes and go home, and later to have himself checked to see if he should be caught and brought in again or not. I'm putting it as crudely as I can.

Then came a reform movement within medicine, starting in the late 1950s and early 1960s, which made the doctor aware of treating the patient rather than his symptoms. And, as Arney and Bergen argue, good medicine became identified with teaching the sick man who came to the doctor how to recognize *disease* as the source of his sickness, and how to constitute himself as a patient of the doctor, taking coresponsibility with the doctor, and coproducing this strange thing which is health.

I think that this is characteristic of the first stage of the recent health revolution, from 1965 to 1980. When I wrote *Medical Nemesis*, I was mainly concerned with the medicalization which destroyed or undermined the patient's art of suffering, which undermined people's ability to bear their uniqueness by telling them that they were abnormal and required correction or improvement, and which destroyed the art of dying.

A couple of years ago, the British journal *Lancet*, a venerable doctors' journal, asked me to write an article on the occasion of the twelfth anniversary of the publication of *Medical Nemesis*. I began the article by saying I don't care about that book. I reread it and saw that it was nicely written, but today I certainly would not begin the book by saying, "The medical establishment has become a major threat to health." Who cares about that today? What I did not write in that book, and what I did not understand, is that beyond pain, disease, impairment, and death having been expropriated, something even more important has happened: people in highly capitalized countries have acquired iatrogenic bodies. They perceive themselves and their bodies as doctors describe them.

Bob Kugelmann has done this marvellous study on "strain."[157] An idea which comes from the late nineteenth century was transformed by Lockheed, which studied metals during the war, into stress. Doctors immediately picked up on stress. There was no such concept in medicine in 1941 when the war began. By 1945 stress was one of the major conditions with which medicine dealt. They had taken it over from Lockheed's concept of metal stress. People began to perceive themselves according to medical models.

I think that we're now going through another revolution and that this revolution is expressed by people who say "My system can't take it," or "I have to get the right inputs," or "I have to watch the baby in my interior on the ultrasound screen in order to see how that system is working." People more and more interpret their own body feelings according to the model of the computer, and no longer according to the still very traditional medical model of the 1960s.

I think, therefore, that by observing the change from smelly bones to certified bones in the twelfth century, or from a royal icon of a person on the cross to a tortured man hanging there, covered with blood, or from a wedding to a marriage consisting in joint rights to two *bodies*, I can train myself to see, within my own generation, similar changes in perception of what the flesh is.

CAYLEY: When you find the historical origins of things you see around you today, does it suggest to you that there is something organic about our civilization, that it's all contained in certain seeds? Are you using the same metaphor Spengler did when he calls the Middle Ages the seed time of Western civilization?

ILLICH: No, I'm not a Spenglerian. I did a doctoral thesis on the philosophical and historiographic background of Toynbee's ideas, but I'm not a Toynbean. I'm very grateful to the master. And I do believe the following: I cannot understand what happened to the body in the twelfth century unless I carefully look at what had already happened with regard to the understanding of the body in the third century. Here I am assisted by Mme Aline Rousselle.[158] There are people to whom we are grateful for having written books, and this year, one of the five or six to whom I'm grateful is Mme Rousselle, who has written an excellent book on the influence of the texts of Soranus, the Greek physician whom today we would call a gynecologist.

CAYLEY: Soranus lived when?

ILLICH: He lived in the late Roman Empire among the Roman elites, the pagan elites, in this world of extreme cruelty and shamelessness. When I read about the enthusiasm among all classes of society for the gladiatorial matches, I sometimes get a taste of our own world. In this cruel milieu, men and women became afraid of sharing their bodies. Another woman, Giulia Sissa, has written on virginity in antiquity, and makes this point very strongly and clearly.[159] This fear of losing something by intimacy with another being is pagan. People usually say that Christianity led to a negative attitude towards the body. I would prefer to say that this pagan anxiety fitted one *particular* view of Christianity, which jelled into the ascetical behavior of the desert fathers.

I have to be aware of this, as I have to be aware of the inability of Christians to accept what the first generations knew about martyrdom. And I have to really digest it. The difficult thing about looking at things historically is that gaining the next mountain also means gaining the next horizon.

I believe that I cannot understand our characteristically European attitudes towards the body unless I go back to the twelfth century. I cannot understand the desire to dissect the body and anatomize it, or the desire to distinguish clearly between body and flesh, between objectively viewed body and sensed flesh. I cannot understand those beautiful passages from Jean-Paul Sartre about the distinction between your body, my body, and my body in your eyes. I don't follow Sartre, but I find him skilful in raising some issues. According to Sartre, I learn about my body through the image of your body because I come to think of my body, made in the image of your body, through your eyes. This, according to Sartre, makes me feel disgust. There's something very true there, but I can't follow Sartre in the sense that I don't feel disgust.

I cannot interpret Sartre's views on the body, any more than I can interpret his fanatical a-theism, which is also a "no," without looking at what happened to the body in the twelfth century. But it is not my principal task when I teach to show how the contemporary body came to be. My main aim is to introduce my students to a very foreign, barely reachable body, in the hope that they will begin to extend the incredulity they feel in the face of this foreign body to the body they take for granted, the body equipped with two appendages which enable them to engage in locomotion.

CAYLEY: In a lecture you gave here at Penn State last night about the perversion of the ideal of hospitality into the reality of hospitalization, you said that you had felt unbearable anguish when forced to confront certainties. Why?

ILLICH: I didn't say "unbearable anguish." I quoted Erich Fromm and said "*almost* unbearable anguish."

CAYLEY: That's true. Excuse me . . .

ILLICH: We were taking about the appearance of the need for places where people who don't fit can be sent. I suggested, as an exercise to help them really understand what I am saying, that during the next vacation they spend two months at an orderly's job in a hospital, preferably a state hospital, or in an operating room, or as a janitor there. I also suggested that they could go to a hospital and sit with dying AIDS patients. By *living* through their deaths, they would understand in what milieux certain crucial moments of modern man are experienced, in alienated space, where strangers "care" for them and minister to their so-called — yes, that's what they call it — *needs*. I love my friend John McKnight's statement that "care is the mask of love."[160]

So I told the students, you cannot grasp what it means to live in the modern world unless you simultaneously abstain from two temptations. The first is what I called "apocalyptic randiness," a term I learned from Freimut Duve, a German politician.[161] This is the atmosphere which can be easily created when very serious and committed people are at their third whisky and one tells about the Iraqis poisongassing Iranians, and the other says, "I know something better. Do you know how much poison gas we have?" And somebody else says, "I know of something even better. Do you know what kind of gas they're now developing?" That's what I call apocalyptic randiness. *Abstain* from it with great discipline! On the other hand, also abstain from romanticism, any kind of romanticism, in order to be able to face the kind of society we live in and have created, in order to be able, but barely able, to bear the anguish of looking at it.

CAYLEY: But once one has laid bare these certainties and become aware of "needs," "care," "development" — whatever these cherished concepts are — once one has investigated them, once one has seen how recently they have appeared, how epoch-specific they are, how destructive they may be, what next? Is your counsel really to live in the dark?

ILLICH: No. Carry a candle in the dark, *be* a candle in the dark, know that you're a flame in the dark. I always think of Helder Camara. When we first met he was the Catholic auxiliary bishop from Rio de Janeiro and at that time one of the shrewdest politicians I had ever seen. I helped him write a speech he was to give in English at Fordham University on the carnival in Brazil. He arrived in New York wearing a black suit, even though he had never worn a black suit in his life, always his cassock. I asked my brother to pick him up at the airport. Helder had said to me, "Tell him I look like a defeathered bird," *passaro desplumado* — a tiny little guy, almost completely bald, without flesh, skin and bones, with a deeply lined face, radiating goodness, a childlike wizard . . . Now, how did I get to Helder Camara?

CAYLEY: A candle in the dark . . .

ILLICH: Ah! . . . I remember being with him in the Palacio São Joaquim when he had just founded the world's first bishops' conference to oppose Rome — but *totally* at the service of the Pope, as he always insisted. This must have been 1962, and we were living together there. He had an appointment with a general and said to me, "Ivan, I want you to sit in the back of the room while I have this meeting." This general was one of the founding fathers of Pro Familia in Brazil and later on one of the most cruel torturers. Helder already knew what would happen.

He had a conversation with him. After half an hour, he let the general out of his study and flopped down on a chair next to me. Complete silence. And then he looked at me and said, "You must *never* give up. As long as a person is alive, somewhere beneath the ashes there is a little bit of remaining fire, and all our task is" — and he put his hands, funny, skinny hands, around his mouth and blew and said, "You must blow . . . carefully, very carefully, blow . . . and blow . . . you'll see if it lights up. You mustn't worry whether it takes fire again or not. All you have to do is blow." We became very good friends. You see, he was considered dangerous, terribly dangerous. Who could consider that guy dangerous? It tells you what the world considers dangerous. During the military regime, he was the archbishop of Recife, in the northeast. He had already been archbishop for five years at the time what I'm about to tell you happened. It was a year after they had delivered his closest collaborator, with signs of horrible torture, dead at his doorstep. He lived in a little sacristy, in a suburb of Recife. He had given the Palacio Arcebispado — the Archbishop's Palace — for some social activities. The little room we shared was just big enough for two hammocks, hung crosswise. I arrived at six o'clock. At 6:20 there was a knock. He went to the door and took out some pennies. Twenty minutes later, there was another knock. Same story. I asked, "What is this?" He said to me, "Ivan, you look at it tomorrow." And I saw that the street, in the evenings, and well into the morning hours, was crawling with extraordinarily ugly cripples. Two days later, I said to him, "Helder, tell me . . . what *is* this?" He said to me, "Prisoners they let go from various places, and then bring here to knock at my door. Two already have told me, 'Sooner or later, I will not be satisfied with what you give me and I'll kill you.'" Helder looked at me and said, "*Deus e grande,*" God is great! In spite of all his foolishness, and statements I couldn't agree with on liberation and such stuff, Helder is for me one of the great examples one can emulate.

As for practically answering your question about living in darkness, it's difficult to tell modern people, young people, that they shouldn't be afraid of being a little candle, a light that others light up in *their* life. People are used to electric bulbs and switches. The metaphor of light doesn't work without darkness.

CAYLEY: Your answer uncovered a dimension in my question that was deeper than I knew. I had meant to ask about the consequences of discrediting so many of the concepts on which our world depends.

ILLICH: But the point is that these aren't concepts. Aristotle had very good concepts, and Plato had different concepts, and Porphyry, when he interprets Aristotle, has different concepts again. Knowing this is what I call being a well-read person — something we have to demand from anybody who wants to risk the trip into this world of plastic words and categories instead of concepts, this world of noncommittedness, this world of no inner orientation in which we live. It is very difficult to look at it critically. You can stay with Thoreau, or with William James, who still gives you concepts. But today's world is conceptless in the sense that meaning, common meaning, precise meaning, is more and more washed out from the words we use. Words are increasingly used like plastic elements, like Plasticine. They fit everything. But *you* are not conceptless as long as you read a book. That's why I would rather have a few students from whom I can demand that they read and talk to me in the language of the author, rather than many who only classify the author for the citation index.

CAYLEY: Since you were talking about Helder Camara, I also wanted to ask you about someone whom you said the other day was important for you — Jacques Maritain. How and when did you know him?

ILLICH: Maritain entered my life quite early and became very important for me while he was ambassador in Rome and had a little seminar there, at the embassy. He made me go back to another great friend whom I acquired in a way only through him, Aquinas. The *Gothic* approach, both narrow and precise, and extraordinarily illuminating, which Maritain had to the texts of St. Thomas, laid the Thomistic foundations of my entire perceptual mode. I don't know whether, if I submitted myself to the judgement of Thomists, they would accept this, but I experienced Thomism — no, *Thomas* — as I discovered him through Jacques Maritain, as the architecture which has made me intellectually free to move between Hugh of St. Victor and Kant, between Schutz — or God knows what strange German — and Freud, or, again, into the world of Islam, without getting dispersed.

Sitting here with you in this strange situation, discussing memories, is making me whimsical. Let me tell you a story. Do you know who René Voillaume was?

CAYLEY: I don't.

ILLICH: The founder of the Little Brothers of Jesus, the most important new order in the Roman Church in the immediate postwar period. It didn't remain that, once it outgrew the first 120 people, but the first 120 were an incredible lot. They sought a contemplative life as the lowest kind of workers, in groups of two or three, dispersed all over the globe. You can say it was too much of an elite. Their founder, René Voillaume, was a man of great importance for me in the 1950s, and during the 1960s he came to see me every now and then in Cuernavaca and took a rest with me for a few days.

One day, I woke up from my siesta — in my office, which was also my bedroom — and there on the chair, having dropped in by surprise, coming from I don't know where and going somewhere else, sat old Voillaume. A few years earlier, I had picked up a full leatherbound set of the Editio Leonina of the works of St. Thomas, a monster set which I found in the Lagunilla, the flea market of Mexico, for a dollar a volume. I enjoyed this possession and had fallen asleep with one of the rather obscure volumes open on my belly. This must have been in 1966 or 1967. So Voillaume said to me, "What a pleasure to see a younger man today still *studying* Thomas Aquinas with devotion!" And I said to him, "Mon père, it's more like a linguistic exercise, a beautiful walk up and down through mental cloisters . . . and for the sake also of the language." And he said to me, "Not for the truth? Quelle horreur! et entre les élèves de Jacques Maritain . . ."

You want to know what Jacques Maritain has meant for me? It is this: to have gotten beyond his intention and discovered Thomas as a magnificent shell, and as a great person and mystic.

He sent me a copy of his last book, *Le Paysan de la Garonne*, the sad meditation of a man who sees not only the world but his church going to the dogs. I have a copy lying somewhere in Mexico which he sent me. In it he scribbled a dedication full of great, great sadness, which gave me the feeling he looked on me as a traitor.

CAYLEY: Why?

ILLICH: I would excuse Maritain to a certain degree. I don't think he was thinking about me, but about newspaper articles and clippings he got about me. There were people in Chile, more than in Italy, who made out of his "integral humanism" a Christian democratic ideology. President Frei of Chile was an outstanding example. And Maritain in turn found, as a very old man, relevance in being a political theorist. Since I am so full of deep respect, I would rather not comment on what can happen to old men.

V
The Last Frontier of Arrogance

CAYLEY: Your book *Shadow Work* appeared at the end of the 1970s just at the time you were beginning to teach at Marburg. How did you come to the idea that you express in the title essay of that book?

ILLICH: *Shadow Work* was my reaction to what I saw happening in the Society for International Development, founded by Gunnar Myrdal. I got in touch with it first when Lester Pearson asked me to give the main address on their tenth-anniversary meeting in Canada, in 1968. I spoke about "Outwitting Developed Nations." Then in 1978 or 1979, Paul Streeten invited me to speak at a conference of the Society of Development Economists. I wanted to address them about what I called the colonization of the informal sector, the economization of unpaid

activities. I saw an attempt by economists and therefore also by administrators to get hold of unpaid
activities and improve their quality and their contribution to the economy. It seemed very important to
me, economically, to make a distinction between
culturally determined human activity in the subsistence sphere, on one hand, and, on the other, unpaid
activities into which people are forced in a commodity-intensive society in which the upgrading of commodities into something useful requires very
specific labor inputs which are not paid. It was then
that I wrote *Shadow Work*.

I also wrote this in reaction to what I thought was
a nonsensical and self-defeating discourse of the
then more radical women's movements who
claimed pay for housework and demanded an equal
share of the employment cake, which I foresaw
would become smaller during the next decade. It
was there, with *Shadow Work*, that I made my first
attempt to shout for some reasonableness in this, for
me, extremely important and significant attempt by
women to study their own condition. I must say that
I was surprised at how my work was received.
Obviously, I didn't know how racist sensitivities
had become by then, and how male academics of the
highest caliber would begin to respect female racism.

CAYLEY: Could you say a little more in detail what
it was you saw happening that made you want to
draw this distinction between subsistence and
shadow work?

ILLICH: People have always labored, worked,
sweated, and toiled, but the idea that paid employ-

ment is the only dignified way in which people can engage in unpleasant activities began to become recognizable about 150 years ago. It was already pretty general in Western societies 120 years ago. The idea began to spread that work which is done by employees who get a paycheque is productive. Any other kind of work is re-productive, or constitutes an exploitation of the person who does it. During the nineteenth century this idea translated into a social distinction between the poor males compelled to go out for employed work and the females of the species who had to be protected by being put into a domestic sphere where they could engage in household activities which people like Marx called re-productive activities, activities re-productive of the labor force. In fact these new categories of political economy were very weakly founded in history. Nevertheless work was increasingly identified with *paid* work, and all other work was considered some kind of toil which could be identified through only one characteristic: that it was *not* paid, or not properly paid. One completely overlooked the fact that the commodities made by wage labor required further labor to make them into *useful* things. Commodities, purchased and brought into the family through the expenditure of wages, required more and more programmed and predetermined inputs in order to become something useful. And these forms of labor became mandatory.

It is true, water was brought rather cheaply into the house. By 1920, half of all American families had an inside toilet and shower. One usually thought that women didn't have to carry buckets of water up the street any longer. In addition, families could use more water than ever before and could be cleaner. But as Mrs. Schwartz-Cowan has shown so clearly, the amount of work women henceforth had to perform in the household in cleaning bathtubs, washing toilets and bathrooms, running the washing machine, and perhaps in going out to earn the money to buy it was much greater than women had expended on the water-related activities which were expected from them, or imposed on them, in previous societies.[162] Which type of activity women prefer — standing with other women at the common water supply for hours while they chat and engage in powerful gossip, or each one being locked in her own bathroom, cleaning the floor — I leave up to them to decide.

My argument was that the kind of labor input required to make commodities into immediately useful things had to be studied as an economic activity, even though its payment would be ridiculous. It was a necessary consequence of the separation of the place of production from the place of consumption. The availability of unpaid labor that would add to the product the amount of human activity necessary to make it useful was the only reason why wage labor could be paid in the first place. I called this unpaid contribution shadow work, and I pointed out that, due to the polarization of social sex characteristics in the nineteenth century, it was initially more incumbent on women than on men. It now also touches men more and more. Men, as Jean Robert has put it, have to put their labor force in their car or take it with them on the subway, to bring it to the place where it will be used. But they don't get paid for this effort of carrying their labor force to work. I said that in a commodity-intensive society the human labor put into a use value is split up, one part is unpaid, the other paid, and it's the unpaid part which creates the possibility of paying wages.

CAYLEY: It was around this time that economists were beginning to identify and study the informal economy.

ILLICH: Yes, and on the twentieth anniversary of the Society for International Development I gave a speech in Colombo, at their general meeting, where I called the colonization of the informal sector the last frontier of arrogance.

CAYLEY: What does this colonization consist in?

ILLICH: Experts for self-help being sent out by the World Bank and by all kinds of well-meaning alternative organizations telling people in the villages and *barrios* how they can become self-employed. Have you ever heard a more masturbatory concept? There was an American aristocrat in the Kennedy administration who said — somebody showed me the transcripts but, stupidly, I didn't make a note of it — that perhaps one should not speak of development as self-help. He suggested that his colleagues in the State Department look up what the word had meant in New England until quite recently.

CAYLEY: Do you have the feeling that there is a genuine confusion about this?

ILLICH: I think that the ideologues of alternative development, the Green Party people, and lots of assistance organizations which think of alternative futures are missionaries of this confusion. I do think that the majority of people all over the world — and this is different than fifteen years ago — know that neither they nor their children will ever have paying jobs. The president of the International Labor Organization has said that anybody who thinks in terms of a future with full employment is not an optimist but nuts.

But there is a difficulty when you ask me these questions. When I wrote *Shadow Work*, ten years ago exactly, it was very difficult to speak about the hidden or submerged economy, and to forge classifiers by which different activities that are unpaid could be put into different boxes. Today, there are departments doing this, and we don't want to discuss this any longer.

CAYLEY: Well, so far in this conversation, we are having this persistent difficulty. I bring up one of your older books, from *Deschooling* to *Shadow Work*, and you say, "Well, one spoke this way in 1978, but now everything has changed." I can see why you would not want to be attached to the fruits of your labor, I can see why you would not want to be a captive of your former statements, I can see why you would call them pamphlets and see them as written specifically for an occasion. But I feel you go too far in denying their relevance today. I would still pass these books to others as currently valuable, not as something like "This is a curiosity that Illich wrote in 1975."

ILLICH: Well, there are other people in the past who wrote for their time and are still read with joy. I'm deeply honored if you consider me a classic, but I don't want to live like one. I want the privilege of going a few steps further and asking questions in which I'm interested, about which I'm curious. I want to tell my friends that I've elaborated considerably on what I said then. I've clarified it and qualified it. I want to say, "Yes that's an interesting direction, but now you should go and look somewhere else." You must shut me up if I become an old blabbering guy. It happens to people in their sixties sometimes that they think they are going on when in fact they're just spinning their wheels.

A few minutes ago you saw me groping for an answer because I didn't want to use the word *value*. And then I did, because you had asked me a question about history, and about what I had formerly written, about use values and vernacular values. Reading and rereading my key authors of the third quarter of the nineteenth century, I have become increasingly aware of the question: What happened when the good was replaced by values? The transformation of the good into values, of commitment into decision, of question into problem, reflects a perception that our thoughts, our ideas, and our time have become *resources*, scarce means which can be used for either of two or several alternative ends. The word *value* reflects this transition, and the person who uses it incorporates himself in a sphere of scarcity. So I wouldn't speak any longer about vernacular values, even though I don't have a better word. I would speak about what other people call cultures, as arrangements by tradition, in a given geography, at a given time, through which a group of people *excludes* conditions of scarcity or, more precisely, limits the appearance of conditions of scarcity to very narrow, very specific aspects of their daily life. You *may* barter, or engage in commerce on Saturday, between sunrise and noon, in the market, or you may do it in the bar and in the brothel. What other people, therefore, call culture, I call rules for the limitation of scarcity within a given social arrangement.

I wouldn't dare, any longer, in an anthropological reflection on the way of life of people, to speak about their values. Rather, I would ask an aesthetic question about the shape in which they perceive the good, the sound in which they address it, the feelings with which they respond to it. I am very happy that I wrote about things such as vernacular values, which can be discussed and applied by people who want to think one step further. But I have to tell them that the next step is not one you can use in everyday discussion. If you exclude values from family life today and try to speak of the good, people say, "Oh, that's an old way of speaking, it's Aristotle's way or at the most recent some fifteenth-century theologian's way." It becomes extremely difficult to know how we should speak about what is important to us, or about what we want.

CAYLEY: I first encountered criticism of the idea of values in a series of lectures for the CBC by the Canadian philosopher George Grant, called *Time as History*.[163] He said that the language of values was the language of Nietzsche, the language in which individuals willed the meaning of their own existence after the death of God.

ILLICH: It is a generalization of economics. It says,

this is a value, this is a nonvalue, make a decision between the two of them. These are three different values, put them in a precise order. But when we speak about the good, we show a totally different appreciation of what is before us. The good is convertible with being, convertible with the beautiful, convertible with the true. For me, the discussion of values is sadly subjective, sadly detached from nature. If I may ask the question, would you say that your wife constitutes a value for you?

CAYLEY: No.

ILLICH: It would be obscene. When you say "I value my children," the question is, How much?

CAYLEY: Is the language of the good recoverable?

ILLICH: Between the two of us, at this moment, yes! I take this strange and uncomfortable conversation between the two of us in front of a microphone to be good, even though I know that we are producing a program and therefore engaging in something of the same order as a public intercourse exhibition. I feel that it is good to talk to you and to take you seriously, even if it's also a game for CBC. I know how to write, and if your questions were written, my answers would be in a completely different language. They would be chiselled and thought out. At this moment, after having spoken for some time with you in this situation, I put myself into what I say for love of you. I try to practise a certain ascetical discipline by which I do not look up my mental index cards and just read off internal writing.

CAYLEY: Why is the microphone, as a repository for our words, different than the paper on which you chisel them?

ILLICH: This is a keyhole, a keyhole to which we expose ourselves, making it possible for somebody to spy on my sitting down, with you, in this form of intense, intellectual intercourse, for an exhibition. We know that the program will be as good as the sincerity of our conversation. But we also know that I am answering rather intimate questions, which are nobody's business, in front of an audience of who knows who? It's a question of shame, a question of delicacy. Can you imagine that somebody would have gone up to your grandfather, stuck a microphone in his face, and said, "Sir, I want to ask you a question. Would you please answer me sincerely?" Your grandfather would have been shocked. He wouldn't have answered a journalist. He would have said, "I'm not a politician, who are you?" Certainly, my grandfather did this. We have gotten used to living among images, as Susan Sontag so graphically described in her book *On Photography*.[164] Kids say, look at that sunrise, that's as beautiful as a postcard! A new generation is so used to having seen everything and heard everything by listening in to the production of programs, or looking at them, that they take reality for another form of program.

I'm full of admiration at how carefully you've prepared yourself and at the good ways you've found to draw me out, as they say. So I've decided that this is good. Therefore, I do it. Now, do you need more discussion about the difference between the good and a value? I don't see any value in it!

CAYLEY: So the good is something you undertake toward me . . . the good is a response?

ILLICH: This conversation between us is good. We

will desire it. We've no need for it. The good is desired, the value is needed or chosen, or picked. Desire has no horizon, needs are made to be satisfied. We live in a world of needs and most people really believe that they have needs. We forget that, as Michael Ignatieff has shown so well, my needs are the result of my having attributed them to others and then saying, me too.[165] It's what René Girard calls mimetic desire, which transforms desires into needs, needs for commodities, needs for products, needs which can be satisfied.[166]

CAYLEY: Well, it's hard to know where to go now, since you've challenged the very basis of what I'm doing here. You've claimed that my listeners are voyeurs who are observing through a keyhole and can't distinguish reality from a program. That doesn't seem to leave any honorable approach open to me as a broadcaster. You seem to be saying that you are doing this in the same spirit that you drive your car: you would prefer to have a speed limit of 20 miles per hour, but here we are, so let's drive the car . . .

ILLICH: Correct! I do drive a car. For seventeen years I was without one. I decided that it was no good, and was without one. Then I accepted work at Penn State University, which is somewhere near nowhere and also distant from the supermarket. I couldn't do anything else but ask Lee Hoinacki to please get me a good car in southern Illinois, where they are particularly cheap, and drive it here.

I know that in order to attend the meeting on water that I will conduct for Wolfgang Sachs next week near Assisi, I will consume as much oxygen as a herd of twenty elephants would consume in their entire life, and not even produce the shit elephants produce. I will be propelled — jetted — to Assisi and, in three days, back. And yet I do it. I try to be austere and draw all my lines. For example, I vowed to myself twenty years ago not to buy a daily newspaper — I, who couldn't go to Mexico without the promise that *The New York Times* would be delivered by air mail every day. It doesn't mean that I don't pick up the paper left on the next seat while the other person in the airplane has gone to the toilet. When I do this I feel a little bit as if I'm peeping. I haven't looked at television. I have refused to be interviewed. But there is a point at which, if you draw your own line, you can make your own exception. You can't find security in austerity, otherwise you are really through.

CAYLEY: You're through when you find security?

ILLICH: The security which comes from vegetarianism. I don't like meat. Other people don't want to eat meat because they don't want to eat cows. But if somebody says, "I will have to embarrass the hostess, she should have known that I'm a vegetarian," I say he would have done better not to have come. That doesn't mean that I don't respect his religious convictions, but that kind of religious conviction deserves civil respect, civil tolerance, not approval.

CAYLEY: Earlier, when you were speaking of values and the good, you distinguished desires from needs. Where does the idea of needs fit into your thinking?

ILLICH: In his little book *The Needs of Strangers*, Michael Ignatieff answers the intent I once announced to write a history of needs by saying it can't be done. And the way he says it, it's true, I agree with him. You can't write a world history of needs. I think you can write a history of needs in the Western tradition in the last two hundred years, a sociogenesis of what we call needs. I agree with Ignatieff, that the place which the term corresponding somewhat vaguely to what we call needs had in the discourse of Shakespeare or Augustine or Aristotle is so different from the place it has in our discourse that you can't reasonably compare the two. If I'm asked to speak about this in a few words, I always recommend to my students a book by William Leiss, called *The Limits of Satisfaction*.[167] Twelve years after having been written, it's still a jewel. He bases himself on the Marxist assumption that needs — he calls them commodity-intensive needs — arise from a transformation of wants into demands for commodities, which in turn become entitlements. Seemingly, from the way you smile, you have a need for toothbrushing equipment. That need demands a brush, toothpaste, water, and perhaps some more little devices. Your need for morning tooth cleansing isn't satisfied without this package. And you can go a step further. You need an advisor on how to compose the different elements — since each one, by itself, is not satisfying — in order to produce the satisfaction of your need for mouth care.

Needs in modern society are fractured. They can't be met individually and can only be met through professional advice, which tells you what constitutes the satisfaction of a need that you don't experience. We are now at the moment when needs are

being intensively transformed into knowledge requirements. The doctor diagnoses the condition you
have, but no longer prescribes what you need — he
isn't stupid enough to believe that you need it, that
you can feel it, that there is some subjective experience — rather, he orders what is required for this
condition. Therefore, when you ask me about needs,
I have to speak under circumstances in which needs
are quickly disappearing from society. During the
late 1980s, they are being replaced by requirements.
People speak about their energy requirements. A
student was here last week. I wanted to offer her a
second glass of the cider that you buy from the
Amish around here, and I said, "This is good cider,
have some." "Oh, no," she said, "my sugar requirements are met for today. I don't want to get into a
sugar high." The idea that all people have specifi-
able needs which can be identified and classified
and then ought to be satisfied represents a break
with a very different perception of the human condition, a traditional perception of the human condition which took for granted that some things are
necessary and can't be changed but must be accepted. In this traditional view the cultivation of
desire and the regulation of desire in the context of
necessity was the principal personal ethical and
moral task for everyone, and for the community.
Needs, therefore, are neither necessities that cannot
be changed, nor desires that can't ever be satisfied.
Needs, in the sense in which I want to discuss them,
when I speak about needs for education, needs for
medical inputs, needs for transportation, needs for
income, result when technique is accepted as a

means to change, to abolish, the necessities which the human condition imposes.

CAYLEY: For example?

ILLICH: The fact that I can't go every day to do something at a distance of more than five miles from my home. The alternative is the vehicularization of space and, simultaneously, the assumption that what I wish ought to be satisfied by the consumption of passenger miles, rather than by walking or just living with the desire.

I go on a pilgrimage, I desire to arrive at its end, and at its end I know that I've just begun. This was the experience of a pilgrim to Santiago in the twelfth century.

CAYLEY: I understand what you've been telling me, about desire having no horizon. What I haven't understood is the idea that we may have passed beyond the boundary of the era of needs into an era of requirements. Obviously there's something to your example of the young woman who has so thoroughly internalized —

ILLICH: That she's a system.

CAYLEY: — a sort of hygienic discourse about herself, that she responds to your offer of another glass of cider in terms of her sugar requirements.

ILLICH: She was also a sexologist. She expressed her sex needs.

CAYLEY: Not her sex requirements? I don't quite understand the point of this distinction between needs and requirements.

ILLICH: When people speak to me about the needy, I answer, "That's none of my business, I don't care for them" — putting very specific stress on the word *care*. The needy, for whom I ought to care, I leave to philanthropists or politicians. I would like to act as a Samaritan picking up a beaten-up Jew, as a Palestinian who picks up his Jew.[168] But I do not intend to care for the needy.

When I speak about this, when I say I don't care for the needy, people say to me, "But what about the people who are dying of hunger at this moment in Ethiopia?" When I answer that I don't care about them, they immediately begin to speak about basic caloric requirements, or, even worse, they give me a list of basic requirements without which their life can't go on. This happens more and more to me. Ten years ago, people still answered me by saying, "Think of the hungry." Now the Ethiopians are no longer hungry. They are human individuals whose most fundamental, existential requirements have not been met.

The moment you begin to think about the hungry in terms of calories, in your own fantasy you become a systems administrator. You become somebody who feels that he has the power, or at least ought to have the power, to turn lifelines off and on, because he who can turn them on can also by not doing what he ought to do turn them off. The fantasy that Ethiopians are dependent on what we send them implies a tremendous vanity. I cease to think in terms of an individual hungry mouth into which a piece of bread will enter, and begin to speak in terms of tons, without my necessarily having either the intention or the capacity to take a piece of bread and share it with somebody else. And this happens in a society in which hospitality has become well nigh impossible. Here, in the North, in America and Canada, we live in a society where you can occasionally put up somebody at home when he comes through to give a lecture, or he is on a trip, but compare this with what you see all over the so-called Third World, where it is quite normal that a household accommodate "guests" who stay for years. The old remain there, the children come back there. The divorced girl, or the girl who went into prostitution and now has to cure herself of syphilis, comes home as a matter of course. Compare this with a world in which not even obvious hospitality for old people is offered, and huge economic problems are created by the frightening prospect — as people see it — that by the time I reach eighty-five there will be five times as many people of eighty-five as there are today. So what do we do? We speak about managing requirements, survival requirements.

CAYLEY: There's something I understand and something I don't understand in what you're saying. I understand what you're saying about hospitality. I see that our world is all sewn up, that we don't have time for the simplest things, and we can't afford the most ordinary things that everybody in the world can afford. But I'm still perplexed by your distinction between needs and requirements.

ILLICH: I believe that during the mid-1980s there has been a change in the mental space in which many people live. Some kind of a catastrophic breakdown of one way of seeing things has led to the emergence of a different way of seeing things. The subject of my writing has been the perception of sense in the way we live; and, in this respect, we are, in my opinion, at this moment passing over a watershed. I had not expected, in my lifetime, to observe this passage.

Now you can always pull out some sentences or paragraphs in which I expressed a sense that we are moving towards it. But I did not think I would be alive in the generation which would get beyond this watershed, beyond this gulf, and then be able to look back on how beautiful the world was in which people still spoke about the needs of strangers and not the requirements of strangers. As romantic and detestable as I often find it, it was still a world in which people of good will created a sense of guilt in many Americans because their needs were met and other people's needs were not met. We have now moved into a situation where a subjective connection between a person and what he needs has been washed out, and has faded.

When I first participated in some of these professional meetings on demography thirty-five years ago, I was stimulated to look into the appearance of the concept of population. Populations are not that old a concept. I found it very difficult to adapt to the population concept. But something else has happened now. We are not speaking any longer about populations in the old sense. We are speaking about systems, and the elements of a system. You can tell me that technically the statistical tools used in both types of discourse are the same. I do believe that the metaphors by which they are interpreted are new.

CAYLEY: So just what is it that you think has happened? You seem to be saying that needs at least imply persons, while requirements is a systems concept that implies only a machine-like interaction. But I'm lost, really.

ILLICH: Good . . .

CAYLEY: You mean that's a start.

ILLICH: And please remember that the term *machine* got a completely new meaning when Alan Turing, for lack of another ordinary language term, began to speak about what became the computer as the universal machine.[169] This is a pure abstraction, a function which adjusts its internal state to its last calculation, a black box. Anybody who wants to use the term *machine* to designate a pen, a watch, a steam engine, or a motor and that black box as beasts of the same kind — in any way of the same kind — hasn't understood what has happened and has no capacity to understand what has happened.

VI
The Double Ghetto

CAYLEY: Why did you write *Gender*?

ILLICH: I had finished *Shadow Work*, which contains, in my opinion, one of my crucial articles on language, the one on Nebrija, one on technology — the one on Hugh, where I make the claim that a twelfth-century thinker was the first and last one to have an alternative philosophy of technology — and one on the history of poverty and work, which establishes the concept of shadow work. I came to the conclusion that I had to go one step deeper. I had to raise the epistemological issue of modern European modes of perception. I had to get into the question of the epoch-specific apriorisms which generate not only our mental conceptions but also our sensual perceptions and the feelings in our hearts about what constitutes social reality. Social reality I define as that which we will never challenge and we will never want to wish away, such as the fact that we sit in a three-dimensional room, that Mary is a woman and you are a man, and so on.

Now this was the period during which my curious reading habits had made me discover a new branch of scientific enquiry, a field which some people pretended constituted something apart, a new view of reality. This view was based on the claim that in our society women, like black people, constitute a minority, or the claim that up to now scientific enquiry has been pursued from a white point of view, from a rich point of view, from a male point of view. In other words, I discovered feminist so-called science.

I avidly read into this material and stumbled, in German, on two little articles. One claimed that what had happened to the social role of women, historically, during the middle of the nineteenth century, had been happening during the 1960s and 1970s to the role of the underdeveloped. During the middle of the nineteenth century, women's work and men's work, according to this theory, had been separated, women in the house and men in the factory, women for unpaid and men for paid work, women for reproductive work, as they called it, and men for productive work. And, in a similar way during the 1960s and 1970s, the activity of the ordinary man in the North became productive work in specialized places, producing high-level incomes, while work in the poor countries became reproductive work, mostly done in or near the home by men and women who were incredibly underpaid compared with what people got in the rich countries. In this article, a German woman professor, Claudia von Werlhof — now professor of sociology in Innsbruck — spoke of the "hausfrauization" of the Third World.[170] And having been engaged in the development debate I found, in this thesis, finally, a new, surprising, imaginative, and historically significant idea.

Second, I ran into an article by Barbara Duden, a colleague of von Werlhof's. In this article, the author claimed something which I think historians by now take for granted, but which at that time constituted a surprise for me. I had not seen it stated anywhere else by historians of the nineteenth century. She said that that change which others describe as the coming of capitalism and the generalization of a capitalist mode of production she could describe as in fact a polarization of activities between reproductive women and productive men. This also generated an entirely new view of the physical, bodily existence of men and women. Men became generators, women, reproductive organisms or, precisely, wombs stuck on top of a pair of legs. I detested this crude image and the purple language in which the article was written, but it made a key point. The modern category of work, defined as something which either men or women can do, has a historical beginning.

Duden and I later on became very close friends and collaborators. But at that moment, I was surprised by this statement and began to read widely into the history of how work has been perceived. *Shadow Work* resulted. And in writing this polemical pamphlet, it became clear to me that the history of modern work or, more precisely, the archaeology of our mental and ideological conception of work, had not been written yet. Why? Because I observed that, no matter which pre-nineteenth-century society I looked at carefully enough to make such a judgement, no matter into which strange, so-called primitive culture I moved, a line ran through the tool kit of every one of these societies, separating tools men may grasp from tools women can grasp. A line ran through all the spaces of daily life — in the house, around the house, in the village. In some spaces at some hours you would find only women. In other spaces you would find only men. It's possible that at another hour you would find men in spaces which otherwise were occupied by women. But there would be this demanding gender line which runs through every society; and therefore, in a traditional society, in a precapitalist society, it is impossible to speak about abstract work for which one can just hire workers without regard to whether they are men or women.

Therefore, what other people had described as the coming of capitalism really could also be described as a demise of the gender line and the creation of the completely new image of the human worker, of whom half have a bulge in the blue jeans and the other half don't. This is the observation from which I started, crudely and brutally described.

I then got together with a few other people and went through hundreds of books in anthropology, historical anthropology, law, and history, and everywhere found my suspicion confirmed, that, until quite recently, until the sixteenth to the seventeenth centuries — and in the Church a little bit earlier, in the thirteenth century — there is no talk about human beings. Customs are those of men, or those of women. Society is conceived in terms of a locally defined, dissymmetric complementarity of two fields, which designate those who are in them as that society's men and that society's women. In no two societies is the definition the same. I was simply so surprised, rendered so curious by what was for me at least a discovery that I spent a year reflecting on it. And since in that year I had this regents' lectureship at Berkeley, I wrote up the lectures so that the students could prepare themselves before I arrived. The book came out of that.

CAYLEY: You claim in that book that the wage gap between men and women —

ILLICH: In modern times.

CAYLEY: — in modern times —

ILLICH: Since work has been degendered, and sexualized.

CAYLEY: — has remained the same, and even tended to increase.

ILLICH: At that time, I had to dig out the data because during the preceding fifteen years feminists had constantly complained about the gap but had *not* demonstrated that there was a close relationship — in all the developed countries — between the increase, during the 1960s and 1970s, and feminist activity.

CAYLEY: How do you explain that?

ILLICH: Counterproductivity, as in medicine or education.

CAYLEY: You must say more . . .

ILLICH: Just as education has produced more stupefied people, and just as medicine has created more complaints, so feminism, as practised during those twenty years, has aggravated the wage gap. Today, I think, most people admit this. Feminism created new opportunities, new chances, for a small minority to rise, while not changing anything in the basic distance between the rich and the poor, so that by the end of a twenty-year period of feminist struggle, the distance between the typically underpaid and the typically highly paid woman was as great as that between low-paid men and high-paid men. I think that discrimination on the job ceased for the few who made it and became more intense and more conscious for those who didn't make it.

CAYLEY: But why does this show counterproductivity rather than the stubborn resistance of the patriarchy against which feminism must continue to struggle?

ILLICH: I didn't claim that it showed anything about patriarchy. I claimed that it showed something about sexism. I tried to distinguish between gender and sex. Gender creates in all societies two fields, two complements which are dissymmetric. In the public sphere men usually dominate women. I have absolutely no doubt of it and it disgusts me. In European, Mediterranean cultures I call this patriarchy. But this is not at all the same thing as the discrimination which can exist only where there is a *claim* that men and women are equal, so that every woman who finds out that she gets a bum deal, or any sociologist who finds out that women as a group get a bum deal, can speak about discrimination. Discrimination happens when somebody who officially is claimed to be an equal in fact finds out that she is not treated as a man in her place would be treated. I tried to make a clear distinction between sexism and gender, and I claimed, in that book, that science is profoundly sexist, not primarily because it is biassed — by being practised mostly by men who look from a male point of view — but primarily because it is an attempt to view reality from the point of view of the human being.

For all the other books I have written, I have been able, long before writing the book, to make a clear forty-minute statement of the argument in a lecture. I did this for *Medical Nemesis* in *The Lancet*, for *Deschooling Society* in *The Saturday Review*, and I did it for other things in *The New York Review of Books*, but with *Gender* I never succeeded in preparing a forty-minute presentation on why I wrote this book at that time, or what point I wanted to make which was relevant to the discussion of the moment. I therefore learned how to argue my point. And I argued it with people who had read my statement and questioned me on the text. In fact, for years I have found it impossible to accept invitations to lecture on what I mean by gender. I can do this in highly technical circumstances — with anthropologists, with sociologists, with economists — that is, with people who don't know why this is important for me, with people who engage in value-free discussions and therefore don't care what I tell them. In front of people who cared, I could discuss it, but I couldn't put it into a lecture that would satisfy me.

CAYLEY: Why? Does that make you suspect that your thesis was cloudy? Or was it just because of the deep prejudice against you?

ILLICH: No. The category of the human being is such a profound certainty of post-Enlightenment thought that my claim that this is a recently engineered social construct is simply unacceptable. I can give my evidence, and my strongest evidence is certainly from tools. There is no way — so far at least — to falsify my statement that the tool kit is split, especially when you are as careful as I was to recognize that there are many characteristic types of exception. For example, during the last three hundred years in a certain Styrian valley, women make the second cut of the grass, using the scythe, which otherwise is strictly reserved for the men. Or, in a given valley of France, when the oldest pig is being killed, the man will select it for slaughter, while for all other pigs it is the woman who makes the selection. I was able to distinguish, with the help of Yvonne Verdier's beautiful book on gender in a village, eighteen distinct activities during the day of pig slaughter, each assigned exclusively to men or exclusively to women.[171]

In order to make my point about this separation of human activities, and the gendered nature of all activity that is cultural and human, I had to distinguish carefully between the purpose of the actions which sociologists and anthropologists usually discuss, and what is observable in the action, namely, the grasp of a tool in a describable gesture. When I say bread-making or bread-serving is a female activity, I do not know exactly what I am talking about. I have taken a category which exists today and projected it into the past. When I look more closely and say that the knife is applied to the well-baked bread before it is served — by the woman, or by the man, in a given society — then I am describing the use of the hand in the grasping of tools. So these tools are gendered, but in each society differently. For instance, I know that for the Slavonic area, men cut the bread towards themselves and women cut it away from themselves, and you can't find a single exception!

CAYLEY: I don't think that anyone disputes your evidence. Even your critics acknowledge that gender has existed. The question, I think, is, So what?

ILLICH: This is my argument: If gender existed, in the sense in which I use the term, there were, in popular culture, no human beings. The human being is a construct of the law or of religion. The human being, then, can be sexed, of this or that kind. And I claim that most anthropologists and sociologists deal with sexed human beings and assume that human beings have always been sexed. Gender is culturally determined. It defines men as belonging to the beings who behave in one way and women as those who behave in the other. It does not really know the construct of the human being.

CAYLEY: Yes, but for feminism, this construction of the human being is liberation.

ILLICH: Yes.

CAYLEY: These gendered domains you describe are simply arbitrary limitations on human freedom to be whatever we would like to be.

ILLICH: Agreed. I have no question of that.

CAYLEY: But I'm asking what you think is lost by the replacement of gender by sex.

ILLICH: Certainly, the relative protection of women within the gender sphere of the woman. Empirically, wherever gender gets lost, if you statistically analyze a population large enough, you'll find out that on any characteristic which is both measurable and valued, women have a bum deal. I do not try to *explain* this. I wrote it in 1982. I began my book by saying please look at the evidence. It is obvious that whenever gender gets lost, we move into a sexist society. And it is evident that sexism, defined as the competition of a woman for a man's tools, was excluded, by definition, in a gendered society. For practical purposes, the only point I wanted to make was to beg people to please look at this!

It's amazing how quickly things change. When I used the term *gender* in 1980, and told my publisher, Pantheon, that I wanted to write a book with that title, they told me that the only thing anyone understands as gender is the article you put in front of a noun. In certain special sciences, it means gender as distinct from species. I do know, my editor said, that some anthropologists also identify gender and sex.

Then I went back to the library — in 1980 — and looked at feminist literature. It was all a question of sexism. Sex and gender were used identically. A few people had begun to speak about the social aspects of women's behavior as gender and their physiological differences as sex. One year after my book was published, in 1983, the two major indices for scientific literature in the United States introduced, for the first time, as a new word in the subject index *gender*. Today we take its use for granted, but as a completely arbitrary way of speaking about the social reflections of sex, in a certain kind of literature.

At the time the book was written, I had another deep hope. At that time, I was strongly convinced that out of the women's scientific movement, out of the women's studies movement, would come a radical questioning of the categories with which society is examined, and has been examined for the last twenty years, or even the last hundred years. I wanted to make my small contribution and say, "Look here, you have a chance — the first chance which I could see — for a *radical* questioning of the categories of economics, of sociology, and of anthropology."

I know what it means to be treated as a Jew. The exalted feminist professors in Berkeley treated me not simply as a Jew but as a Jew who had engaged in explicitly anti-Aryan activities. They made me realize why it would have been impossible for a Jew to speak in Germany — say, in 1934 or 1935 — about racism as a category. Now, maybe, this is all funny, if you look back on it . . .

CAYLEY: When I asked why the loss of gender was to be regretted, you said, first of all, that it exposes women to humiliation.

ILLICH: Yes, but not the humiliation women became particularly sensitive about, that of patriarchy, a very old category. If I'm not mistaken, the humiliation which results from the loss of gender is that of discrimination.

CAYLEY: But this is only the beginning. You also suggest that with the loss of what you call the ambiguous complementarity of gender our whole way of knowing the world shifts.

ILLICH: The book which got published as *Gender* constitutes a small fraction of the papers I wrote at that time, for myself and a couple of friends. In those papers, I examine the break between the past, which I can explore as a historian, and the modern industrial present, in which I live and in which I can test my sociological or anthropological categories, in order to give them the appearance of scientific tools. I began then to be concerned with the same thing with which I am completely occupied today. I began to investigate the discontinuity between past and present which has resulted from the transformation of our mode of perception. In the demise of gender I found *the* most profound and *the* most radical change which has taken place during the epoch in which modern science and engineering have come into their own.

Up until that time, for instance, I was truly convinced that it was possible to speak about the human body. I still remember when a woman who has had considerable influence on me, Norma Swenson, of the Women's Health Collective in Boston, after a lecture at Harvard asked me just one question: "Professor Illich, have you ever seen a human body?" *It hit me*, believe me.

For a long time I had been interested — we can come back to this, if you want — by the fact that the I, the ego, has no grammatical gender in any language in the world. There seems to be an exception in a dialect spoken in Hadhramaut. I don't know that dialect, but it has been called to my attention.

Let it stand, it proves my rule! Suddenly, I could understand why. It was obvious that when *I* speak in an oral society everybody immediately knows whether it's a man or a woman because the voice is gendered. But we aren't born with a gendered voice. Psychologists tell us that it is the influence of our society that shapes our voices as male or female. In Madagascar, "men have to speak this way" [falsetto], and "women have to speak in a different way" [affected bass]. Yet there is no spoken language in which, when you hear it, you can't immediately understand whether it is a man or a woman speaking.

I became increasingly convinced that the deepest change I could observe between then and now, between a prescientific, preindustrial, pre-commodity-intensive past, and our present worldview as examined by Gehlen,[172] was the transition from one type of duality to another. It is quite clear that "two" can be conceived of in two different ways. When I say one, two can mean primarily, emotionally, conceptually the *other*, or it can mean one more of the same. Here I was helped by G. E. R. Lloyd's great study on polarity in classical Greece.[173] It seems to me that in all preliterate societies, or prealphabetic Western societies I can study, the first way of conceiving duality shaped the depths of consciousness. There is me and there is the other; there is the microcosmos and there is the macrocosmos; there is this world and the other world; *here* are the living and *there* are the dead; and, in the most profound sense, I *am* a man, and these others, women, are shaded for me, muted for me, other for me. There might be a search for a distant unity in which the world would disappear. But otherness, even at the height of intimacy, was what gave ultimate consistency to what we today call consciousness, to being here.

With the seventeenth century — or, as I can argue later, with certain religious ideas of the twelfth century — *the* human being, *the* self, *the* individual, became the model of our thinking. And then an entirely new way of seeing the other came into existence: he is an other with a black skin; the post-Cartesian inside is a special zone within a general space; people who speak English are a special group in humanity where others speak French, or German; I am a type of human being who is not constructed in the same physical way as others — you are blond, I am dark, you are a woman, I am a man. This loss of the idea of otherness involved the collapse of what as far as I can see is constitutive of all traditional language and culture and thought. The tension between dissymmetric complementarities was collapsed into an a priori abstract notion, which then finds accidental distinctions. *Now* I can understand why the people to whom I spoke as engaged members of a movement didn't pick me up on this kind of reflection. It wasn't for them!

CAYLEY: I presume the loss of gender is not absolute. But, if you're right, to the extent that it is lost, this loss ought to be fatal to the imagination.

ILLICH: You say supposing that the loss is not absolute. The greatest difficulties I encountered when I wrote the book had to do with how to speak about what I called the rests of gender, those things we can recover in a very personal relationship of friendship, which must replace what was formerly a culturally defined relationship between men and women. We become conscious of what makes us able to survive. Without the recovery of these gender rests, we're really locked in a double ghetto without any access to what makes poetry or imagination between the two of us possible, and at the very same time excluded from what we seek in sexed society, namely, equality as human beings. There can't be a relationship between two human beings! It certainly has nothing to do with what Plato called friendship.

CAYLEY: You gave the lectures that were published as *Gender* in Berkeley. A journal called *Feminist Issues* later published a series of papers given at a symposium held after the lectures. What happened?

ILLICH: A group of seven senior professors of Berkeley organized a witch-hunting trial to which I was invited a week after my lectures were over. I was told from the beginning that while each of them would speak for twenty minutes, I would have ten minutes to answer the seven of them. I was accused. The papers were published, as you say, and a copy of the journal was somehow sent to me. It's one of those journals where you may pay a certain amount and reproduce it. I said to myself, Well, this is really an opportunity to make people aware of what I have said by sending this out. So I had a thousand copies made, and a list made, but then I said, No, a gentleman doesn't do this.

I know that this attitude will probably be interpreted as sexist, but I wanted it to show that a man doesn't try to meddle in the gossip of women.

CAYLEY: The women who argue against your position in *Feminist Issues* point to the fact that gender very frequently occurs under circumstances that are patriarchal and actively misogynistic.

ILLICH: Yes . . .

CAYLEY: So there are many gendered societies where ambiguous complementarity is a bit of a euphemism for suppression, segregation, and shunning of women by men.

ILLICH: No question.

CAYLEY: And this leads to a question, I think. Is this . . .?

ILLICH: Is this any better?

CAYLEY: Well, yes, all right.

ILLICH: If you carefully read my book, you'll see that I leave this question up to women who have to experience discrimination. I ask them to make that judgement, once they have understood my distinction between patriarchy and discrimination. For instance, there is a tremendous difference in modern society between being born to poor parents and having learned in school that the reason why I have remained poor is my having failed in school — especially once you have understood that if you are born to poor parents the probability that you will fail in school is enormously higher than if you have been born to rich parents. Therefore, as an outside observer, not subject to feminist discrimination, or *machista* discrimination, it is my conviction that I live in a society in which the traditional Italian, Spanish, French, German, English patriarchal subjection of women has been compounded with an entirely new interiorized discrimination, which was unknown previously. And I am *angry* — I was then, at least, deeply angered — furious at seeing the position of modern woman as worse, as far as I could understand, than the position of women any time before. And I was also angered, though much less so, by the belief of a little bunch of women who believed that by improving their own *personal status* through outlawing discrimination, women would be helped.

CAYLEY: I think the problem is partly that you're understood to be holding up the past as an ideal.

ILLICH: No, the past is a foreign country, as Lowenthal points out.[174] I'm not endorsing the past. It's *past*, it's *gone*. Even less am I endorsing the present. I'm subject to it, I'm in it.

CAYLEY: But people see traditional society as a closed society, and I think they feel that you're recommending a return to a closed society.

ILLICH: I'm neither a romantic, nor a Luddite, nor a utopian. I tell them, please look, try to understand how these people lived, felt, laughed, cried, moaned, shouted, fought, bit each other, stripped trousers or shirts from each other. Look at it! That's how people lived here, and somewhere else they lived in a very different way, in hundreds of different ways. But there were certain commonalities, no matter how they lived. They had at least this one assumption that I'm discussing now, namely, gender. And then look at how we live. We don't have the assumption about gender. We can't go back to it. Wherever the money economy was kept at bay, gender prevailed. Exchange relations were excluded from the village or household through the existence of gender. What women could do men couldn't do, and what men could do women couldn't do. They depended on each other. There was a mutual dependence built in wherever gender reigned. Look at it! I'm not endorsing the way I live now. I personally find much of it terribly sad. I end my book by saying quite clearly that I have no strategy to offer. The book was not written with strategic intent. I refuse to speculate on the probabilities of a cure for the regime of sex. That's not my task. Each one of us will have to invent, in friendship — in which I believe — his own anodyne, medicine, or ray of hope. I will not allow the shadow of some brilliant future, of something which is to come, to fall on the concepts with which I try to grasp what is and what has been.

I'm not one to dream about a fully sexed, totally degendered population of cyborgs, cybernetic organisms. Whom do I want to imitate? I don't demand that other people follow the ascetic and the poet in meditating on death, and in the meditation find enjoyment of the present, an exquisite aliveness, which is absent among people who close their eyes to death. So I stand looking backwards, not forwards to what will happen in the next ten years. I look backwards, to the sad loss of that perceiving duality, which is gone. I have no fantasy about it coming back.

I strongly suspect that a contemporary art of living can be recovered. I believe in the art of suffering, in the art of dying, in the art of *living*, and, so long as it is in an austere and clearsighted way, in the art of enjoyment, the art of living it up. I accept the double ghetto in which I'm stuck. I take the term *double ghetto* to honor Barbara Duden. The book grew out of a fight with her, which became a conversation. She coined it. We are caught in the ghetto of the economic neuter, which obligates me to recognize as barely recoverable that sense of otherness which is constitutive for people around me in a Mexican village, and, simultaneously, to renounce the relative comfort, the easygoing nonchalance, the superficiality of economic sex. The only hope for the life which I'm seeking rests upon rejection of sentimentality and openness to surprise.

CAYLEY: *Gender* is, in many ways, an essay in economic history, so I wonder if we could turn now to a figure who crops up increasingly in your later writings, *Homo economicus.*

ILLICH: *Homo economicus.* That would be in my yellow cards.

CAYLEY: Is he in there?

ILLICH: Certainly he's in there, in three or four places. I always want to live detached from all things, and last year my filing case got lost in an airport. And there I realized, to my great surprise, that not because I was a poor man but because I was an *old* man I could say, well, I can live on without it. But here it is again!

CAYLEY: It came back . . .

ILLICH: *Homo economicus.* I pull out the cards only symbolically, to tell you that *Homo economicus* is not a concept which grew in my garden. I use the term in the way in which Louis Dumont uses it. Dumont is by now an elderly sociologist who lived for a quarter of a century in India and wrote a huge study on the caste system there. He argues very strongly that our concept of the individual never penetrated the spirit or the conceptual frame of the Indian subcontinent.[175] He then came back to Europe. He had been made very sensitive by his Indian experience; and, looking, if you want, as a very sophisticated Brahmin would look, he tried, through a commentary on the texts of Mandeville, Hobbes, Locke, Marx, to describe how economic man had come into existence in Europe.[176] He described how society became a net of individuals who depend on each other for the satisfaction of their needs and how an image of man appeared in which he is born needy, with wants which can be satisfied only through recourse to commodities.

So I really have to send people back to read Dumont, and even more importantly, to read René Girard, whose reflections on mimetic desire cast a new light on Dumont's work.[177] Girard proves through his study of certain novels of the last century that *Homo economicus* comes into existence only from the middle of the nineteenth century. I begin to be a person who can desire only what I see you and others desire. Desire becomes mimetic when it's no longer my fantasy but the imitation of the other's expression of his need through which my need will be shaped.

CAYLEY: When does the economization of society begin?

ILLICH: Aristotle relates his shock at the fact that his fellow Athenians have begun to behave like *kápeloi*, which means sausage vendors on the forum, who let prices go up when there is much demand and no more fried sausage is available and let them drop when they want to sell off the last already burned remains of their sausages. He was deeply worried by the fact that decent, virtuous Athenians behaved that way. Karl Polanyi analyzes this story and points out that no author before him had taken Aristotle's telling of it seriously.[178]

Polanyi made me understand, through a seminar he held on this subject for several years in the early 1940s, at Columbia, that there is nothing natural about the law of demand and supply, changing prices, that this is a highly sophisticated technique, almost as sophisticated as the idea of picking twenty-three signs for twenty-three clusters of sounds and beginning to call them an alphabet, and writing with them. These are tremendous break-throughs. This technique was invented by Phoeni-cians, appeared in Athens, and then spread all around the globe.

Marketing, according to Polanyi, must not be con-fused with trading. Traders, who, like diplomats, arrive with products of a foreign land which they exchange at a politically fixed rate against other goods, are millennia older than merchants, who use markets to render scarce commodities that are sup-posedly in demand.

When people today ask me what I mean by the history of scarcity, I speak to them about what others call culture. Anthropologists take for granted the concept of culture. I remember that only twenty years ago when I used the term in German, I had to say *Kultur*, but in the American sense. Otherwise, Germans understood something else. And in France, I would say *la culture, dans le sens Américain*.

What other people call culture, I would understand as unique arrangements by which a given group limits exchange relationships to specific times and places. You may engage in these activities on Saturday, when the market is open from six in the morning till noon, or down at the brothel, or over there at the bar, but otherwise, we don't want any of that.

For a couple of millennia after Aristotle most European cultures remained market-resistant. Markets were carefully regulated and kept in place. The story of *Homo economicus*, the story of commodity production — not simple commodity production, but, as Marx would say, industrial commodity production, capitalist commodity production — is the story of the last 250 years. For instance, there has been a total transformation in the perception of space. Formerly the space of one kingdom was different from the space of another kingdom. The weights and measures were different, here and there. When a good passed from one kingdom to the next, it actually changed in nature. The idea of circulation was absent. Harvey spoke about the circulation of blood, but when I carefully read him he tells me that blood circulates as Aristotle said water circulates, and then he describes distillation, not circulation! The idea that something can return to its source without changing its quality is an idea which becomes thinkable only together with vast commodity circulation around 1680. In 1650, old Harvey still defended himself against Descartes, who described the heart as a pump. "No, I don't want to describe it that way," said Harvey. "The blood doesn't circulate in that way." Thirty years later, *les idées circulent en France*, traffic circulates, commodities circulate. So I'm speaking about a *long* history during which a certain number of our current certitudes slowly take shape, and these certainties are all requirements for living in a world where everything ultimately can be purchased for a buck. And if it can't be purchased for a buck, it's called a *value*, which is nothing else but what dollars can't yet buy.

CAYLEY: You spoke of Polanyi and his seminar at Columbia. When did you encounter him?

ILLICH: I stumbled across Polanyi. It always seems to happen that way. One knows of a book, one has seen it quoted, one has looked it up. But one day I said, My goodness, what have I been losing by not having read this book twenty years ago? Polanyi became particularly important for me when I wrote the key chapter in *Medical Nemesis*, the chapter on counterproductivity. I didn't write that book on medicine to speak about medicine, but to discuss the counterproductivity of commodity production after a certain level of intensity in supply is reached. I just used medicine as an illustration.

Polanyi became important reading for me in 1976 and 1977. I had him translated into a couple of languages where he was not yet available. Later, my work was picked up by Dr. Yoshiro Tamanoi, professor of economics at Tokyo University. He had translated Polanyi and wrote me asking if he could translate *Gender*, because it seemed to him a very economic book. Through my friendship with him, Polanyi became even more important for me. I have a group of four or five friends, three of them Japanese, for whom the further elaboration of Polanyi became a very major undertaking. For example, Makoto Maruyama is now at the University of Toronto doing his doctorate on alternative monies. He's much more competent and clearsighted on this issue than I would be.

Doctor Tamanoi died. I had the honor of burying him — but that's not the right word — presiding over the ceremonies at his cremation. I loved the man and respected him. Makoto is his successor. I would trust him to continue this conversation.

CAYLEY: What did you mean by saying Polanyi needs further elaboration?

ILLICH: Well, the same thing is true about Chayanov, as Teodor Shanin has pointed out.[179] Chayanov was killed by Stalin for his thinking about the relationship between Soviet communism and the peasants. He is now becoming the great prophet and is being quickly edited in Russia, where he was proscribed for forty years after his death.

It's funny that in this very liberal world, some of the most significant men and thinkers are, after a short period of fashion, pushed into an eclipse. Of course, you can find them in libraries, but not always so easily. Elie Halevy was the first man who really understood that *Homo economicus* is a totally new construct. He was a French historian of the English working class, writing at the beginning of this century. He wrote a book on radical philosophers, making a strong point that with Bentham, more or less, there is a break in European thought. This break hasn't been explored to its depth because what is thought and discussed afterwards would formerly have been considered, under all circumstances, *im-*

moral.[180] This is a book which Polanyi considered fundamental. But Elie Halevy is unavailable in France. One can find only a few copies in strange libraries of his full book on radical philosophers. In the United States, he is never read and is practically unknown. I'll bet that, in another ten years, he will be "must" reading in departments of economics, which will have discovered in the meanwhile that they are dealing with fantasies.

CAYLEY: In your work on gender, and in your history of scarcity, you seem to be concerned with the disappearance of boundaries and of roots. Yet you yourself move easily between cultures; and when you were talking about multilingualism the other day, you disparaged the idea that people's identities are threatened by living in overlapping cultural realities. Is there a contradiction here?

ILLICH: When I talk to you in English, I'm distinctly different in my expression than when I talk to you in French. People say that even my gesture changes, but certainly my expression, and I don't mean just the muscles of the mouth, but the eyes. And, since words have taste and atmosphere and something which can be touched about them, the sensual reality in which I live at that moment is different in English and in French, and in German it would be different again. And when I quote in a German lecture one of my darling passages from Seneca or Abelard, for a moment I pull people away from the sensual experience of German and ask at least those who have the ability to share a bit of the power and conciseness of that Latin. When I dance the waltz, my body is a different body than when I dance the cha-cha-cha or the tango, which I don't know how to dance.

I do believe that it is precisely rootedness which gives you ease in multilingual expression or participation in dancing intercourse with very different cultures. Only when one's roots are cut or denied or considered as something secondary does the search for the so-called identity, for some kind of inner fitting of the individual upon itself, become an important fantasy.

CAYLEY: How can this mobility of which you speak be distinguished from the decentered personality which one finds in postmodern thought?

ILLICH: Roots . . . knowing that soil exists only insofar as you are within a horizon and a true horizon always roots you in soil even if it's the soil of the desert through which you walk.

CAYLEY: So mobility, which is not rootlessness, depends on the substantial existence of things within a horizon, which enables us to belong to them, and not on some fantasy core to our personalities, which you regard as a Romantic illusion.

ILLICH: When the old Estruscans or Greeks wanted to found a city, they drew a furrow the way the clock runs around an envisioned space. And that furrow became symbolic of the meeting place of heaven and earth, outside and inside, horizon and soil. Always, each one of these meetings was conceived as a marriage, a sacred marriage. Rootedness has something to do with the full awareness that we bear asymmetric complementarity within us, that we are one insofar as we are the meeting of two that fit but aren't mirror images.

CAYLEY: Identity grows stronger as the world becomes more spectral, in a sense.

ILLICH: Identity becomes a necessary refuge for those who live in a spectral world. That's true. But I'm not speaking of identity. I'm speaking of rootedness, of awareness of lying in the hands of another, of contingency, and of being myself because I'm constantly being created and sustained. That's the mystery. But it's very difficult to speak about these things which seem to have been obvious and unquestioned during a thousand years of Western tradition.

VII
The Mask of Love

CAYLEY: I want to begin today by asking you about some people. The first is Michel Foucault. Did he have any influence on you around the time you wrote *Limits to Medicine*?

ILLICH: No. Foucault became important for me, for a while, in the late 1970s, when I met him for the first time in Paris. We had a very long conversation at the point at which he had just gotten beyond the first volume of his history of sexuality and had become stuck, trying to find his way into the next volume of this multivolume project.[181] I argued that I could not see sexuality in the modern sense of something common to women and men yet with a different plumbing — to use Erich Fromm's phrase — as something constituted before the penitentiaries of the twelfth century. After this conversation, I went on to read seriously his previous work. At the time of *Medical Nemesis*, I had taken notice of him, but he had not influenced me.

CAYLEY: That's interesting, because I assumed that he had . . .

ILLICH: You *might* be right. I let things penetrate me and very often I'm not aware where my ideas come from. It has often happened that I have had an idea which I thought was original and, therefore, needed testing and checking out, and, in the process, I have turned up the source from which I had taken it, even if it was a source I had known only indirectly.

CAYLEY: I wanted to ask as well about a man whom I think you loved very much and learned from, Paul Goodman.[182]

ILLICH: Yes, I loved Goodman very much, but not from the beginning. In 1951, as a twenty-six-year-old man newly arrived in New York, I went to a public debate. This strange person arrived and fascinated everybody with his way of presenting himself. I was just then having my first experiences of sitting through cold turkey with neighborhood kids from Washington Heights, and this guy carefully phrased his proposal that New York *immediately* decriminalize all substances you can ingest, because otherwise the city of New York would become an unlivable city within the next few years. He had recently played a major part in getting a law passed which recognized that the state should not interfere with the private activities of consenting adults.

Well, I was shocked! I would not have suspected that within three or four years we would be good friends and that during the last part of his life he would spend considerable time with me in Cuernavaca. I consider Goodman one of the great thinkers I've known, and also a tender, touching person.

CAYLEY: Was he at CIDOC a good deal in the late 1960s and early 1970s?

ILLICH: Yes. Did I tell you the story of Goodman in 1969 and the little guy who defined himself as an anarchist? Every day Valentina Borremans, who directed CIDOC, closed down all language teaching and seminar activities for an hour and gave even the employees the time off. Those who wished could gather under a big tree on benches which accommodated three or four hundred people for what we called the daily circus. Goodman had agreed to give four lectures in this forum. I had asked him to state a theme for his talks, and he had chosen the law. On this day, he was to speak about the majesty of the law.

There was a little red-haired, woolly-headed kid who felt that anarchistic testimony was very important. I had caught him stuffing forks down into the toilet. I just looked at him and said, "Come, let's take them out together," and didn't tell anybody about it. But I knew the guy. Well, this guy gets up and says to Goodman, "We had expected something better from a man like you than to talk about the law at a time like this." He said much nastier things which I can't remember and won't repeat. Goodman began to cry. When finally his tears had stopped, he looked at the kid and said, "I guess we have come to the point where you have to be an anarchist to understand the dignity of the law."

Goodman once said to me, "I have never written a line unless I was sure either that I had said it or would say it as it's written." And that impressed me, of course, because I've never written a line which I have the feeling I could have said. And people don't notice the difference between my speaking and my writing. They aren't aware how much, given my destiny, speaking obliges me to read off internal lines. This conversation with Goodman was one of the reasons why later I got so much concerned about the impact of literacy on the mode of being of our Western culture.

CAYLEY: You mentioned this anarchist. Did it often happen that you were mistaken for a sort of free university?

ILLICH: I never worried for what I was mistaken.

CAYLEY: When and why did CIDOC end?

ILLICH: In 1973 I came to the conclusion that all that I had wished to achieve by having started the center in 1960, and then totally done it over in 1965, all which I had absolutely wanted to do and that could be done, had been done. And because of the funny image created, the physical danger to my collaborators had become something which it was difficult to take responsibility for — you must remember what Latin America was at that moment. I also understood that the place would not be able to save itself from university-like institutionalization. Groups of professors from Stanford, Cornell, and other universities wanted to take over the place. This would have meant that the sixty-three people who, under the leadership of Valentina Borremans, actually ran and made the center, none of whom had a college degree and most of whom had not finished elementary school, would have been replaced by a new bunch of internationals.

And I saw a danger coming, because of the Mexican government's policy of sustaining the peso. I trusted my inherited financial instinct enough in 1973 to convince myself that the oil boom could not sustain the growth rate projected by the Mexican planning institutions. And I predicted that the support of the peso would lead to a very bad crash and to insolvency. Meanwhile life in Mexico would become increasingly expensive. I have never taken grant money, gift money, except for tiny things — I wouldn't refuse a cookie. CIDOC's independence was predicated on the difference in salaries between the U.S. and Mexico. We offered intensive language instruction, five hours a day for four months in groups of three. We paid Mexican high school students salaries they couldn't have gotten being high school teachers in Cuernavaca, and charged Americans prices which were high for Mexico but extremely low for the U.S. Thus, through economies of scale, we were able to cream off enough to run an institute for advanced studies, and a library.

In 1973 I saw that our ability to do this was threatened. Through this managed peso the difference in incomes between Mexico and the U.S. would become too small to sustain this policy. So in 1973 I asked the administration of CIDOC — I never held any office, I never exercised any power, I never signed anything during these fifteen years in Mexico, I always acted through unquestioned influence, but not through the exercise of managerial power — I asked them to get together and gave them a three-day seminar on international economics. I got assistance at this meeting from two or three outstanding Mexican economists, and convinced the group of sixty-three that it was in their interest to accept my plan that, for the next two years or for as long as it would take, income above expenditure would not be spent on books or airplane tickets but would go into a fund. When the fund reached one and a half times the salary mass of a year, it would be divided into sixty-three equal parts, people would go home, and we would close the institution. We then did it on the tenth anniversary, the first of April, 1976, with a huge fiesta at which hundreds of people from town were also present. Some of the language teachers split up the school into several different ones, the library went as a gift to the most responsible library there, at the Colegio de Mexico, and from one day to another it was over.

CAYLEY: Does a vestigial language school remain?

ILLICH: When I began this, I chose Cuernavaca as a place already so touristy that any damage which outsiders could do to a Mexican town had already been done, so we wouldn't have to feel guilty about the presence of the Peace Corps types and missionaries whom we would attract there. By 1980, there were seventeen competing language schools in Cuernavaca.

CAYLEY: I also wanted to ask you about another of your associates at CIDOC, Paulo Freire. There was a group of us in Toronto at the end of the 1960s who thought of you and Freire as a kind of one-two punch from Latin America. But there's a footnote in

Gender where you treat, not Freire as a man, but his idea of conscientization quite sharply.[183] I wondered, what had happened?

ILLICH: Paulo I met in the early 1960s in Brazil. From 1960 on I had felt that something parallel to the center I got going in Cuernavaca — for the discouragement of volunteering activities — ought to be established in Brazil also. And so I founded a place in Petropolis, near Rio de Janeiro. The now deceased John Vogel, who had been in Brazil for a long time, took the place into his hands. It played a strange, important role before and after the military takeover in Brazil. I myself went there as the first student to learn Portuguese.

Then Helder Camara took me over for a month and a half. He made me read at least one book by a Brazilian author or about a Brazilian author's work every day — people forget sometimes that he was a demanding reader and intellectual — and then in the evening he sat down with me and that author for hours of conversation right across the spectrum of Brazilian politics, literary genres, mentalities. He then sent me out, mostly by bus, for a two-month trip through what he wanted me to know of Brazil before I opened my big mouth. I've *never* had a tutor like that! And people wouldn't expect Helder to be a tutor like that.

Well, one of the men I had to meet was Paulo Freire. We hit it off immediately and became good friends. Then, a year and a half later, he was in the military police jail. On the very next day, I went to Teodoro Moscoso, who had been one of the five members of the board of higher education in Puerto

Rico, where I served with him. I knew him very well. He was then the administrator of the Alliance for Progress, and asked for two heads, that of Paulo Freire and that of Francisco Julião, the peasant leader. The CIA reported to Moscoso at the Department of State that these two were as dangerous as Castro! I didn't ask why. With that kind of people, you won't get very far anyway.

I then brought him to Cuernavaca, and there we edited and published his first book outside of Brazil. We made the first translations of his writings and circulated them throughout the world. I was certainly very much impressed by what I saw Paulo's teams do. *Deschooling Society* has a few pages which give testimony to this. But I moved from the criticism of schooling to the criticism of what *education* does to a society, namely, foster the belief that people have to be helped to gain insights into reality, and have to be helped to prepare for existence or for living. Adult education then tries to push itself and make itself obligatory. This became for me the thing I wanted to analyze very critically. Therefore, despite its good and solid tradition, it was I who moved away from the approach for which Paulo had become the outstanding spokesman during the 1960s and early 1970s not only in Latin America but all over the world.

Our friendship has remained tender and completely untouched. And I think a good biography of Paulo would show that he has remained quite independent from the Marxist Christians at the World Council of Churches who have adopted him as their idol and have manipulated his image. I remember

Paulo with immense affection, but also as somebody who more and more wanted to save the credibility of educational activities at a time when my main concern had become a questioning of the conditions which shape education in *any* form, including *conscientizacão* or psychoanalysis or whatever it might be.

Now, I hope that nobody interprets such a split in our fields of interest, which at a certain moment began to diverge, in that silly political way in which people are always considered as opposing each other. In the analysis of ritualized and graded school education, Paulo was for me a very solid point of passage and remains a dear friend.

CAYLEY: You spoke a little the other day about this passage in your thought from criticizing schools to analyzing the assumptions that make education in any form possible. Perhaps this would be a good time for you to say a bit more about it.

ILLICH: The simplest way of explaining it would be to speak about Wolfgang Sachs. He's twenty years younger than I and, I don't know how, he got interested in my work and did a good, solid critical thesis on *Deschooling Society*. When that thesis was nearing completion, he came to Cuernavaca to meet me, and was there in my seminar. He invited me, if I were ever to be in Germany, to his mother's, because she knows how to make a very special apple cake. I liked him. So I went to visit his mother, and she told me that her son was not in München but in Tübingen at that time. I went to Tübingen — this was some years ago — on Pentecost. It was a glorious day, one of those days when Germany is really flowering and you think of Goethe and the German Romantic poets. For a couple of decades I had practically not spoken the language. It was a funny, enjoyable weekend.

From then on a group of people formed. They are now middle-aged and serious, but they were then students, and they took me to task for the damage I had done through *Deschooling* by identifying what other people call education with *that* institution. They said that nongraded rituals, rituals which assembled either fewer than fifteen or more than fifty people at one time, rituals which did not require thousands of hours of attendance, were increasingly becoming the modality by which the commodity called education was pushed down people's throats. Therefore, a criticism had to be mounted of the implicit human costs of destroying informal education and replacing it by adult education and in-service training and so on. I took them seriously. And insofar as I was still interested in education, what I went through in the mid-1970s was an attempt to make people understand that the alternative to schooling, when it becomes adult education, could be more oppressive than schooling itself, that the alternative to schooling through home education by parents might be even more horrible than schooling. This was something John Holt very quickly understood. I could then give up talking about it because he took it over with his newsletter and his association.[184] This was a beautifully monomaniacal guy, someone you occasionally went to see, just to touch him, to make certain that he did exist! And there he was with his paperclip on his shirt, strengthening his fingers for playing the cello, which he learned as a man of forty, while you talked with him, a guy who put on a green helmet when he went into the subway so he would not be disturbed and could listen to whatever recording of poetry he wanted to enjoy that day.

So this was an important stage for me. The next stage came when I began to say that it was not the myth-making ritual used to make people believe in education which I wanted to examine, but the milieu, and the set of social assumptions, within which the idea of education can arise. This was the beginning of my interest in writing a history of scarcity. I have never succeeded in doing this under one cover. But I have brought together a couple of dozen collaborators, each one pursuing his own line of inquiry in this field.

I began to speak about education as learning under the assumption that the means for this purpose are scarce. If I had only one desire, it would be to get across to the people who study education, researchers *on* education, that they should study not what happens *in* education, but how the *very idea* of this nonsense could have come into existence.

CAYLEY: Let's talk about some of these assumptions. For example, there's a passage in *Gender* where you talk about how the idea of reform has been misunderstood.

ILLICH: Excuse me, but do you know what this feels like? It has just come to my mind. In the twelfth century, priests began to assist at the deathbed. It hadn't happened before. People died, but the priest didn't have anything to do with it. Then, in the twelfth century, the priest comes to the deathbed. By the thirteenth, he has taught the dying how to make their final confession.

I knew that there was something strange in this activity in which we are engaged here. And suddenly I've realized that you are making me set out on a life-long confession, a re-evaluation, what the preachers in the last century called the personal judgement, as opposed to the final judgement on the day of the resurrection of the dead . . .

CAYLEY: Yes? Now, shall I read you the passage?

ILLICH: Yes.

CAYLEY: You say that ideas like conscience and confession, and the Church's whole machinery of social control, are a perversion of the original Christian idea of reform, which reflects an attempt to bring about a renewal of the world by means of one's own personal conversion.

ILLICH: One of the *great* and overwhelming fortunes of my life has been the teachers I've had, and among them, Gerhart Ladner is one of the foremost. He is a professor of medieval history, mainly of the history of images, of iconography, in the Middle Ages, a very learned man who in the early 1960s wrote the first volume of a work which will probably remain unfinished.[185] The second, he might finish as a gift to me. For the third, he's too old now, he'll die before he writes it. His book deals with the idea of reform. Reform, in Latin, means turning around, like a wheel, *revolutio*. In this first book, Ladner looks at the end of antiquity, Roman antiquity, and notices that three characteristic types of *revolutio*, turning around, or *reformare*, putting back into form, can be conceived. The first is the idea of going back to Paradise, to the moment of the creation of the world — the hope or expectation that we're moving forward, into a thousand years' kingdom, which justifies any holocaust or any destructive social development which is necessary to reach it. The examples, of course, are mine, not Ladner's.

Second, there is another form of renewal, which is periodic, the greening of the world every spring. But then, in late antiquity, Ladner sees a new, fundamental assumption about the possibility of renewal arising, which comes from the Hebrew biblical idea of *shub* Christianized. This idea animates the practice of the Christian monks, particularly Irish and Scottish monks, who go out to strange desert islands and leave the world without leaving life. They make themselves responsible for turning away from their culture and from its assumptions and towards the kingdom of God, towards something new, for which they are willing to turn themselves inside out. He follows this example of the monks because it is an extreme representation of what early Christianity demanded: self-renewal, the renewal of the person, which God will perform, as the major *social* task of a Christian community. Ladner as a historian asks the question, How does a historian deal with the sudden appearance of an idea as *discontinuous* with all previous ideas as this? As a historian, how does he grasp it? It's not legitimate for him to say, Well, God came and revealed it. That's not within a historian's frame of reference. He has to face the fact that a new form of perception and behavior, which is unprecedented, surprising, unexpected, and unexplainable, is simply . . . *there*.

Now I have read and reread that volume of Ladner. During the mid-1960s, when all those well-meaning people from South and North America came to my seminar talking about revolution, I said, "At least read the Introduction and a set of pages of your choice in that book before you come." When I gave this seminar in Mexico, I examined people and eliminated from the class those who hadn't done their reading of Ladner to my satisfaction. Many just accepted it as a duty. They couldn't figure out what this crazy man wanted. It was then, and with regard to this concept of Ladner's, that I began to reflect on the appearance in the first millennium of Christianity of normative ideas which are radically new, and belong to a new gestalt, different from anything known elsewhere or previously. And I began to wonder if their history could be studied, if it would be possible to follow their historical evolution.

Then, slowly, from another direction, I came to ask myself about these young people who sat in front of me and talked about revolution and about the need for renewal today, to which they were committing themselves. I remember the atmosphere in the mid-1960s. It's difficult to make people today believe that this was not sentimentalism, not mere fantasy, not mere escapism, not mere anger and hatred. There was a real sense of renewal then. It was not romantic, in the sense of trying to go back to Paradise. It was, for many of the best, *not* apocalyptic, though of course there were Stalinists around, some among the Students for a Democratic Society. And it was not simply Reich's *Greening of America*, or Esalen.

There were people who were searching for renewal. They sought this renewal through giving themselves totally to the possibility of making a new society, right now! I asked myself, Where does this idea come from? And I reflected, within this spirit of renewal, on how one could avoid ending up in the well-known American tradition of utopianism. So I began, for the first time in my reflections on history, to go back from a present experience and ask, What are the antecedents of today's revolution? of social change today? of the possibility of desiring social change? And I slowly remounted the ladder until I found, in Ladner, this early certainty which had so surprised him, that the most important service to the world and to others consisted in turning around one's own heart.

Since the 1970s, always growing stronger, this has remained a motive of my research. Powerful and unprecedented ideas, brought through Christianity and through the Gospel into Western history, have been perverted into normative notions of a cruelty, of a *horrifying* darkness, which no other culture has ever known. The Latin *adagium, corruptio optimi pessima* — there's nothing worse than the corruption of the best — became a theme in my reading and reflection. Most of my concern with the Middle Ages is precisely to observe the process of flipping by which a notion which goes beyond what I find in any other culture in bringing out the glory of being you and me is then institutionalized by the Church and becomes something more destructive and worse than anything I can find anywhere else.

That's the reason why this summer with my young friend Manfred Werner, I took once more in my hand the attempt to write a history of the invention of the marriage *bond* in the twelfth century as one example of this. In the early twelfth century, the idea appears that a man and a woman are so radically equal, so human, that they can make an absolutely bilateral, symmetrical contract by saying yes to each other. *This* creates a bond between them, a bond acknowledged by a *vow*, even though Christians are *not* to swear, according to the New Testament. And God is called as a witness to transform this sacramentally into a contractual relationship in heaven. This is the sacrament of matrimony! All societies know weddings: "You have a daughter, I am an old man and have a son . . . Hey, don't you think it would be nice to become in-laws, you and I? . . . Let's use these two guys to make our plans . . . Oh, and by the way, I have noticed that they already sleep together . . . Much better . . . So we avoid any disaster." That's typically what weddings were in all societies. Jack Goody, that marvellous English anthropologist who classified African marriage, family, kinship patterns, came back and said that after twenty years, he realized that there was no precedent for this idea of the marriage contract.[186] It would have been unimaginable that two people could go and see a priest, and the next day she could say to him, "Listen, I want you to meet your father-in-law."

The *idea* that such a thing can exist is something revolutionary, but also of *unspeakable* potential destructiveness. I'm concerned with how unprecedented, glorious attempts to discover what you and I can do and be, when institutionalized, can become evil and destructive beyond anything one could imagine.

CAYLEY: I want to follow that one step further. The other day you said, I think in reference to starvation in the Sahel, "I don't care." I want to know why you refuse "care," in that sense.

ILLICH: When we use the term *care* in modern English, it is extremely difficult to make it mean love without demeaning love. Professional care predominates, medical care, care for the pupil in school, taking care of your car, take care! or, he is so *caring*. John McKnight quite rightly called care the mask of love, the *ugly* mask of love.[187] Of course, it's a very good old English word, which has been used for centuries; but, if you examine the literature of this century, you'll find out that care in the sense of the so-called caring professions is a rather modern phenomenon. These have very effectively, very strongly, changed the everyday usage of care. So I'm suspicious when somebody bases morals on care. Professions who learn how to provide professional care in a very peculiar situation usually have very strong public backing. For example, they can establish what care a blind person needs as a minimum. They can set standards, and then test all those people who have difficulties with sight, and then define who is blind. As was shown twenty years ago, half of all people in the U.S. who can't see have not been defined as blind and don't get care for the blind, while half of those who are defined as blind can read the newspaper every day. It's a fact! My own long-dead mother was one of them. She had a black nose, because *The New York Times* rubbed off!

So, professionals define what constitutes minimal care, who requires it, and then how it will be given. They decide what universal certificates people have to have before they are allowed to touch a diseased person, or teach this blind person how to walk with a cane. In the setting of care having become very much a commodity, when somebody says "I owe care to this person," he says, gratuitously, "I'll generate, I'll make, I'll produce the commodity which really a professional ought to give in that case." So, having become very suspicious of care that is the banner of the caring professions, considering caring professions as intrinsically disabling, I become incensed when somebody as beautiful, as loving, as alive as this friend to whom I made the remark you quoted asks me, "But don't you care for the bloated-belly children on their stick-legs, for those afflicted with kwashiorkor in the Sahel?" My immediate re-action is, I will do everything I can to eliminate from my heart any sense of *care* for them. I want to experience horror. I want to really *taste* this reality about which you report to me. I do not want to escape my sense of helplessness and fall into a pretence that I care and that I do or have done all that is possible of me. I want to live with the *inescapable* horror of these children, of these persons, in my heart and know that I cannot actively, really, love them. Because to love them — at least the way I am built, after having read the story of the Samaritan — means to leave aside everything which I'm doing at this moment and pick up that person. It means taking whatever I have with me, in my little satchel of golden denarii, and bringing the guy to an inn — which then meant a brothel — as that Palestinian did to the Jew who had fallen into the hands of robbers, and saying, "Please take care of this guy. When I return I hope I'll have made a little bit more money and I'll pay you for any extra expenditures."

I have *absolutely* no intention, if I'm sincere, of leaving this writing desk, these index cards, these files, or selling that little antique Mexican sculpture which I bought for a dollar but which might be worth $500 if I find the right antiquarian in New York, and taking that money to go to the Sahel and take that child in my arms. I have no intention, because I consider it impossible. *Why pretend that I care?* Thinking that I care, first, impedes me from remembering what love would be; second, trains me not to be in *that* sense loving with the person who is waiting outside *this* door; and, third, stops me from taking the next week off and going and chaining myself to the door of some industry in New York which has a part in the ecological disaster in the Sahel.

CAYLEY: If you refuse care for those outside of your immediate reach, are you left with anything like what one would normally mean by a politics? Or is this in fact a refusal of politics as we usually understand it?

ILLICH: What an enormous jump you want me to make! The future, in the context in which you now speak, is in the hands of God. The big bang might be now. I can't let anybody insure either the material or the spiritual future for me. I know I live in a world where the greater our ideals are, the greater the insurance companies will become. This includes the Church. It's an insurance company, to a large extent, for virtue, *Christian* virtue, for love . . . surviving. And, in a strange way, it is! Because without it, we wouldn't have tradition, and we couldn't go back to the Gospel.

As far as politics goes, I'm not condemning anybody who continues to think that democratic politics can be continued. In the tradition of the Western world I, radically, in my roots, have chosen the politics of impotence. I bear witness to my impotence because I think that, not only for this one guy, there is nothing else left, but also because I could argue that, at this moment, it's the right thing to do. Today, politics almost inevitably focusses attention on intermediate goals but does not let you see what the things are to which we have to say NO! . . . as, for instance, to care.

VIII
Walking the Watershed

CAYLEY: I would like to talk today about Hugh of St. Victor. Perhaps we could begin with your remark in passing the other day that Hugh was the first and last man in Europe to have an alternative philosophy of technology.

ILLICH: Well, it ought to be clear by now that careful, systematic reflection on what constitutes a tool suddenly appears in the twelfth century. A tool is the physical shape given by man to something natural for the purpose of getting him from intention to end. My two main sources are the *De Variis Artibus* of Theophilus and Hugh's fantasy dialogue with the King of the Brahmins, the natural Christian from India, Dindymus. Hugh was Flemish and must have travelled as a very young man to somewhere in

eastern Europe and gotten his early monastic training there. I see him wandering back to Paris just
when the scandal around Abelard's unmanning had
taken place and establishing himself in that rela-
tively new order called the canons regular. These
were no longer monks, but people who lived in
community in town, for the purpose of *docere verbo
et exemplo* — to teach by speaking and giving an
example of how one lives in a city. Five years later,
he is already made the Master of Studies in that little
cloister of St. Victor, which was then just outside
Paris, on what today would be the Left Bank. He was
an intensely visual type — everything resolves into
light. He who reads is searching for light, he who
loves is enlightened by love. In his doctrine, he has
three pairs of eyes: the eyes of the body, with which
he grasps physical things; the eyes of the mind, with
which he understands what's really in these things
and what relates them to each other; and the eyes of
the heart, which must slowly open and with which
he once looked into the invisible, unspeakable, unlimited light of God.

Now, living with that kind of concentration in all
his reflections on light, he feels that the worst thing
that has happened, as a consequence of disobedi-
ence in Paradise, is an obscuring, a shadow, which
has fallen between man and the creation in which
God has placed him. God made the world in such a
way that man would fit into it perfectly. Adam and
Eve were the only beings God created who were not
protected by thick fur against the cold, and by scales
against thorns, and who didn't have good claws but
only hands made for picking fruit. God told them to

respect certain rules, or ecological limits, as we would say today. There was one tree they were not to break, because if they broke it, they would destroy — according to Hugh — the beautiful harmony and balance of the universe. So what did these two do? According to Hugh, Eve, out of curiosity, and Adam, out of love for Eve, broke a branch from precisely that tree and ate that apple.

The consequence according to Hugh was foreseeable. The balance of the universe changed, and man was left with a body designed for Paradise. His body "changed" into one which was made to bleed by every thorn and which needed shoes, into one which felt cold and needed spinning and weaving and woollens. So Hugh developed a philosophical theology of technology in which technology is an activity by which man, thanks to what God has given him in creation, recovers part of what he has lost through his ecological intervention, which was sin.

When in the early 1970s people began to talk about ecology, and about having to live in a world into which modern technologists have introduced disorder, I somehow had a faint remembrance that I'd heard a story like that before. Very quickly, I picked up in my Migne — Migne's collection of the Church fathers — the two passages, one in the *Didascalicon* and one in this conversation with Dindymus, where Hugh presents this idea. And then I began to wonder, Who else had spoken that way? Who else had spoken of sin as a destruction of the fit between mankind and nature? Who else had spoken, more importantly, of technology as a remedy, as a *recovery*, a partial recovery, of that which would have been the best condition for man to live in during his whole existence? And, of course, I came back to Hugh.

Now, when you look at modern philosophies of technology — the best way to do this is to consult Professor Carl Mitchum's bibliographies on the philosophy of technology[188] — you'll find a great number of different theories about what techniques, what tools, what technology are all about. But, strangely enough, they all share the idea that the Bible has forced Western people to think of technology as a means to dominate nature, while the *only* explicit treatment I find of tools in the first twelve hundred years of Christian thinking is Hugh's idea of what he calls mechanical science, in which he sees technology as a remedy.

CAYLEY: I know very little of the literature that you're referring to, except for some of Lynn White's writings.[189]

ILLICH: Then you know something of technology in the Middle Ages.

CAYLEY: And you're saying that most contemporary thinkers share White's view that our technomania is rooted in the Christian Middle Ages.

ILLICH: Yes, in a flip over from Hugh's thinking, which never became general. For him, tools are a search for a remedy. Tool-making is a kind of penitential activity, an effort to make the sin with which we are born, which we have inherited, a little less unpleasant by reducing cold and hunger and weakness. Within fifty years, by the thirteenth century, technology was already treated — in thought and not only in practice — as a means to subdue the earth and was spoken about in that way.

I've looked carefully at the reception of Hugh's work. Hugh of St. Victor is one of those thinkers who in modern times have been little looked at. In the Middle Ages, you know about Albert the Great, you know about Thomas Aquinas, you even know about Abelard. But Hugh's book on the method of study, the *Didascalicon*, is unknown today. It was not always so. It was written around 1140, and it was one of those four basic textbooks that every cleric had to read as part of his education until well after the Reformation. Southern, the historian, says that the end of the Middle Ages was when this ceased to be a textbook, along with the *Glossa Ordinaria*, the *Commentaries* of Peter the Venerable, and Gratian's *Commentaries on Law*.[190] Hugh's book, as I've said, deals with technology, but I haven't found a single commentator, from his immediate successor in St. Victor in 1170 until modern times, who has recognized Hugh's brilliance in devising a way in which one can speak about technology as a theologian.

CAYLEY: Why do you prefer Hugh's way of speaking to its alternatives?

ILLICH: The overwhelming view of what tool-making means can be summed up in the phrase "making the world a better place to live in." But Hugh says — if I understand him correctly — that tools are an assistance to remedy a little bit the damage we have done to the world. It's a humble view of tools.

CAYLEY: So this remedial approach is self-limiting, as opposed to a more open-ended attempt to establish —

ILLICH: Something better than the Creator provided. People say that there's a danger when I speak
this way. It provides fodder for fundamentalists. But
I say that I will not be blackmailed because one or
another person might appropriate me for his fantasies or ideology.

CAYLEY: You're working at the moment on a book
about Hugh and the history of reading.[191]

ILLICH: Yes, but allow me to introduce this topic in
a somewhat more general way. If anybody asks me,
"Ivan, what is it that you would most like to stimu-
late during the next year and a half of your life?" —
it's in that kind of horizon in which I see my life —
I would answer that I would like to get a certain
number of people to think about what tools do to
our perception rather than what we can do with
them, to look at how tools shape our mind, how their
use shapes our perception of reality, rather than how
we shape reality by applying or using them. In other
words, I'm interested in the symbolic fallout of tools,
and how this fallout is reflected in the sacramental
tool structure of the world.

And I don't want to make just this point, I want
to go a step further. I would like to explore a series
of approaches through which this question has been
raised and studied in different branches of so-called
knowledge in order to find where these converge,
and to what degree the convergence of existing research is distant from the question I want to ask. And
then I would like to attempt two or three alternative
approaches to the exploration of this fundamental
question. This is the way — we've talked about it —
in which I again and again try to proceed. Now, since

I do this with friends, who come to me rather than imposing it from a platform, I have had to select a few specific questions in which I have just enough competence to suggest a model approach. And one of them is this. I ask myself, What is *the* — perhaps only one of several, but certainly for me *the* — most interesting technology that shapes the space one usually calls Western culture, as distinct, say, from Chinese culture? The obvious answer — and here Father Walter Ong has been my main modern living guide — is the alphabet.[192]

We live in a world in which we take for granted that there is a device, a tool, which can record speech. Speech can be so recorded that after very simple training even an idiot, who doesn't even know what one calls the language whose dead sounds have been recorded on the page, can go there and with eyes and mouth resurrect them. This extraordinary and unique technology was invented by Phoenicians and adapted by the Greeks into what it is today. Invented just once, it has spread throughout the world. The Japanese, when they write, note ideas. Traditional Jews and Arabs, when they read, engage in an act of exegesis by which they breathe the spirit — *ruah* — into the three written consonants which stand for each idea, bringing bones together with bones so that these little words stand up again. The alphabet is a phonetic code, which is prior to any idea and allows every idea to be represented. Most of the concepts with which our philosophy is constructed are based on the existence of this technology. We couldn't have them without it.

Speech persists in writing. In order to imagine

yesterday's sentence, still present — which is fundamental for Greek thought — I must imagine
yesterday's sentence recorded somewhere so that it
can be resurrected. The winged word, the bird
which has passed, has been put on a skewer somewhere. This also changes the idea of memory. Memory is a tablet on which something is written, it's a
storeroom where these dead birds are stored and can
be picked up again. It is *not* remembrance in the
sense in which Plato still knew it. Remembrance,
according to Plato, is the sense of something that has
once been in my heart. I follow its trail to the river
of remembrance and try out driftwood. I find a piece
that fits more or less in the space which was left
empty by what I feel has been there. I know it's not
the same, but I treat it as if it were the same. That's
my version of how Plato distinguishes remembrance from memory.

Thought requires that the technology of writing
be interiorized. Even if I don't know how to write, I
know that some people can write, and that's the way
they do it. Memory requires it. Rhetoric is planning
out and storing the sentences which I'll use under
certain circumstances somewhere in my memory
palace, in my interior space, where I can go to grab
them and fit them to my discourse. Lying — the
divergence between what is in my mind and what
is in my mouth, with the intent to mislead you — is
a *literate* concept. Literature is a lie. Chaucer in *The
Canterbury Tales* disguises his fiction with the story
that he is relating a conversation he has overheard.
We teach our children to tell the truth, suggesting
even to the little illiterate toddler the difference be-

tween the thoughts which are already scribbled in his heart and what he has said.

So, I'm interested in the history of the shaping of Western thought — or the frame for Western thought — through the existence of the technology of the alphabet. With a friend, Ludolf Kuchenbuch, we have made this, during the last four years, into a project. As soon as Ludolf was appointed to a full chair of history, he said, "In this chair we will teach older European history, from the beginnings to the late Middle Ages, and we will teach it as a sequence of distinct shapes given to European space by different users of the alphabet."[193]

I have sought to investigate one of these major changes that I see happening in the twelfth century. This is the origin of my current writing. What I have done is to go to these friends whom I've already told you about. I'm very much aware of the fact that it's not an objective reason which leads me to speak about those friends when I want to make a point. I speak about them *because* they are my friends. History looks to me the way a couple of dozen people whom I've come to know in the past allow me to see it through their eyes. Hugh of St. Victor wrote the book that is called *Didascalicon*. The word means teaching tool. There's a subtitle, *De studio legendi*, On the art — no, on the commitment? how should I translate it? Study means today what your kids have to do when they come home from school. If you look it up in the Oxford Dictionary, it still means commitment, engagement, effort — on the effort of reading, let me translate it for the moment.

I have not interpreted this very well-known

twelfth-century text, as others have done, as an introduction to the corpus of four years' curriculum in the pre-university cloister — Hugh mentions a lot of titles, whom one should read and in which order one should read them. Instead of taking this book as a summary on clerical education, I analyzed it with two questions in mind: What can this book tell me about what Hugh actually did when he engaged in that activity he calls reading? That is, what did he do, materially? What did he do, psychologically? Not, what did he read? but, what did he *do*, in his own mind, when he read? And, second question: What *meaning* did he give to the things he did when he read, using his eyes, shifting his eyes from line to line, reading out the verses?

This led me into a careful analysis of what a page looks like around 1120 and what it looks like around 1150, ten years after Hugh's death. I compared the reading of Hugh with the reading of half a generation later, what I call the generation of Peter Lombard. Peter Lombard is a man about fifteen years younger than Hugh, who came in his thirties, already a well-known teacher, to listen to what turned out to be the last two years of Hugh's lectures in Paris. So it makes sense to compare these two. I compared the physical appearance of the two pages they read. And what did I find? There are about twenty or twenty-five changes between the early medieval page and the late medieval page. Obviously, all of them are not observable between 1130 and 1150 as changes everywhere in Europe on every page. Early medieval lines are "Indian file" lines of letters — there are no distances between words. I would ask anybody who doesn't believe what I shall say to sit down at a typewriter and just type a line without putting spaces between the words and then try to read it. He'll make a very simple experiment. You can't read it unless you read it aloud. You can't read it unless you put actual silences, audible lines, between one word you have discovered in that sausage and another.

When I compare a page from the early twelfth century with a page from the late twelfth century, I observe a profound change. In the late twelfth century, I find characteristics which as a modern reader I take for granted — a couple of dozen characteristics which are generally absent in the early twelfth century page and certainly are missing in the time of Bede, the time of the early Carolingians. The most remarkable change, which first happens in the eighth century, is that there are distances between words. A word fully written out or abbreviated is followed by an empty space. The Romans did that occasionally when they chiselled out texts on stone. But, in writing on parchment, up until the eighth century, there are no such distances. There is no possibility, practically, to read it with your eyes alone. You have to read with your mouth for your own ears. Hugh says that clearly. There are three modes of reading, he says: reading for my own ears, reading for the ears of somebody else, and reading with your eyes. But he's the first one who says this.

The division of word from word is only one condition for reading with my eyes. I am used to texts which come in paragraphs. Paragraphs become a standard feature in the twelfth century. I'm used to a book with title headings for which I can search, written with a different font. This idea of writing titles, distinguishing them from the rest of the page, comes from the twelfth century. Sub-paragraphs appear. The numbering of paragraphs and verses becomes standard. Pages, of course, cannot be numbered. That can happen only with the printed book, where page 73 always begins with "and they . . ." You couldn't do this in a manuscript that you copied. Texts taken and copied from another book are now put into a different color, which means that quotation marks appear. Stars appear, which refer to a footnote, which tells you the source from which something has been copied.

Since books can now be looked up, rather than simply remembered, it becomes possible to quote: this is taken from Augustine, such and such a book, chapter seven, verse three. People began to be able to quote Holy Scripture in this way a hundred years earlier, but now it becomes standard practice. This makes it possible to put out an index, and a table of contents, so that you can enter the book at a certain chapter and, after searching a bit, find what you're looking for. The book becomes — to speak this horrible modern language — randomly accessible. But much more important, the alphabetic index is invented. The alphabet, strangely enough, from Phoenician times had the same sequence — alpha, beta, gamma; a, b, c; aleph, beth, gimel — but nobody, for two thousand years of existence of the alphabet, had used this feature of an ordered fixed sequence to order concepts. During the twelfth century, preceded by a slight attempt in the eleventh, the idea appears of ordering concepts alphabetically. In a book on animals the lion and the leopard are put next to each other. But even in the thirteenth century, Albert the Great excuses himself with his readers, noting that it is a highly nonintellectual way of putting things together. The lion should go with the ferocious animals, the leopard with the sweet ones like the panther. But, for practical reasons, he finds it *very* useful to put concepts in an alphabetic order, and we take this for granted.

CAYLEY: So he apologizes?

ILLICH: He apologizes for it. When my students don't understand why he apologizes, I take the months of the year and write them down in alphabetic order on the blackboard. Then I take the numbers from one to twenty and write them down in alphabetic order, and ask the students to figure out in which order they are. They usually understand why even we take it as crazy, as maddening, if someone tells us that the months begin with April.

This again made it possible to look up where subjects in a book are mentioned or where biblical passages in a book are quoted. The early twelfth century knows the gloss. Holy Scripture is commented upon by dozens and dozens of Church fathers. The *Glossa Ordinaria*, as it came to be known later on, consists of a huge sequence of volumes with all the comments which the Church fathers had made, for example, about Genesis, chapter one, verse seventeen, for a thousand years. Formerly, the only way to look up something in it was to follow the order of Scripture. Now, suddenly, in the late twelfth century, this book is not just a commentary on some old text — which, perhaps, overwhelms the old text — but is the projection of an order in my mind onto the page where the order of my mind becomes visible.

Silent reading becomes the norm. Reading becomes an activity where the letters, through my eyes, speak to my mind, rather than activating my mouth, making me hear what I read. When I read Hugh, I'm still in the old world. When Hugh speaks about the page, he remembers that *pagina* means a vineyard, or, more precisely, the espalier along which he walks in a vineyard. He still picks and tastes words, like berries. He still sucks words from the page. It's an oral activity, literally, of the mouth and the lips. He still walks through the pages and conceives of reading as a pilgrimage. Reading is not solely a visual activity for him, not an accumulation. Rather, reading is a pilgrimage towards regions ever lighter, towards the light, into the light, until the light becomes so strong that he doesn't go on reading but begins to contemplate. All this becomes totally different by the end of the century. Scholasticism would have been impossible if Thomas Aquinas had not recovered the art of making notes in cursive writing — he belonged to the first generation to make this recovery. We have lecture notes of Aquinas in his own handwriting. Nobody could decipher them. It was a new invention.

CAYLEY: And what is the symbolic fallout of the new reading, of the transformed page?

ILLICH: First of all the clerics, that minority who knew the technique, became convinced that one can speak about a text, an original text. This is not a book but something detached from it, an ideal which is there even when the book isn't, an original from which all others are copies, perhaps incomplete or deformed copies. The idea was that I can project my mind onto a *pergamen* or, by the end of the century, already onto paper — paper was reintroduced into Europe from China through the Arabs. The page could be a measure of what's in me. Hugh is the first who speaks about mirroring oneself in the page. He stands exactly at that point of transition. Therefore, the *self* can be conceived in a new way. There's an interior text. Examination of conscience becomes possible as a reading of the text that is on the inside.

The peasant can't go into the church in the twelfth century without passing the tympanum, that hollow above the door where the last judgement is sculpted. And there sat the judge, deciphering a book of accounts. People know that in the abbey there are account books, even if they themselves can't keep accounts. It is not their *remembrance* of what they owe that counts, but the debt written down somewhere. The devil stands next to everybody, noting down what he does, says, and thinks and transferring it into the eternal account book. Torture appears as something distinct from punishment. It's explained in the thirteenth century as an attempt to find out the truth by reading into people's hearts.

The relationship between person and community, person and person, is conceived of in terms of a text. I can act in context. Some changes which I learned to notice from Marshall McLuhan, but which he wrongly ascribed to print culture, appear much earlier, without the technology of printing, on the manuscript page of the late twelfth century.[194] At that moment, the new individual emerges, that individual whom we have, in our conversation, referred to as capable of establishing a tie with an individual of the opposite sex through a *copula*. In Latin, *copula* means the verb which ties subject and object.

CAYLEY: So, the marriage bond —

ILLICH: Is a *copula*!

CAYLEY: And is, therefore, a literate concept.

ILLICH: Absolutely. We spoke about contract and about the image of the text. A *writ* comes to have the last *word* in law. Imagine what a change in communitary perception that means. In popular culture the oath was the ultimate statement and ultimate empowerment. A man grabbed his testicles and *cursed* himself conditionally, invoking horrible divine punishment on himself and his oath-helpers if things were not as he said. A woman grabbed her hair and did likewise. This was replaced by a piece of paper you could hold in your hand. Possession, which is something you do with your behind, possessing land by literally sitting on it, turns into property, which you hold in your hand as a writ.

This change from an oral public to a literate public happens without any increase in the percentage in the total population capable of using the pen. This is the reason why I speak of *lay* literacy. The impact of the alphabet and its use on the popular mind is quite independent from the success of clerics in transmitting the skills of pen-holding or spelling. Reading is something you can do through your own eyes, or through somebody else's, as in South America today. Writing can be divided into *scribing*, which some technician does, and dictating, which the ruler can do without ever having held a pen. He becomes a dictator. The peasant can employ a notary and dictate to him. And the notary can betray the peasant as much as he can betray the ruler.

CAYLEY: I want to get to what this transformation can show us about what is going on today, but I'd like to ask you first about your essay on the Spanish grammarian Antonio Nebrija in *Shadow Work*. What you describe there seems to belong to the same history you've just been relating.

ILLICH: What a funny thing to compose this mosaic we're making out of stones broken from readings and writings which were set in a different context, within an actual biography.

CAYLEY: Maybe it's something like what Albert felt about the alphabetic index. I am similarly embarrassed by my procedures . . .

ILLICH: The technological creation of the visible page, going hand in hand with the intellectual perception of texts — something we take for granted — is the step which I wanted to analyze in the twelfth century. In the late fifteenth century, within the same history of basic assumptions, I wanted to analyze the emergence of what we today take as much for granted as the text, namely, language. In Spanish, language can be distinguished from speech more easily than in English. *El habla de la gente* and *la lengua* are clearly distinct from each other, even today. This was not so around 1400. This was not so in 1492. The year 1992 is a year which people will celebrate, with great solemnity, five hundred years of America. I think that five hundred years of *Homo monolinguis* is a *much* more important event.

Columbus discovered territories between Spain and Japan whose existence people had suspected but hadn't really known about. Or, if they knew, they thought they were islands. He discovered a huge chunk of land. But in the very same year Antonio Nebrija, his contemporary, engineered the idea of language, and he says so.

Who is Nebrija? He comes from a family of converted Jews. He is someone who has written one more very good Latin grammar, and a Latin dictionary because he wanted to improve the Latin taught in Spanish schools. Nebrija approaches the queen twice, just as Columbus does. The first time Columbus went, asking for ships, he was thrown out. The second time, he got them. Nebrija went a first time and told the queen he wanted to do something much more important for her reign, namely, transform or, rather, create out of the many *hablas*, the many speech forms of the Spanish peninsula, a language, as much a true language as the three languages we have received from God — Latin, Greek, and Hebrew. The three languages, Majesty, you can see hanging on top of every crucifix, where Pilate has the reason for Jesus' death written on a tablet. In order to do this, Nebrija says to the queen, he intends to transform, transmute the many valuable bits one can find in the mouths of Spaniards into one artifice — which will be the new Castilian — which he intends to create with his grammar. The queen, through the mouth of one of her assistants, makes him understand that she considers this a glorious undertaking but can't quite see the point of it because she, majestically, is the ruler over many people, each one in perfect command of his *habla*, of his speech, of the *territory* of his speech.

She is also the foundress of one of the first nation-states. And she is the one who has called in the Inquisition to get rid of the useless nobles in her court and replace them with lawyers, technicians. She wants to create an *administrative* state. She doesn't want to rule, but to govern. The transformation from rule to government begins at this very moment. So, Nebrija says to her, Majesty, in order for your people to obey you as they ought to — under these new circumstances — you must have a means, an instrument, a tool, to address them in one language through which they hear directly what you say. It is for this reason that with my grammar, I will teach them correct speech and also put in your hands a means to give them what a ruler owes the people whom he subdues, law and language. Now that our ships travel west — this was written while Columbus was on his way — you must acquire the power to give to these people the Castilian language in which you can govern them and subject them — through language.

I love that three-page introduction with which Nebrija wants to prepare a second visit to the queen in order to have her adopt his grammar, as she accepted to equip Columbus with his ships.

CAYLEY: How do these changes, in Hugh's time or in Nebrija's, bear on what you see around you today?

ILLICH: I'm now in my sixty-third year. During the last fifteen years, I've seen around me a change of which I become aware each time I study the two changes to which you just referred, but somehow it seems much deeper. I see a new conscience, a new consciousness, a new self.

I study history in the way a necromancer goes back to the dead. I leave it to others to tell me about the sociogenesis of the world in which I live, of the certainties with which I live, of the word fields within which I move. I want — if it's possible at all and always knowing that it's like switching to a dream state — to find the dead again. A good necromancer knows how to make them come to life, but he knows how tempting they are. Therefore, he draws a circle around himself, a magical circle, and takes those who engage him into that circle because otherwise he might be taken away by the dead. I would like, as far as it is possible, to be a visitor to that which has been and is no more in order to sharpen my eye for those few things which emerged and became that which I have to live with.

When I recently had to give a class here at Penn State, I began the class with a poem from a Chilean, Vicente Huidobro, who wrote mostly in French and who died in the 1940s. "*Je suis un peu lune et commis voyageur* — I'm a bit moon and a bit travelling salesman, and my specialty is finding those hours that have lost their clock. There are hours which have drowned — *les heures qui sont noyées* — and there are other hours which have been eaten up by cannibals, and I even know a bird which drinks them. Others have been made into commercial tunes. But I am a bit moon and a bit travelling salesman, and I look for those which have lost their clock."[195]

It is in that sense that I wanted to go back with Milman Parry, with Albert Lord, with a lot of students of epic orality, into the hours when the epos got drowned under literacy, under literate notation, when Homer was changed from an epos to a poem that could be written down.[196] It's for this reason that I go into the palaeography of the middle of the twelfth century, to see how the sounding and singing pages — this is how the page was conceived — which vibrate in my heart, because my mouth has sung them to my ear, became projections of my thought, and texts in which others could perceive the structure of my thought. I want those who are willing to study with me to engage in the exegesis of these old texts, to move into this *foreign* milieu, to move into the magic circle which is surrounded by the dead who for a moment come alive as shadows, as skeins. I want them to move as precisely as possible, following the technical routes which historians with their dictionaries, reference books, and critical editions make possible. The reason why I lead them there is because I want them to re-emerge with me — perhaps because that dumb phone rings — back into the present, not to abdicate but to assume fully the destiny that places me at this desk, in this milieu today. And here I see a similar change happening around me. I'm afraid for the text of the twelfth century, the mirror of Aquinas' thought projected onto the paper covered with his scribbles, from which he gave the completely new kind of lecture out of which the *Summa Theologica* came.

I see that this perception of the page as a mirror *of a mind* is now being eaten up by the word processor. Morris Berman, a sensitive man, speaks about the cybernetic dream state.[197] I don't like the expression entirely. I would rather speak of the cybernetic nightmare state of the twenty-first century which we are cultivating in our universities, as a reality to which you become sensitive, when you have visited with me the twelfth century, or the end of the fifth century before Christ, in Greece, or other moments in the history of literacy. You will become aware that we are moving into a new stage. I don't want to speak in terms of the future but in terms of the dazed look I see on the face of students who ask me, "Dr. Illich, what data do you have? Couldn't you tell me about the *program* which you are following? How did you *plan out* your approach? What is it that you want to *communicate* to me?" I then feel that I'm drowning with an hour which has passed, that I've lost my clock.

CAYLEY: Do people really think of themselves as books in the twelfth century, or really think of themselves as computers now? Are these epistemic breaks, as Foucault calls them, really as catastrophic and as total as you say, or is there perhaps more underlying continuity? This is the thing about which I'm not quite convinced; I'm persuaded by what you say, but not quite convinced.

ILLICH: There is something terribly sad about training young people always to seek the average, the average tolerance of *all* ideas. Such spiritual indecision is the very contrary of walking the middle way, of the ideal of *mesotes*, of prudence in Christian terms. I like to walk along the watershed and to know that left and right are *profoundly* different from each other and contradictory to a high degree. The world of sex holds together only because of the rests of gender, which survive in it and sprout in it. The world of cybernetic modelling, of computers as root metaphors for felt perception, is dangerous and significant only as long as there is still *textual literacy* in the midst of it. Transportation systems can function only as long as people have legs to walk to the car and open the door. Hospital systems can make any sense only as long as people still engage in that totally nontransitive activity which is living.

I wish I could find a way of never appearing like a preacher who focusses your attention on the scenery on only one side of that watershed. As I walk along, thinking and exploring, I try to find my way between two dissymmetric but complementary fields, dissymmetric but profoundly unlike fields. Once thinking becomes a monocular perception of reality, it's dead.

CAYLEY: I was talking yesterday with our mutual friend Lee Hoinacki, and he told me that he thought you were "doing theology in a new way." There were some lectures lying on the table which you had given at the McCormack Theological Seminary in Chicago. I picked them up, and noticed that you began by emphasizing that you were speaking as a historian, not a theologian. The critical distinction seems to be that if you spoke as a theologian, you would —

ILLICH: Start from revelation which you must accept before you can follow me.

CAYLEY: So the position of the historian is part of your embraced powerlessness.

ILLICH: Yes! That you got right!

CAYLEY: It seems to me that in a way, your work is a form of iconoclasm, a form of image-breaking that clears the way for surprise and for mystery.

ILLICH: For mystery and for what in the Old Testamentary tradition we call the attempt to walk beneath his nose. *In facie tua* . . .

CAYLEY: I don't know the phrase. Beneath the nose of God?

ILLICH: Yes, beneath the nose of God. God has a nose as big as mine, seemingly. Lee, who knows me very well, knows that I haven't tried to do anything else. That's the key for what I've written in my life. You know, people read *Deschooling* twenty years later. Let them look for Thomas Luckmann's book *The Invisible Religion*, and they'll see where it all began.[198] When he speaks about "church" and "faith," I simply put in "school" and "education." At that time, I still identified education with the faith. I wouldn't at this moment.

Yes, my work is an attempt to accept with great sadness the fact of Western culture. Dawson has a passage where he says that the Church is Europe and Europe is the Church,[199] and I say *yes*! *Corruptio optimi quae est pessima*. Through the attempt to insure, to guarantee, to regulate Revelation, the best becomes the worst. And yet at any moment we still might recognize, even when we are Palestinians, that there is a Jew lying in the ditch whom I can take in my arms and embrace.

I live also with a sense of profound ambiguity. I

can't do without tradition, but I have to recognize that its institutionalization is the root of an evil deeper than any evil I could have known with my unaided eyes and mind. This is what I would call the West. By studying and accepting the West as the perversion of Revelation, I become increasingly tentative, but also more curious and totally engaged in searching for its origin, which is the voice of him who speaks. It's as simple as that . . . childish, if you want, childlike, I hope.

CAYLEY: You're saying, I think, that the perversion and the preservation of Revelation are bound together in the history of the West.

ILLICH: Absolutely. That is what the human condition is after the crucifixion. You can't take the crucifixion away if you want to understand where we have arrived at.

IX
A Generation Rid of Stuff

CAYLEY: *H2O and the Waters of Forgetfulness* began as a lecture in Dallas. How did that come about?

ILLICH: I was sitting at my desk in Mexico, puzzling out some passages in my sources with my miserably limited Greek, when the gardener called me to the other building where there is a phone. It was somebody from Dallas, asking me if I would come to talk. "I don't want to talk, what's it about?" "Well, we're having a meeting, celebrating water." "What? I'm just sitting on the waters of Lethe, a river which washes away memories from the feet of the dead, and carries them into the pond of Mnemosyne, where poets can go occasionally, in an altered state, and pick them up and bring them back to sing them. So what do you want?" "Well, you know, there is a large number of Mexicans living in a certain area which is to be washed away to build a central lake in Dallas." So I asked them to explain, for a few minutes, what they were doing and said yes, who says A must say B. If I say Mnemosyne and Lethe and so on, I must say yes to Dallas!

They sent me the records of a seventy-year-long discussion on whether there should or should not be a lake in Dallas. Dallas wasn't 130 years old, and for seventy years they had discussed that issue. Was it feasible financially? Would it contribute to commerce? How would it affect the environment? On each of these points, they had been looking at the pros and cons for seventy years. About one thing, everyone was certain: a lake would be beautiful.

So I got photographs of Dallas for as far back as they existed, which included those seventy years. It was quite clear that there was a little brook, or some kind of spring, which might have supplied a lovely small lake in a central park seventy years ago. But they were planning now to use the lake also as a reservoir for recycled toilet sewage, and to create fountains and waterfalls and reflecting surfaces with that goo which was, chemically, H_2O, but for the imagination was something *utterly* distinct from what water meant in all the sources I was just then reading.

Now I had been asking myself, How can I introduce Gaston Bachelard into the conversation among my acquaintances, especially in the English-speaking world?[200] This is a strange man. You spoke about Foucault. Bachelard certainly influenced me much more than Foucault. He was also an epistemologist, but an epistemologist who asked a question which, in my opinion, goes much deeper and is much less fashionable than that which was asked by Foucault. Foucault makes us understand that conversation — discourse — is the *stuff* from which social reality is made. We should become aware that things are what emerge in an epoch's discourse. He speaks a lot about what he calls power.

Bachelard has a quite different project. Where Foucault is among many who in a very peculiar and practically applicable way speak about what emerges as discourse, and then shapes those who participate in it, Bachelard wants to go deeper. He wants, *very* presumptuously, to deal with the historicity of the deep imagination. There, in a dark, subtle, deep way, we also conceive stuff, that stuff which can gurgle, and chant and sparkle and flow and rise in a fountain and come down as rain. In other cultures, that stuff not only comes down as rain but also comes down as the souls of women who have died and who seek reincarnation. That's how it's imagined among the Lacandon Indians in the south of Mexico. In India that stuff flows around the sun as *soma*.

That's where a distinction comes in between stuff and surface qualities, sparkle or stench, perhaps. It's a distinction between that which, at least in old times, people believed they could actually sense with their inner senses, their *phantastikón*, their inner eye, ear, touch, ability to embrace, and, on the other hand, that which appears to their outer senses.

Now there is a Canadian whom I met in Kingston, who, when I asked him at a faculty meeting, "And what do you do, sir?", answered me, "I want to make *stuff* a subject of philosophy." I wish I could remember who the man is, but I owe it to him that since then I've been thinking about it. Now I want to do this *history* of stuff, because I believe that in this world into which I see the young generation now moving, it is not only their voice they are losing — by imagining themselves according to the model of the computer — it is also that they are emerging as a generation *rid of stuff*.

Now water is one of the traditional four stuffs from which our Western universe is made. There are other universes, in other bodies, world bodies, which are made of five or of seven elements. Ours is made of four, and water is one of them. In this little booklet, I wanted to raise a question about the historicity of stuff and the possibility of studying it.

So I gave my speech in Dallas, and tried to convince a civic crowd, in a short and simple way, that it's strange to agree on the presumption that recirculated toilet flush, H_2O, coming out of a factory, could be the stuff out of which they would create the new beauty around which their city ought to be organized.

Then I sat down and wrote, for a friend of mine, a little pamphlet, a long letter, which was then published as *H_2O and the Waters of Forgetfulness*. I tried to trace the history of the *stuff* of water, and to get at the age-old ambiguity of water, which is a surface and a depth, which can wash off dirt from the skin, by flowing, but also purify the depths of the soul with just a touch. These are totally different activities, washing and purifying. And this gave me an exceptional opportunity to speak about a stuff which at this moment is escaping us socially.

CAYLEY: If we take, let's say, the question of baptism, then water — a natural stuff — is used to perform and signify a supernatural act. So this would be an example of how the stuff of water is conceived by the deep imagination.

ILLICH: I find it very strange to go to a tap, from which something comes out that is still called potable water but children are told, "Drink from the bottle in the icebox, don't drink that stuff from the faucet," and then to take this and baptize a child with it. That's how things are. That's what it means to live today surrounded by people baptized in that stuff. I'm not questioning baptism. I'm simply saying, Look at how humiliating it is, how horrifying it is, to live today. You will then learn how to appreciate the moments of flame and beauty.

CAYLEY: Are you saying, then, that when industrialization goes beyond a certain intensity, producing H_2O, a cleaning solvent, this kind of water loses its imaginative resonance with the result that, in a certain way, a baptism can no longer take place because there's nothing to baptize with?

ILLICH: I'm *not* saying that, definitely not. I'm saying something else. Other people worry about the human organism not being able to find, sometime in the middle of the next century, any more of the appropriate kind of H_2O to make it work. I'm talking about the deadness which sets in when people have lost the sense to imagine the *substance* of water, not its external appearances but the deep substance of water. That deadness might be worse for those who live on than the diseases which will set in — the AIDS analogues which will appear because there are too many organic phosphate residues, or God knows what kinds of radiation-bearing elements in the goo which comes out of the tap. I'm speaking of the deadening of the imagination through the loss of water as a substance, as I spoke about the deadening of the imagination through the loss of the text as a reflection of our mind and *its* inner organization. So far, I have been able to recognize every book that was composed on a computer.[201]

CAYLEY: Truly?

ILLICH: Yes. I remember the first time it happened to me, with Hofstadter's *Gödel, Escher, Bach*. Somebody who was enthusiastic about it gave me that book in Berlin. I was fascinated by it, but couldn't get into it. So I asked myself, What *is* this? I had just heard about word processors, and I suddenly said to myself, It must be written that way, in paragraphs which didn't come out of an inner flow. It's like reorganizing a river by taking a piece of it from here and putting it somewhere else, if it seems to fit. I then read the introduction and saw that the guy was proud, and grateful to the computer for having helped him to write the book. Even today, I can discover this in books.

So I made a vow — just as twenty years ago I made a vow not to buy a daily newspaper and have kept to it — not to type into the computer anything, any sequence of sentences, which I had not first written out with a much newer invention, the felt-tipped pen, which is so soft that you can even write on a moving Mexican bus with it.

CAYLEY: A child builds his imagination by his encounter with stuff. The child whose face is in his food is building his imagination. Now I've never seen it, but I've heard that children will sometimes try to get inside television sets to reach the stuff they see there.

ILLICH: A horrible image . . .

CAYLEY: Yes, it is a horrible image, but it may be a myth because I've never actually seen it.

ILLICH: I know that it's not a myth. I arrived at my grandfather's place in Dalmatia, when I was three months old, along with the first loudspeaker. For his world he was a very learned man. And he ordered that the loudspeaker be opened up because he wanted to see who was sitting in there! December, 1926, Dalmatia. *Si non è vero, è ben trovato*, as the Italians say.

CAYLEY: Father Tom Berry once said to me, "Imagine that we lived on the moon. What would our imaginations be like?"[202]

ILLICH: What would water be?

CAYLEY: Perhaps, in a way, we're moving towards living on the moon.

ILLICH: That "we," I don't care about. I'm concerned with you and me, him and her, them and us, the we who want to celebrate the stuff in a drop, even though the drop has become only symbolic of water, since it comes out of a tap. And here you have my reason for my violent *no* when you said that you can't baptize with it.

CAYLEY: Yes.

ILLICH: Have you done everything you want to do?

CAYLEY: Yes, unless you want to say a final word.

ILLICH: No. I got into this out of foolish trust, full-hearted trust. I did it once — never again! — and instead of being a useful interviewee for you, in the old way, which I thought I could be, I had a unique experience besides making a new friend. *Laus tibi, Domine*!

X
A Cosmos in the Hands of Man

CAYLEY: In 1988, you addressed the Lutheran Church in America and told them that life might be the most powerful idol the church has faced in its history. You gave them a very, very strong warning. To what did you owe your awareness of this question?

ILLICH: I really owe the sense of sudden horror which overcame me when saying the word *life* to Dirk von Boetticher, a young man from the Lake of Constance, who studies medicine. For quite a few years in a row he restricted his medical studies to half a year and stayed with me the other half, following my classes and studying philosophy. During this time he began to study the ways the word *life* was being used in German, but also French, Italian, and English advertising, compared to the way it was being used in the discussions of the Bundestag and the major churches. It was at that moment that I began to suspect that *life* was an amoeba word. And that shook me.

CAYLEY: What is an amoeba word?

ILLICH: I take the term from the work of Professor Uwe Pörksen of Freiburg, a linguist and medievalist.[203] During the second part of the 1980s, he came to the conclusion that there are certain words in all modern languages which ought to be labelled in a special way when they are put into a dictionary. A dictionary will tell you that a certain word in its common meaning means this; in its antiquated meaning it means something else; when you combine it in a particular way, it becomes vulgar; in another sense it is technical. He came to a conclusion that one major category of word usage had been overlooked, and for it he created the term *plastic words*. A plastic word, an amoeba word, he found, is a term which has about twenty-five precise characteristics — Pörksen's very German — and he doesn't admit any word into this egregious category unless it fits all these twenty-five. A plastic word has powerful connotations. A person becomes important when he uses it: he bows to a profession which knows more about it than he does and he is convinced that he is making in some way a scientific statement. A plastic word is like a stone thrown into a conversation — it makes waves, but it doesn't hit anything. It has all these connotations, but it does not designate anything precisely. Usually, it's a word which has always existed in the language but which has gone through a scientific laundry and then dropped back into ordinary language with a new connotation that it has something to do with what other people know and you can't quite fathom. Pörksen puts *sexuality*, for instance, into the category of amoeba words — or *crisis* or *information*.

He has found these words in every language. There's only a couple of dozen, and they're always the same. When I came to Pörksen and said, "Uwe, I think I've found the worst of them, *life*," he became very silent. For the first time in my life, I had the impression that he became angry with me, disappointed in me. He was offended. And it took about six months or nine months before he could speak about that issue again, because it is just unthinkable that something as precious and beautiful as life should act as an amoeba word. I came to the conclusion that, when I use the word *life* today, I could just as well just cough or clear my throat or say "shit."

CAYLEY: You called it an idol when you spoke to the Lutherans. Are all amoeba words idols or does this one have a peculiar property?

ILLICH: Perhaps I should explain what I mean by idol. An idol, in the theological sense, is a creation of man's hands, as the Bible says, in front of which we worship, and to which we attribute a power which transcends our own. In the Bible, in the Psalms, that lord whom we address is called the Lord of Idols, "*Deus deorum dominus est.*" That's the reason why in Mexico, when I say my prayers, I always bow towards Popocatépetl and Iztaccíhuatl, the Masters of the Valley in which I live.[204] I want them to behave like the idols or spirits you can see in Romanic churches on the capitals — the dragons, the whales, and the mermaids. They all are there in the Romanic church, to carry the building which represents the whole universe, the cosmos, which lies in God's hands. In modern usage, I would think that terms like *freedom*, *democracy*, *liberty* tend often to be used as if they were idols. But nobody would attribute substance to them. And now we come to what Boetticher pointed out to me. When I speak of *a life*, I give it a substantive meaning. I'm saying, this here is a life. By doing this, by giving to *life* this substantive meaning, I transform the being whom I would call a person into a life. Now, nobody has said about himself "I am a life." Can you imagine "I'm a life too?" No. "Life" is always spoken about as something which another person is. So I began to research the origin of the term *life* in this substantive usage as *a life*. And I found out that this usage is radically modern. I can't find people speaking of somebody else as "a life" until the 1960s, at the very earliest. This left me as dumbfounded as it had left Uwe Pörksen surprised, and I began to reflect, Where does the substantive use of *life* come from? It quickly became obvious that it cannot be found in the Brahmanic tradition, the Hindu tradition, the Taoist tradition, or any extra-European tradition. Of course, life is there, just as it is in the Bible. In the Bible the word with which God is addressed also connotes in Hebrew *aliveness*. But the origin of the idea of a person defining himself as *life* lies in a conversation between Jesus and Martha, the sister of the public woman Mary Magdalene, whom Jesus had gone to visit because their brother Lazarus had died. And in that conversation, Jesus said to Martha: "I am life."[205] And from that moment on, in Western history, in Western languages, *life* in the singular — *a life* — life *tout court* which we can have or not have, refers to a relationship with Jesus. For much more than a millennium, it was quite clear that people can be among the living and be dead, and other people can be dead and have life. This is not simply a religious statement; this was a Christian message which became an everyday, ordinary assumption. If, therefore, today, we use the term *life* for a zygote, a fertilized egg, which is to be implanted in the uterus, we abuse the word for the incarnate God. For this reason, when I had to give the talk you mentioned to a large group of Protestant ministers in the United States, I began the talk with a curse, a formal curse, a curse in the strongest sense in which you can curse, by saying "To hell with life!" three times. And these guys looked at me. I said to them, "That was a theological statement, which I'll now explain." To turn an attribute created by that man in Galilee to designate himself into an object which you manipulate, for which you feel responsible, which you manage, is to perform the most radical perversion possible.

CAYLEY: I'd like to come back to that, but I'd like to ask you first for the evidence of how you see this word being used now in the discourse of law or politics or medicine, or bioethics, or ecology. You choose.

ILLICH: I'm almost embarrassed to pick the text for the exegesis. As a man who works with history, I'd like very much to answer a question like yours by taking a text and then perhaps a second text and saying, Look at how the word is used here and then look how it is used here. And I want to take a serious text, not "There is more life in Coca Cola," or "This washing powder enhances your life," or the body-count approach, in which, since the Second World War, "lives" of American soldiers are lost or saved. These are superficial. One could call them folkloric bad taste. Since you are interviewing me here in Germany, I cannot help referring to a proposal which lies at this moment in front of the German parliament to extend the protection of the constitution beyond the present formulation, not to persons but to lives — intrauterine lives — which begin from conception. I assume that Germans are not so foolish as to let such a thing pass. But the fact that there is a whole faction in the Bundestag standing in favor of this might give you an idea how serious the abuse is.

There is also the bioethics boom. I remember when, in 1976, the University of Montreal asked me to come up there to help establish a center of medical philosophy. It became then of course a center not of medical philosophy but of medical ethics. There were then only two such centers, the by then seven-year-old Hastings Institute and the much more horribly bureaucratic Kennedy Institute. Fourteen years later, in Chicago, I had to address the representatives of an association which included twelve hundred commissions or centers for bioethics.

"Life" has become a way of speaking about what were once respectfully called persons. Doctors were in charge of persons whose sufferings had to be relieved. Now they have become managers in charge of lives "from sperm to worm," as good old Bob Mendelsohn called it.[206] By including *life* in an ethical discourse, you inevitably give the semblance of ethics to an unethical context. *Life*, as the term is used in this context, has nothing to do with ethics. The term is now used in the United States principally by these hospital commissions for bioethics, which are a refuge for doctors and unfrocked clergy with degrees in theology or philosophy, to justify the most distasteful and impudent manipulations of people by their medical staffs.

On this side of the ocean it is frightening to see the degree to which this construct has entered juridical discourse. I'm speaking of the Continent, not of England. I am afraid that in Germany this has something to do with the fact that every Jew whom Hitler killed also was a life. It's the old sense of guilt which allows this strange conflation. However, the texts to which I particularly want to draw your attention are the papal statements on life. I'm aware of the tradition of careful formulation of official documents in the Roman Church. These documents must be read with an attention that other documents, outside of constitutional law, don't normally require. And among them I find a statement from that year about which you talked, 1988, by the man who presides over the commission which was formerly called the Holy Office of the Inquisition. He is a German cardinal, and was in his youth a remarkably famous theologian. In this document, Cardinal Ratzinger says first of all that it is a scientific fact that, from the moment of conception, a new life comes into existence. Second, he says that human reason, unaided by faith or revelation, can recognize in this life which comes into being at the moment of conception the existence of a human person. And third, he says that for a Christian, this human person is the most helpless and therefore the most deserving brother of Christ, or in Christ.

The first statement claims in a papal document that I have to start reflection on the basis of a scientific fact. The term *scientific fact* was introduced, to the best of my knowledge, into conversational English, German, French by that predecessor of Thomas Kuhn — who cribbed only part of what his predecessor had to say — Ludwik Fleck.[207] Fleck was an interesting man from Poland. In 1935 he wrote a book entitled *The Genesis of a Scientific Fact.* In this book he showed that you can analyze what happens in a laboratory not only as a discovery of truth but also as the creation of facts by definitions. In other words, observations are imposed by paradigms rather than being self-evident appearances. I find it extraordinary that, fifty years after Fleck, the man who is in charge of the protection of the traditional purity of the faith begins his argument by saying, I oblige Christians to believe in something which is based on a scientific fact. Now, scientists, biologists, would say that, in the genetic information of a newly fertilized egg, there are some characteristics which cannot be found in any other cell of the mother organism. His Eminence connects the appearance of some new element in the genetic information with the creation of a life. He therefore translates a scientific statement into ordinary language and thereby completely falsifies what the laboratory data warrant.

He then makes a second step and says, What I have just told you to believe as a scientific fact, reason can recognize as a person — a person without legs, without arms, without eyes, a person without face whom I can't face, a person whom nobody in ordinary life can see, a person who can appear only in certain types of electron photographs as something totally unlike anything which I know as a person. He goes on and says that, as a Christian, you must deal with this person as your neighbor in the likeness of Christ, as your weakest neighbor.

This is most surprising for me, because this statement is signed by a very intelligent theologian, who in his youth wrote a book on brotherhood in Christ in which he clearly states that, from a theological point of view, in his opinion, no human person can be really treated by me as my brother in Christ but he with whom I share the eucharist. The same man who in his youth made this, for me, extremely fundamentalist statement which can barely be tolerated even in traditional Roman Catholic discourse, today defends the interests of the Roman Church as a political agency by claiming that I must treat something which has no face as my brother. I have dealt at some length with this text because it so clearly reveals how profound is the confusion that reigns at this moment and how powerfully amoebic words, plastic words, which can take on any shape and any meaning, have entered high-level discourse and are being imprudently used as the basis for normative statements.

CAYLEY: Life has also become an unquestionable certainty of popular ecology, where it is said that life on earth is something we ought to protect and foster.

ILLICH: In your conversation with Wolfgang Sachs, which you have published,[208] he distinguishes clearly between three types of ecology: boardroom ecology, street ecology, and the quite separate and supposedly scientific endeavor of studying the interrelationship between different grasses and flies in a meadow. Boardroom ecology is typified here in Germany by Ernst Ulrich von Weizsäcker, who has written a brilliant, very well argued book about how to preserve life on earth by planning and engineering and political management.[209] In this discourse life seems to have the function that the holiness of family life had in the 1960s, or the dignity of women. It's a concept which is used in a purposeful and disciplined way as a slogan, as a designed slogan. This would be true from the Brundtland Report to the Brazilian legislation about the global importance of protection of the forests through new types of engineering and harvesting. In street ecology, those kids whom I saw going processionally through a university town in the United States carrying banners and shouting "We don't want global warming! We are for life!" use this term in a sentimental, wishy-washy way, in which we don't know exactly whether they are for bears or for teddy-bears. On the third angle of the triangle, in scientific ecology I don't think that the word appears. In any case it has no content, neither in the boardroom nor on the streets nor in the lab.

I have the strong impression that what the word evokes at this stage is fear and an imprecise sense of "I *ought* to be responsible." It therefore implies manageability not of what's good but of what we want to conserve. It emphasizes survival, not aliveness. Erich Fromm in the 1960s told me that there is no more necrophilic word than *survival*. He was a very intelligent man, you know — people forget that sometimes.[210]

CAYLEY: What did Fromm mean by this?

ILLICH: Well, Fromm had a strange idea about personal character and social character, which we don't want to go into now, and one of the three most important vectors he analyzed was that between a person who loves life and a person who loves death. The person who loves death he called necrophilic, death-loving. And, at a time when I was still completely unprepared to reflect on the appearance of *life* in public discourse, I suppose it was in 1969, perhaps in 1970, he came back to Mexico from a short visit in New York and told me that the word which had most frightened him was the term *survival* — the *survival* of the human race, the *survival* of certain parts of the human race, the *survival* of cultures. He compared this usage with the ancient Egyptians' efforts to build pyramids where their king's soul would survive, and called it a terribly necrophilic term. Only years later did I grasp what he might have implied.

CAYLEY: Survival is necrophilic because it's a purely defensive concept — it affirms nothing?

ILLICH: It affirms nothing and it means I'm constantly thinking of death. I'm fixated on death. I consider whatever I'm doing at this moment or whatever I decide to do with others as prolonging the stay of the world on death-row. *Survival* implies "let's make one more petition." I can't help seeing death-row as the best metaphor for the psychological attitude of people who make survival into a fetish.

People who speak about survival — this is my experience, I have no studies to prove this — speak not out of finely developed senses of smell and taste or a feeling for atmosphere, they speak out of a terminology and as a result of a propaganda, which goes through the head and not through the heart. After all, ecology has become a major educational institution, a major formative influence in our society, a major distributor of key concepts by which we can speak about what's important as survival and justify as love of nature a purely intellectual closeness to plants or to trees or to meadows.

CAYLEY: *Life* is a highly abstract, really the most abstract, term. Does it lend itself to manipulation for this reason?

ILLICH: Yes, but it is so abstract that in order to make it into an object of manipulation you have to create emblems which are essentially powerful. The word *life* is so evidently rootless in science, and patently deprived of any common-sense correlate. It can be a person or a child, or a cell, or a pre-infantile form in the uterus, or a bear, or a bee, or a molecule. Who knows what you speak about? It's so obviously rootless that it could not acquire powerful connotations unless it were tied to some kind of emblem. I'll never forget when this struck me for the first time several years ago, in the kitchen of an apartment where some six or seven graduate students lived together. On the icebox door two pictures were pasted. One was the blue planet and one was the fertilized egg. Two circles of roughly the same size — one bluish, the other one pink. One of the students said to me, "These are our doorways to the understanding of life." The term *doorway* struck me profoundly.

This stuck with me for quite a few months, until, for a totally different reason, I again took down a book of Mircea Eliade.[211] Eliade has been, for many of us, a teacher of religious science, the study of myths, and the scientific study of religion. He headed the editorial team which created the encyclopaedia of religions that now stands in every university. He is not the most important of my teachers in that field, but I have always been full of admiration for him. And, going through this book, I came to the conclusion that better than anybody else whom I had studied, he brings out the concept of *sacrum*. The term *sacrum*, the Latin noun corresponding to our *sacred*, has been used for a long time by religious scientists to describe a particular place in the topology of any culture. It refers to an object, a locality, or a sign, which within that culture is believed to be — this young lady was right — a doorway. I had always thought of it as a threshold, a threshold at which the ultimate appears, that which within that society is considered to be true otherness, that which within a given society is considered transcendent. For Eliade, a society becomes a conscious unity not just in relation to neighboring societies — *we* are not *you* — but also by defining itself in relation to what's beyond. Now, we live in a society where that which is beyond is not officially recognized as religious. In fact, when people speak

of American civic religion, they usually lower tran-
scendence into something which cannot be understood in terms of the religious symbolism of the
churches or organized forms of religion. Eliade's
sacrum is the doorway to the absolute other, the
place of self-revelation of the holy or of God, or of a
power.

I began to reflect on whether these two circles, the
blue one and the red one, were not the *sacrum* of our
time. They are different from other *sacra* because
they are pure science, they are not objects. They are,
to speak with Cardinal Ratzinger, emblems for scientific facts, results of technological instruments. As
Wolfgang Sachs says so beautifully, the most violent
view ever obtained was that of the earth from the
outside. Imagine how many tons of explosive went
into separating a Hasselblad camera from the earth
so that they could photograph the earth from the
outside. We now claim that we can see the earth from
there when, in fact, we only have a photograph of it.
Imagine how much violence was done to women,
how much shameless violence, in order to photograph the zygote. Remember in what a powerful
way the traditional and probably necessary division
between here and there is abolished, both when we
look at the earth from the outside and when we look
at the unseen in pregnancy as something already
visible here. These two colored circles are results of
the transformation of activities, which are called
scientific so that they can demand high funding, into
images which can be used in propaganda, and now
become thresholds, doorways, to something which
nobody sees, something which makes sense for no-

body — life here and life there; a life pink, life in general blue; pink light, blue light — the ultimate for which any sacrifice can be justified.

As a perversion of the statement by the incarnate God, "I am life," the construct *life* belongs to hell, if there be one, and we would have to invent it if there weren't to say where it belongs. These two images are the threshold through which *life* justifies total global management. It's justified because of the sacredness of this nothingness.

CAYLEY: So these two objects are in that sense quite literally anti-Christ?

ILLICH: I have always abstained from making apocalyptic statements or interpreting the apocalypse. I don't want to get into that kind of fundamentalism. I'd much rather stay in history. But I cannot help seeing in what you refer to a resurrection of nature, a horrible resurrection of nature, and I'll explain why. Mrs. Carolyn Merchant has spoken about the death of nature.[212] She has done so by dividing history into pagan, Christian, and modern phases. (May she forgive me for simplifying.) All our Western traditions of philosophy, pre-Socratic and thereafter, assumed that nature is alive — not is *a life* but is *alive* — that nature is a matrix, a womb. *Natura a nascitura dicitur,* nature comes from giving birth. Nature, pagan nature, gives birth to very different, let's call them, gods. Then came Christianity and that extraordinary world perception that lasted from the proto-Christian period through the latest Middle Ages, in which nature's aliveness was given a reason. The Greeks couldn't decide if nature had a beginning or not. Christians *knew* it was created by

God — they had learned that from the Jews. The world was created by God and maintained alive in God's hands. The aliveness of nature, therefore, had its roots in God, who was life. Then, Merchant says, with the various philosophical steps that led to the Enlightenment, the idea of nature's dependence on God was abandoned. With the disappearance of the idea of continuous creation in God's hands, in God's womb, nature lost the reason for its aliveness. Nor could it recover its Greek pagan aliveness, which had been extinguished and forgotten. The Renaissance could not resurrect the gods as a source of nature's aliveness or as transmitters of nature's aliveness to different groups of beings. She speaks, in this sense, of the death of nature as the phenomenon which founds modernity. She thereby becomes able to define a question which has troubled modernity without being formulated in this simple way: If nature is dead, how to explain life?

The word *life*, not *a life*, but *life*, appears for the first time in natural sciences around 1801 and 1802 in Germany and in France. Zoology and botany during the eighteenth century were essentially classificatory sciences. To overcome this limitation, biology was created. Jean Baptiste Lamarck introduced the term into the French language and began a fruitless search for a definition of life that went on for thirty or forty years and then died out. By 1840, 1850, you won't find any biologist looking for life anymore.

CAYLEY: Why?

ILLICH: Simply because there's nothing operationally verifiable in that term. Within biology, the plastic nature of that term was discovered 150 years before Uwe Pörksen created the technical term *plastic word*.

CAYLEY: I would like to return to the question of life as a *sacrum*. What would be an example of a *sacrum* in religion?

ILLICH: The Kaaba in Mecca, Jerusalem, Mount Zion, the Holy City, Buddha's steps in stone — a yard long. A totem pole is a sacrum. So is the navel of the world at Delphi or in the Lake of Mexico.

CAYLEY: Golgotha?

ILLICH: I would argue strongly that Golgotha is precisely not a sacrum, that, theologically, faith in the incarnate word sacrificed on the cross is not a religion and cannot be analyzed within the concepts of religious science. If there is something analogous to a *sacrum* in the Christian tradition, it is the tomb; and Christian holy places are built around an altar, a table, which stands on top of an empty tomb and is covered by a cupola. It is at this place that Christians remember a historical event and expect one by which history will be closed. This historical event is part of sacred history, from creation to ascension, which will be concluded by the coming-again of this real person, who is Christ. The empty tomb had a powerful, structuring influence on fifteen hundred years of Western history. I find the emptiness into which the blue and the red thresholds lead much more frightening, because what stands behind these thresholds is not just emptiness but nothingness.

Our Western tradition eliminates the *sacrum* through Christian architecture — architecture which is an affirmation of the faith which celebrates the remembrance of a historical event. This event is the Last Supper, but analogically also the transit of the Red Sea. This, in a sense, makes our Western religion nonreligious, although I would of course refuse any connection with Harvey Cox's idea that this is, therefore, a secular tradition.[213] It is only within this Christian tradition, after the death of that nature which lies contingently in God's hands, that the cultural space is created in which then *a life* can appear as an object of management and perhaps as an object which can even be produced, such as artificial intelligence. I felt this very strongly when I participated in a seminar recently which brought together two or three Japanese informatics theoreticians with a number of German professors in the fields of informatics, communications sciences, and systems management. My German-cultured, Goethe-reading colleagues were all tempted to assign some special meaning to what they are doing. The Japanese seemed unaware of any meaning which is either threatened or re-enhanced by what they do.

CAYLEY: So to make this more explicit, what is it in Christianity that allows the concept of life to appear in its wake as what you earlier called a "horrible resurrection"?

ILLICH: The social eclipse of Christian life and the elimination of the life of Christ from culture — I'm not talking here about churches — created an empty space. If this did not actually call *life* as a construct into being, it at least permitted the idea of man taking charge of man and of the cosmos. When I hear of "a global management," I, as a reader of mostly twelfth- and thirteenth-century documents, cannot avoid translating this into Latin, as a cosmos contingent on man, a cosmos in the hands of man, and as a delivery of what we formerly called persons into the hands of man. Here you have the ultimate realization of the idea that man makes the world. The idea that everything can be made derives from the heritage of Francis Bacon, and the more powerful this idea becomes, the stronger grows that strange word *responsibility*. Responsibility no longer means primarily legal accountability, for which the word was used for a long time. It now means moral responsibility for something, rather than legal accountability to someone. It is therefore closely related to the social assumption that we can make the world what we want it to be and what we think it ought to be. By claiming that we are responsible for the world, we also imply that we have some power over the world; and, by being convinced that we should pursue our so-called scientific endeavor of remaking the world, we enhance our need to believe that we are responsible for it. If we can be responsible for life, we imply that we can improve it, that we can recover it, that we can save it. In this sense what appears in these two doorways is a resurrection of man-conceived, man-made life in a dead nature. Life becomes the ultimate purpose of history. We spoke earlier about the fact that, according to Carolyn Merchant, early modern thinkers had to face the question: What is life in a dead world? The new question that now comes to us is: What is the *stuff* of a world in which we are responsible for life? And, by this question, we claim that we can make this world live. *Make it* in all the three senses this word has in English.

CAYLEY: Three senses?

ILLICH: Fabricate, shape, and then the vulgar sense in which one says "he made her."

CAYLEY: When you referred earlier to your German colleagues and how they differ from Japanese people with the same interests, you seemed to imply that it's quite impossible for Western people to think about these questions outside of a Christian heritage, even though they think after Christianity. Is that true?

ILLICH: One of the funniest experiences I've had this fall derives from the fact that a group of teachers and professors here at the university got together a couple of years ago to discuss the idea I developed twenty years ago of convivial tools. They studied the impact of this idea on various theoreticians and philosophers of communication and information. This led me to the insight that in the last twenty years things have radically changed. You cannot speak of systems as tools because the operator is always part of the system. They helped me greatly to clarify something I've been studying with Professor Carl Mitchum at Penn State for the last three years. We've conducted a seminar to ask ourselves about the concept of *tool,* and our ability to group things in this category, which appeared in the thirteenth century. Thanks to these Bremen colleagues, I see that this historical concept now is being overshadowed by systems.

Now, one advantage of this funny experience in Bremen was that two different age groups of what you could call systems philosophers, people who consider systems a kind of being which they want to analyze, philosophically and historically, came to dinner on alternate nights. One group is in their forties and one group is about twenty-five to thirty. The ones twenty-five to thirty are thoroughly aware that they are at home in things which the older ones are constantly in awe of. The older ones, for example, are fascinated by hypertext, which is a concept utterly unlike anything the last six centuries have given us.[214] The young ones laugh at them but, at the very same time, these young ones are aware of the fact that the seventeen-to-twenty-three-year-olds, who are their pupils, whom they call only the "computer kids," have an even more straightforward, non-problematic approach to things than they do. These thirty-year-olds, as good German academics, still have to reflect on the impact of this new epistemology on their imaginations, on their senses, and on their fantasy. Johannes Beck is fascinated by the generation gap between middle-class kids — but who isn't middle-class here in Germany? — now thirty, and those now eighteen, because those now eighteen might as well be Japanese.

CAYLEY: You seemed to say earlier that Western people cannot think outside of a Christian heritage even when they have consciously forsaken it, and that life as a substantive can appear only as a sort of demonic parody of life more abundant in Christ. About these kids you seem to be saying the opposite.

ILLICH: What I said earlier is true, at least in a shadowy way for the thirty-year-olds. The twenty-year-olds don't give a damn, even though one or two of them are sons of families of Lutheran pastors.

[*The second part of this interview was recorded a week later. Illich said he was dissatisfied with what we had recorded on the first occasion. I invited him to begin our second session by telling me why. He did so by first briefly reviewing the history of his thinking about life.*]

ILLICH: My reflections on the use of the words *a life,* or *life on earth,* have had several stages. There was a time in the 1960s, under the influence of Erich Fromm particularly, when, with great innocence, I insisted on the possibility of living the world apart, as little plants can destroy thick walls with their roots. I stressed aliveness and celebrated awareness without any fear that the word *awareness* could be replaced by *life.* Then came the 1970s, during which my attention was particularly drawn to "medicalization" of society, medicalization of the mind, and medicalization of the entire physical environment. This made me reflect on the destruction of the ability to die and the replacement of my death by medicide, the medical decision that in this particular instance no further attempt at resuscitation should be made. In *Medical Nemesis* I tried to discuss, as one of the major three cultural consequences of medicalization, the constitution of an amortal society — a society which cannot face dying, which has to pedagogize dying, as Elizabeth Kübler-Ross does with her terminal education in which you go through your stages as your teacher tells you you ought to,[215] a society in which the mystery and the beauty of living with one's own mortality has disappeared.

I then thought that I had discovered historically how death had come into the world at the beginning of the fourteenth century with the transition from the dance of the dead to the dance of death. Jews, Christians, and Arabs know an angel of death, a messenger who comes and says, "Hey, it's time now." In Jewish legend, he's exactly the same angel who called me once upon a time from the lap of Abraham, saying, "It's time to become flesh in a mother's womb," where, according to this beautiful story, I then spent nine months with a little candle lighted next to my head. The same angel then came and said, "Now it's time to be born," and, just as in the lap of Abraham, so then in the womb of my mother I said, "No, no, it's so good here." And this same angel will come again and tell me, "Ivan, now it's time to come to present yourself in front of the judge." This is Jewish legend. An angel of death was known. In the late thirteenth century, in that period which Huizinga in *The Waning of the Middle Ages*[216] describes so beautifully, so whimsically, the sense of mortality takes on concreteness in a peculiar type of representation which we find in churches of the time, where each man — the peasant with his heavy clothes, the king with his crown, and the bishop with his miter — dances in the arms of somebody else, who is their mirror image, as a corpse. This is called the dance of death.

Around 1340, quite suddenly, the imagery changes. It is no longer each one embracing his own mortality who dances through life but it is a bunch of skeletons dancing at the behest of a piper, who is a skeleton man, holding an hourglass. Death becomes a skeleton holding an hourglass, and a scythe or a sickle, and they dance under his leadership. As I examined these pictures, it became increasingly clear to me that I was in front of an anthropomorphic representation of something which for the first time in history came to be conceived as a force of nature, and not as an intimate limit which I embrace from birth on and throughout my *bios*, my *curriculum vitae*. Death as a force came to be represented in this macabre way at this moment.

During the 1970s, I watched this idea of death as a natural force turn step by step into its mirror image, life as *a life*, life personalized, not in the abstract way in which death had been, but in the zygote, in the blueness of the earth, in the patient whom the doctor has to keep out of the grip of the enemy of that life — death. Then came the 1980s, and I became increasingly aware that what was referred to as *a life* was taking on a shadowy substance: it became *stuffy*, a thing which had stuff. It became, in a modern way, animistic. And physicians began to think of themselves, not any longer as natural scientists in charge of providing relief, repair, and perhaps life-prolongation for persons, but managers of that stuff called life. When I spoke to you earlier, I was still mainly reflecting on how this could come about. In the meantime, especially reflecting on the function which the blue planet and the pink cell have as a *sacrum*, analyzing all this came to seem less crucial. Instead I wanted to emphasize *life* as the transcendent foundation of a world in which we can speak about "lives." Life has become a pseudo god, and a negation of the God who took on flesh and who redeemed us. It is in this sense that I am not fully happy with the way our conversation has gone so far.

CAYLEY: But what you have just said sounds like what I understood all along.

ILLICH: David, we have talked so much with each other, and you have rendered me a unique service by being the one person who has had the guts and my consent to examine what I think in terms of its biographical evolution. You are right, and again you are not right. Yes, I agree with you that I have not changed fundamentally anything I said earlier, but I now see it in the setting of the 1990s which are advancing. And, in these '90s, my nose, my intuition, and also my reason tell me that we might be at a historical threshold, a watershed, a point of transition to a new stage of religiosity. I'm not speaking of the Roman Church or Islam, nor am I speaking of Will Herberg's or Marty's civic religions.[217] I am speaking of a mode of being, of talking, of signalling, and of perceiving in which the creatureliness of the world is strongly accentuated, in which we speak about a fertilized egg as a creature and the rose as a creature without ever thinking about a creator. The term *creature* or *critter* has been detached from the term, the object of faith, to which in our Western tradition it has always been connected. Therefore, increasingly, conversations, especially conversations in the field of ecology, which you have examined, deal with creatures and speak as if God or the Creator would be a reasonable hypothesis. Now, as you remember, five years ago I scandalized these hundred and fifty reverends by saying formally and as a solemn curse, "To hell with life!" Now, with double emphasis, with triple emphasis, I must say, "To hell with God as a hypothesis!" And I see the *sacrum*, the double *sacrum*, the blue and the pink *sacrum*, through which life appears — life which is nothingness — as the appropriate step towards a world mood which conceives of a god who, *faut de mieux*, we have to deal with as if he existed, as if he were there.

CAYLEY: There's a passage in Nietzsche where he says — this is Northrop Frye's paraphrase — that despite the death of God, since we continue to use grammar, we will continue to hypothesize God. Rilke speaks of building God and calls the creative artist the ancestor of a future God;[218] Jacques Derrida, in a paper that he gave in 1964 at Johns Hopkins called "Structure, Sign and Play in the Discourse of the Human Sciences,"[219] says that, even though discourse can no longer be centered on what he calls "the transcendental signified," the idea of such a center can never be eliminated. It's a hollow but necessary idea. These thinkers all seem to me to be part of the same story which you are now telling. Is that so?

ILLICH: It is. I myself would go back to Dietrich Bonhoeffer, that Lutheran pastor and theologian who was hanged on a meathook as one of the so-called traitors to Hitler. He said that a Christian had to speak *etsi deus non daretur*; he must express himself as if there were no God. Harvey Cox picks that up in his *Secular City*, where the idea becomes

frail and talkative. I think today I would say a believer must be a man who, with the whole of his
being and his life, objects to any argument which
takes the shape *etsi deus daretur*, as if God existed —
God is not an *as if*.

CAYLEY: And life, for you, is that kind of a functional
hypothesis.

ILLICH: Thinking about life makes us act as if there
were life, although the scientists never use the term,
and no reasonable philosopher or ethicist would
ever dare to introduce that term without much qual-
ification into his argument. We are here in front of
the emergence of some ultimate justification for let-
ting ourselves be administered by a clergy, a managing clergy, a planning clergy, a dictatorial clergy,
worse than anything we have ever thought about.
You know how much I love and admire George
Orwell. Here Orwell's message comes to an end. We
would need a new Orwell to speak about what we
are now discussing.

CAYLEY: We are now at the end of communism,
which was a perversion of Judaeo-Christian myth.
It's interesting that no one seems to notice the dictatorship of this equally perverted version of Judaeo-
Christian myth which concerns you.

ILLICH: Not at all, not at all. You began this interview by speaking about the statement I gave to the
synod of Lutheran bishops who had founded a new
church by uniting three previously distinct corpora-
tions and who wanted me to speak about the
church's concern for resources. I said, "You people
have to watch out, the most important resource we
are now creating is life. Don't fall into the trap of

defending it in the name of the gospel and of God."
I then had an opportunity to speak to a Lutheran
academy in Germany on the same subject. In neither
place did I get the impression that one person understood what I was speaking about. This is the
puzzling thing for me, that whenever Christians
today participate in the life of the church, whichever
church it be — for the Roman Catholic Church it's
even clearer — they are deaf and dumb to the issues
I can so easily discuss with you. It's a very painful,
puzzling thing, and has something to do with bu-
reaucratization I think, and with security.

CAYLEY: You are genuinely puzzled?

ILLICH: Yes, I'm puzzled. I have no answer. I mean,
I can't drag in the devil because that would be a
diabolus ex machina. I don't want to engage in some
kind of complex theology of the corruption of the
best which becomes the worst. I can say strongly
that, at a basic level, issues touching upon the historicity of medical care, of education, of transportation, of monetarization of wage labor, can't be
discussed and are not discussed in any Christian
church as an issue of agenda, the public agenda, and
I don't know anybody there who even participates
in the conversations which go on around the world
on these subjects. On the second level, which is the
historical source of these ideas in a perverse trans-
mutation of a Christian vocation and message, I
have not even found a first conversational partner
within any of the established churches. And, when
I go onto the third level, and ask myself if this
blindness has something to do with a peculiar transformation of our senses in modernity, I often have

the impression that, the more traditionally I speak, the more radically alien I become. This is the issue I've been discussing this whole year. I base all my argument on a Christian-Western tradition in which the inner senses and embodiment were seen as the result not only of creation but of the redemptive incarnation, but I still feel only distance from the concerns of popes and Protestant councils.

CAYLEY: I haven't heard your lectures on the inner senses, but I wonder if this idea is germane to the subject we're discussing?

ILLICH: In the first thousand years of Christianity, Christians assembled around a table called an altar and built above an empty tomb, where they celebrated the absence of God, who had become flesh, because he had by now risen to heaven, where he wanted to go. The pictures they painted were icons — that we still know from Russia and from Greece — frames within which a certain motif was represented and which had the purpose of making the invisible present to the heart, to the inner eye, of the person who stood in front of them trying to pray and to adore. After Giotto in the West, they increasingly represented scenes from the Gospel. During the Renaissance and during the Baroque — just think of St. Ignatius, whose five-hundredth anniversary was just celebrated — people used these pictures to make real scenes really present in front of their inner eyes, and they distinguished these representations of the past from illusions, fantasies, dreams, or fancies. Today I live in a world in which most people see by command. Whatever they know, whatever they learn in school, whatever is communicated to them by the media, has been carefully planned and structured. Screened images tell them how to see, what to see, and what not to see. We live in a world in which increasingly people cannot distinguish between seeing as an act that your whole body does, as I now *see* you, and being told, from a screen or a photo, that they ought to see David Cayley. Somebody recently told me, "Yesterday evening we first saw Kennedy, then we saw Bush, and then ET." They might tell me, "And I saw life."

CAYLEY: I would like to return to the subject of ecology, and to ask how you see the increasingly global pretensions of this new "way of knowing," as William Irwin Thompson calls it.

ILLICH: I thought it would be easier to answer this question if I reread your book *The Age of Ecology*. So I did, and it gave me a very funny impression. With a few exceptions, I had a distinct impression that the people who spoke there were engaged in a defensive rain dance. In fact, you know that I can't sleep so well anymore; and, after I finished reading I had a nightmare in which I was at a party you had organized with these ecologists. Thompson was there, and Lovelock,[220] and there were several ladies. We were performing a dance to keep away the obvious, the evidence of the obvious, that, as long as you think about the world as a whole, the time for human beings is over, and has been over for a long time. I felt very strange at this dance because it reminded me of something I talked to you about once. In 1971, when I began to write *Tools for Conviviality*, on the multidimensional thresholds beyond which human endeavor becomes destructive of a human mode of existence, I broke down. It was the only time in my life that something which is probably called a "depression" has hit me very deeply. I don't think I would have gone on writing if I had had a son of my own flesh in my arms. I would have had to join the rain dance.

I think it is a necessary condition for thinking and reflecting, both with meaningful and sensual words and clear and distinct ideas, to know that we have no future. There might be a tomorrow, but we have no future about which we can say anything, or about which we have any power. We are radically powerless and engage in conversation because we want to find out ways of extending our budding friendships to others who, with us, can enjoy the experience of their own powerlessness and our joint powerlessness. The people who speak about Gaia and global responsibility, and suppose that some fantasy *we* should *do* something about it, dance a crazy dance, which makes them mad. I am not an atom, nor am I a beauty. And as much as I love to look at you, you aren't a beauty either — you are this David. A sense of being able to celebrate the present and celebrate it by using as little as possible, because it's beautiful, not because it's useful for saving the world, could create the dinner table which symbolizes opposition to that macabre dance of ecology, the dinner table where aliveness is consciously celebrated as the opposite of *life*.

CAYLEY: This can be heard as a counsel of despair.

ILLICH: No! Of hedonism. I know only one way of transforming us, *us* meaning always those I can touch and come close to, and that's deep enjoyment of being here alive at this moment, and a mutual admonition to do it — please don't misunderstand me, I'm not a touchy-feely man — in the most naked way possible, *nudum christum sequere,* nakedly following the naked Christ, which was the ideal of some of the medieval monks whom I read.

CAYLEY: Why do you believe that responsibility is impossible?

ILLICH: Unless I'm crazy, I can be responsible only for those things about which I can do something, and I can't help laughing about these kids, organized by some of my friends, who walk around the streets of a midwestern town and shout, "We don't want global warming! We are against pollution!" Rain dances.

Responsibility is a word which has been used in law for a long time. You are responsible for having done this action. Not in the eleventh century. In the eleventh century, if you fell out of a tree onto somebody's head and killed him, it didn't matter whether you intended to kill him or not, you still had to pay an amend for what this man was worth to his master. The idea of distinguishing murder from homicide without malice aforethought came later. But anyway, *responsibility* as a legal concept has existed for a long time. As a general concept, as a concept of woolly ethics, it's a rather new idea. In Germany at least, the word *Verantwortung,* which means responsibility, appears only in the 1920s in the dictionaries. Now, what is this *responsibility*? It is a peculiar type of ethics related to a belief that I can do something about the things for which I'm responsible. Now, it is a total illusion that one can do anything effective, anything which will make a difference, about all those things for which people are today being preached responsibility, by Hans Jonas[221] or any other philosopher, not to speak of the demagogues. But *responsibility* catches because it gives people a sense that if that wise man tells me I should feel responsible, then after all, I have some power, I have some influence, it makes a difference how I behave, which, after some reflection, turns out to be phoney. So it's the ideal base on which to build the new religiosity of which I speak, in the name of which people become more than ever administrable, manageable.

So I say let's be alive and let's celebrate — really celebrate — enjoy consciously, ritually, openly, the permission to be alive at this moment, with all our pains and with all our miseries. It seems to me an antidote to despair or religiosity — religiosity of that very evil kind.

CAYLEY: In the 1970s, when I worked at the CBC in Vancouver, there was no recycling. But I had the conscience for it, so I used to bring my car down to the CBC once a week and load up these huge packs of newspapers that were accumulating in our office because we read a lot of newspapers, and haul them off to some recycling depot.

ILLICH: You did the right thing.

CAYLEY: I did the right thing. Now these are picked up in front of my house in Toronto. It's a small thing. I notice, in your house, that there are unbleached coffee filters and degradable detergents and so on. Perhaps, if newsprint is reused, the damage to the forests of Canada will not be as great as it is right now.

ILLICH: That's a prudential statement, which I fully agree with.

CAYLEY: Then what is the distinction between that kind of action, of which you don't deny the possibility or the benefits, and the sense of responsibility you're speaking against?

ILLICH: I object for reasons which I've just explained to calling this a responsible activity. This is wise, this is prudent, this is sensible. But what do you feel responsible for? You can feel responsible — I mean I'm just speaking English — for something you can do something about. If you want to dilute the word *responsibility* to such a point that it means anything which is good and nice and prudential and sensible and meaningful to you, do it. It's a catchword. Acting sensibly has no hook to draw you into a ritual; acting responsibly can immediately make you responsible for your own health and punishable if you don't take care of it.

CAYLEY: So acting prudently or virtuously pertains to my existence. When I behave responsibly, I inscribe myself within —

ILLICH: The system.

CAYLEY: — the system, within life.

ILLICH: Within life, within the ecosystem. You properly regulate your immune system. You engage in the appropriate autopoetic construction of your own balances. It's all abstract stuff which is wide open to management by publicity and graphs and formulas and fashions.

CAYLEY: You and I have talked at times about the Gaia hypothesis, in which the earth is described as a cybernetic system. There is a passage I found very clarifying in your talk to the Lutherans, where you say that such a system is simultaneously both model and reality, which I think is as much as to say that in such a system reality disappears. It becomes "a process which observes and defines, regulates and sustains itself," as you say. The difference from classical science seems to be that in classical science something is observed, while in this new science something observes itself.

ILLICH: The world as a great masturbator.

CAYLEY: Can you expand on this idea of model and reality becoming indistinguishable?

ILLICH: I had a French friend, an outstanding mathematician, who was interested in these questions. He wanted to make a purchase in Hamburg, and I wondered if I could help him. No no, he said, he had the address, and he knew what he wanted to purchase. I wasn't curious, I didn't intrude on him, but somehow, during the conversation with this gentleman of roughly my age, it emerged that he wanted to buy one of those dolls in a sex shop, who did it in such a way that he could regulate it appropriately, and I just wondered if, for him, a woman was a second-class doll or the doll a first-class woman. But I think that's not an appropriate way of answering such a weighty question as you have asked me about the world as a system of self-observation.

You know, David, that questions of this kind are more difficult for me to deal with in 1992 than they were in 1988? Some limit on what can be discussed and what can't be discussed in public is rapidly disappearing. Nils Christie calls it "the disappearance of basic humanity."[222] Orwell would have called it "the disappearance of basic decency." I have become at sixty-five the contemporary of people whose heart has been cut out and rewired, and I love them. I live in a world in which I know that the incarceration rate of the black population of the United States is superior to any other known incarceration rate except at the height of the Stalinist terror in Russia. I live in a world in which fourteen people condemned to death in Taiwan — I'm totally against the death penalty but that's what they still have in Taiwan — were shot while attached to respirators so that their organs could be harvested undamaged and transplanted in Japan.[223] And in a world in which all this becomes trivial, it becomes very difficult to say that for me earth and soil are still the same thing. I want to be able to kiss the soil on which I stand, to touch it. The earth, which is nothing else but a photograph taken by a Hasselblad whirling around in a satellite, is a denial of the earth. One can speak about atheism. One doesn't have a word, *agaia*, but Gaia is an "agaia" hypothesis, an agaistic hypothesis, inimical to what earth is, which is something you have to use all your senses to grasp, to feel. Earth is something that you can smell, that you can taste. I am not living on a planet.

CAYLEY: But why is it different from a hypothesis in classical science?

ILLICH: Misplaced concreteness. Provoked sensuality. Vision on command. Technological imperative transformed into normative responsibility.

CAYLEY: This seems to me to be about the consequences of the theory rather than the theory itself.

ILLICH: I'm really not interested in scientific theories in 1992. That was very interesting in the 1960s and much more interesting when I studied science in the '40s. By now, science in America has become fundable research, and in Germany, it's tasks for which civil service positions can be created. I mean, stop it with that appeal to science. What's wrong with Gaia is that these guys want to be scientific. What the difference is between that kind of science and religion, I don't know.

Endnotes

1. Illich and Barry Sanders, *ABC: The Alphabetization of the Popular Mind*, North Point Press, Berkeley, 1988
2. "Literacy: The Medium and the Message," *Ideas*, CBC Radio, 1988. (Transcript available for $10 from Ideas Transcripts, Box 500, Station A, Toronto, Ont. M5W 1E6.)
3. *The Development Dictionary*, ed. Wolfgang Sachs, Zed Books, London, 1992
4. "Part Moon, Part Travelling Salesman: Conversations with Ivan Illich," *Ideas*, CBC Radio, 1989. (Transcript available for $20 from Ideas Transcripts, Box 500, Station A, Toronto, Ont. M5W 1E6.)
5. "Life as Idol," *Ideas*, CBC Radio, 1992. (Transcript available for $5 from Ideas Transcripts, Box 500, Station A, Toronto, Ont. M5W 1E6.)
6. Illich, *In the Mirror of the Past: Lectures and Addresses 1978–1990*, Marion Boyars, London, 1992, p. 52
7. *In the Mirror of the Past*, p. 53
8. Illich, *Celebration of Awareness: A Call for Institutional Revolution*, Doubleday, Garden City, N.Y., 1969, p. 70
9. See pp. 198, 279–80
10. See p. 101
11. See p. 134
12. Proposal to David Ramage of McCormack Theological Seminary at the University of Chicago

13. *Celebration of Awareness*, p. 42

14. "Part Moon, Part Travelling Salesman: Conversations with Ivan Illich," p. 4

15. All quotations in this paragraph are from Chapter 1.

16. *The Saturday Review of Education* 51 (April 20, 1968), 56–59

17. Illich, *Deschooling Society*, Harper and Row, New York, 1971

18. See pp. 105–107, 242–43, and Illich, *Gender*, Pantheon Books, New York, 1982, pp. 154–55

19. *Deschooling Society*, p. 43

20. *Deschooling Society*, p. 108

21. Raimundo Panikkar has made a parallel interpretation of another myth of two brothers, the biblical story of Jacob and Esau (Genesis 25:29–34). The story relates how Esau comes home famished from hunting and his younger brother Jacob refuses him food until Esau promises his right as the first-born to Jacob. Esau says, "I am at death's door. What use is my birthright to me?" and swears it away. Esau and Jacob represent hunter and pastoralist, oral society and literate society, primitive and civilized, past and future. Tradition has generally concurred with the writer of Genesis, who interprets his story as showing how little Esau valued his birthright. Panikkar suggests that, as the inheritors of the brilliant future promised to Jacob, we have reason today to think better of Esau's grounding in the present. ("History and the New Age," *Ideas*, CBC Radio, pp. 3–4. Transcript available for $10 from Ideas Transcripts, Box 500, Station A, Toronto, Ont. M5W 1E6.)

22. *Deschooling Society*, pp. 106–108, 106, 55

23. Illich later came to see the term *values* as deeply colored by the economic assumption that goods are inevitably scarce. See p. 159ff.

24. Illich, *Toward a History of Needs*, Heyday Books, Berkeley, 1977, p. 56

25. *Toward a History of Needs*, p. 66

26. *Toward a History of Needs*, p. 60

27. *Commonweal*, Sept. 4, 1970, pp. 428–29

28. "The Vanishing Clergyman" was published in *Celebration of Awareness*.

29. *Celebration of Awareness*, p. 102

30. "Part Moon, Part Travelling Salesman: Conversations with Ivan Illich," p. 5

31. Francine Du Plessix Gray, "The Rules of the Game," *The New Yorker*, April 25, 1970, p. 79

32. The quotation is from the Opus Dei paper *Gente*, cited in Du Plessix Gray, "The Rules of the Game," p. 62.

33. See p. 120

34. See pp. 98–99

35. Rules of the Game," p. 91

36. See pp. 212, 213

37. *Deschooling Society*, p. 112

38. Illich, *Tools for Conviviality*, Harper and Row, New York, 1973, p. ix

39. *Tools for Conviviality*, p. 109

40. Leopold Kohr, *The Breakdown of Nations*, new ed., Routledge and Kegan Paul, London and New York, 1986

41. *Tools for Conviviality*, p. 84

42. *Tools for Conviviality*, p. 23

43. E.F. Schumacher, *Small Is Beautiful* (Abacus, London, 1974); Harold Adams Innis, *The Bias of Communications* (University of Toronto Press, 1951); and Marshall McLuhan, *Understanding Media* (McGraw-Hill, New York, 1964).

44. *Tools for Conviviality*, p. 23

45. *Tools for Conviviality*, p. 66

46. *Tools for Conviviality*, pp. 80–82

47. "Part Moon, Part Travelling Salesman: Conversations with Ivan Illich," p. 1

48. *Tools for Conviviality*, p. 53

49. Illich, *Limits to Medicine*, Marion Boyars, London, 1976, p. 116

50. *Toward a History of Needs*, pp. 27, 31

51. *Toward a History of Needs*, p. x

52. Illich, "Body History," *The Lancet* (Dec. 6, 1986): p. 1325

53. *Limits to Medicine*, p. 133

54. See p. 141

55. *The Lancet*, pp. 1325, 1326

56. *Toward a History of Needs*, p. 69

57. *Toward a History of Needs*, pp. 75–76

58. Karl Polanyi, *Trade and Market in the Early Empires*, with C.M. Arensberg and H.W. Pearson, Free Press, New York, 1957

59. Raimundo Panikkar, in *Interculture* 77, Oct./Dec. 1982, pp. 23–24, relates the following story: "I witnessed some years ago the following dialogue between a boss and an Indian worker who was privileged enough to earn 250 to 300 rupees a month. He was asking his boss in whom he had sufficient confidence and trust for a few thousand rupees loan for the marriage of his daughter. You can cut 100 rupees a month on my salary, he told his boss . . . But the boss was quick in giving him arguments showing the irrationality of his demand. He told him: you cannot repay all that without being miserable for the rest of your life! . . . Finally the man just said, with the feeling of not being understood, 'but the marriage of my daughter is just once in a lifetime.'"

60. Illich, *Shadow Work*, Marion Boyars, London, 1981, p. 26

61. *Shadow Work*, p. 2

62. *Shadow Work*, p. 12

63. Illich, *The Right to Useful Unemployment and Its Professional Enemies*, Marion Boyars, London, 1977

64. *In the Mirror of the Past*, pp. 42–43

65. *Shadow Work*, p. 3

66. *Shadow Work*, p. 4

67. For an account of the shape of the "new commons" in Mexico City, see the remarks of Gustavo Esteva in "The Informal Economy," *Ideas*, CBC Radio, 1990. (Transcript available for $10 from Ideas Transcripts, Box 500, Station A, Toronto, Ont. M5W 1E6.)

68. *Shadow Work*, p. 67

69. The story is recounted in "Vernacular Values," *Shadow Work*, pp. 29–51.

70. See p. 175

71. See Polanyi, *Trade and Market in the Early Empires*

72. *Gender*, p. xi

73. *Gender*, p. 81

74. *Gender*, p. 143

75. *Gender*, p. 62

76. *Gender*, pp. 178, 177

77. *Gender*, pp. 35, 66

78. See p. 182

79. *Gender*, p. 179

80. *Gender*, pp. 178, 179

81. *Feminist Issues: A Journal of Feminist Social and Political Theory* 3, no. 1 (spring 1983)

82. See pp. 169–70

83. Illich, *In the Vineyard of the Text*, University of Chicago Press. Forthcoming.

84. Adam Parry, ed., *The Making of Homeric Verse: The Collected Papers of Milman Parry* (The Clarendon Press, Oxford, 1971), and Eric Havelock, *The Muse Learns to Write* (Yale University Press, New Haven, Conn., 1986).

85. "Literacy: The Medium and The Message," *Ideas*, CBC Radio, 1988, p. 11. (Transcript available for $10 from Ideas Transcripts, Box 500, Station A, Toronto, Ont. M5W 1E6.)

86. Dom Jean Leclercq, *L'Amour des Lettres et le Désir de Dieu* (Aubier, Paris, 1963), quoted in Marshall McLuhan, *The Gutenberg Galaxy* (University of Toronto Press, 1962), p. 89ff

87. Illich and Barry Sanders, *ABC: The Alphabetization of the Popular Mind*, p. 4

88. Morris Berman, "The Cybernetic Dream of the Twenty-First Century," in *The Journal of Humanistic Psychology* 26, no. 2 (spring 1986): 24–51

89. See Ferdinand de Saussure, *Course in General Linguistics* (P. Owen, London, 1964); Andres Hodges, *Alan Turing: The Enigma* (Touchstone Books, New York, 1984); Steve J. Heims, *The Cybernetics Group* (MIT Press, Cambridge, Mass., 1991); and Erwin Schrödinger, *What Is Life?* (Cambridge University Press, 1944).

90. *In the Mirror of the Past*, p. 177

91. See p. 172

92. *Shadow Work*, pp. 75–95

93. This and following quotations from *In the Vineyard of the Text.*

94. *In the Mirror of the Past*, p. 207

95. *In the Mirror of the Past*, p. 207

96. See p. 241

97. *In the Mirror of the Past*, p. 223

98. Illich, *H₂O and the Waters of Forgetfulness*, Heyday Books, Berkeley, 1985, p. 7

99. *H₂O and the Waters of Forgetfulness*, p. 7

100. *H₂O and the Waters of Forgetfulness*, pp. 21, 22

101. "Declaration on Soil," *Whole Earth Review* 71 (summer 1991), p. 75

102. Alasdair MacIntyre, *After Virtue: A Study in Moral Theory*, 2nd ed., University of Notre Dame Press, 1984

103. *Gender*, p. 5

104. See p. 276

105. *In the Mirror of the Past*, p. 225

106. See p. 270

107. James Lovelock, *The Ages of Gaia*, W.W. Norton, New York, 1988

108. *In the Mirror of the Past*, p. 225

109. "Part Moon, Part Travelling Salesman: Conversations with Ivan Illich," p. 32

110. "Part Moon, Part Travelling Salesman: Conversations with Ivan Illich," p. 31

111. "The Educational Enterprise in the Light of the Gospel," an unpublished lecture delivered in Chicago, Nov. 13, 1988

112. Ann Freemantle is an American writer and and old friend of Illich's.

113. Max Gluckman, *Essays on the Ritual of Social Relations*, Manchester University Press, 1962

114. The distinction between values and the good is developed at more length in Chapter 5.

115. John Amos Comenius, 1592–1670, was a Moravian bishop and an educational reformer and innovator.

116. Wolfgang Sachs now teaches at the Institute for Cultural Studies, in Essen. He is a close friend and collaborator of Illich's. See *The Development Dictionary*, ed. Sachs (Zed Books, London, 1992); *For Love of the Automobile: Looking Back into the History of Our Desires* (University of California Press, Berkeley, 1992); and "The Archeology of the Development Idea," *Interculture* 23, no. 4 (fall 1990).

117. The late Erich Fromm was a close friend of Illich's and a neighbor in Cuernavaca. See *Escape from Freedom* (Farrar and Rhinehart, New York, 1941); *Man for Himself* (Rhinehart, New York, 1947); and *The Art of Loving* (Harper and Row, New York, 1956). He wrote the introduction to Illich's *Celebration of Awareness*.

118. Herbert Gintis, "Towards a Political Economy of Education: A Radical Critique of Ivan Illich's *Deschooling Society*," *Harvard Educational Review* 42, no. 1 (February 1972)

119. Vicente Navarro, *Medicine Under Capitalism*, PRODIST, New York, 1976, pp. 103–131

120. John Ohliger and Colleen McCarthy, *Lifelong Learning or Lifelong Schooling? A Tentative View of the Ideas of Ivan Illich with a Quotational Bibliography*, Syracuse University Publications in Continuing Education, Syracuse, N.Y., 1971. Also available in ERIC (Educational Resource Clearinghouse), ED 049 398 (1-800-227-ERIC). John Ohliger, *Bibliography of Comments on the Illich-Reimer Deschooling Theses* (ERIC ED 090 145). The third volume, by John Ohliger, is available in draft form from Basic Choices, 730 Jefferson #1, Springfield, IL 62702-4830, for U.S. $10 paid in advance.

121. Philippe Ariès, *Centuries of Childhood: A Social History of Family Life* (Knopf, New York, 1962) and *The Hour of Our Death* (Random House, New York, 1981).

122. Valentina Borremans was the director of the Center for Intercultural Documentation.

123. Leopold Kohr, *The Breakdown of Nations*

124. A translation of Illich's *laudatio* is published as the Foreword to the 1986 edition of *The Breakdown of Nations*.

125. D'Arcy Thompson, *On Growth and Form*, Cambridge University Press, 1971

126. J.B.S. Haldane, "On Being the Right Size," in James R. Newman, *The World of Mathematics*, vol. 2, Simon and Schuster, New York, 1956

127. Dorothy Day, 1897–1980, cofounded The Catholic Worker. She lived much of her life at a Worker house in New York City.

128. Joseph P. Fitzpatrick, S.J., *Puerto Rican Americans: The Meaning of Migration to the Mainland*, 2nd ed., Prentice-Hall, Englewood Cliffs, N.J., 1987

129. Uwe Pörksen, a medievalist and linguist, is a friend and collaborator of Illich's. He is a professor at the University of Freiburg and the author of *Plastikwörter: Die Sprache Einer Internationalen Diktatur* (Klett-Cotta, Stuttgart, 1988). The book is unavailable in English. For a digest of the argument in English, see Pörksen, "Scientific and Mathematical Colonization of Colloquial Language," *Biology Forum* 81, no. 3 (1988), pp. 381–400.

130. Daniel Berrigan is an American Jesuit who was then just becoming known for his work in draft resistance and other radical political causes.

131. The organization was called the Catholic Inter-American Cooperation Program (CICOP).

132. A fuller account of these events is given in a profile of Illich by Francine Du Plessix Gray called "The Rules of the Game," which appeared in *The New Yorker*, April 25, 1970.

133. This refers to a papal encyclical called *Sollicitudo rei socialis*, which was released in February 1988.

134. Raymond Hunthausen is the archbishop of Seattle.

135. Gotthold Ephraim Lessing, 1729–1781, was a German dramatist and critic.

136. The poem appears in Robert Lowell, *For Lizzie and Harriet*, Farrar, Straus and Giroux, New York, 1973.

137. *Energy and Equity* was published by Marion Boyars in England and Harper and Row in the U.S., in 1974. A draft appeared in *Le Monde* in 1973.

138. See *Bicycle Technology*, CIDOC Antologia: B6, Cuernavaca, 1973

139. Jean Robert is a long-time friend and associate of Illich's. Swiss-born and trained as an architect, he now works mainly on the archaeology of modern perceptions of time and space. For a recent article, see "Production" in *The Development Dictionary* (see note 116).

140. Illich's friend Gustavo Esteva describes himself as a deprofessionalized intellectual and nomadic story-teller. He left a career in business and government to help found ANADEGES, a network of citizens' groups in Mexico. His article "Development" is in *The Development Dictionary* (see note 116) and he was featured on CBC Radio's *Ideas*, "The Informal Economy," November 1990. (Transcript available for $10 from Ideas Transcripts, Box 500, Station A, Toronto, Ont. M5W 1E6.)

141. Illich, *Tools for Conviviality*, p. 83

142. Jean Marie Domenach is the publisher of *Esprit* in Paris.

143. Joseph Needham et al., *Science and Civilization in China*, 7 volumes in 15 parts, Cambridge University Press, 1954–

144. Donna J. Haraway, *Simians, Cyborgs, and Women: The Reinvention of Nature*, Routledge, New York, 1991

145. Illich's friend Costas Hatzikeriaku is a mathematician and a former colleague at the Pennsylvania State University.

146. "The Rebirth of Epimethean Man" in *Deschooling Society*

147. Robert Brungs, S.J., is the founder of the Institute of Theological Encounter with Science and Technology, at the University of St. Louis.

148. Dirk von Boetticher is a friend who has collaborated with Illich in studying the social construction of "life." He is currently studying medicine in Heidelberg.

149. Robert J. Lifton, *The Nazi Doctors: Medical Killing and the Pyschology of Genocide*, Basic Books, New York, 1984

150. This refers to a conversation between Illich and Berrigan.

151. See "The Right to Dignified Silence," in *In the Mirror of the Past*

152. Marguerite Yourcenar, *Memoirs of Hadrian*, Farrar, Straus and Young, New York, 1955

153. The word *visible* here refers to the accessibility of texts as tools. The point is developed at length in Chapter 8.

154. Barbara Duden, *The Woman Under the Skin*, Harvard University Press, Cambridge, Mass., 1991. A second book, *Woman's Body as Public Space*, was published in Germany in 1991 (*Der Frauenleib als Offentlicher Ort*,

Luchterhand, Hamburg) and is currently being translated into English.

155. O. Lottin, "La doctrine morale des mouvements premiers de l'appetit sensitif aux XIIème et XIIIème siècles," in *Archives d'histoire doctrinale et littéraire du moyen-age* VI (1931), pp. 49–173

156. William Arney and Bernard Bergen, *Medicine and the Management of Living: Taming the Last Great Beast*, University of Chicago Press, Chicago, 1984

157. Robert Kugelmann, *Stress: The Nature and History of Engineered Grief*, Praeger, New York, 1992

158. Aline Rousselle, *Porneia: On Desire and the Body in Antiquity*, Oxford University Press, New York, 1988

159. Giulia Sissa, *Greek Virginity*, Harvard University Press, Cambridge, Mass., 1990

160. John McKnight, an old friend of Illich's, is the director of the Urban Affairs Institute at Northwestern University in Chicago. His definition of care as "the mask of love" occurs in his article "Professionalized Service and Disabling Help," in Illich, Irving Zola, John McKnight, Jonathan Caplan, and Harley Shaiken, *Disabling Professions*, Marion Boyars, London, 1977.

161. Freimut Duve is an editor and a friend of Illich's. He represents a Hamburg riding in the Bundestag.

162. Rosalind Schwartz, *Women at Work*, Institute of Industrial Relations Publications, UCLA, Los Angeles, 1988

163. George Grant, *Time as History*, CBC, Toronto, 1969

164. Susan Sontag, *On Photography*, Farrar, Straus and Giroux, New York, 1977

165. Michael Ignatieff, *The Needs of Strangers*, Chatto and Windus, The Hogarth Press, London, 1984

166. René Girard, *Deceit, Desire and the Novel: Self and Other in Literary Structure*, Johns Hopkins University Press, Baltimore, 1977

167. William Leiss, *The Limits of Satisfaction: An Essay on the Problem of Needs and Commodities*, University of Toronto Press, 1976

168. This refers to the parable of the Samaritan, Luke 10:26–37.

169. Andres Hodges, *Alan Turing: The Enigma*, Touchstone Books, New York, 1984

170. Von Werlhof's thesis is summarized in Illich, *Gender*, p. 65.

171. Yvonne Verdier, *Façon de dire, façons de faire: La laveuse, la couturière, la cuisinière*, Gallimard, Paris, 1979

172. Arnold Gehlen, *Man in the Age of Technology*, Columbia University Press, New York, 1980

173. G.E.R. Lloyd, *Early Greek Science: Thales to Aristotle*, Norton, New York, 1971

174. David Lowenthal, *The Past Is a Foreign Country*, Cambridge University Press, Cambridge, 1985

175. Louis Dumont, *Homo Hierarchicus: An Essay on the Caste System*, University of Chicago Press, 1970

176. Louis Dumont, *From Mandeville to Marx: Genesis and Triumph of Economic Ideology*, University of Chicago Press, 1977

177. See note 166

178. Karl Polanyi et al., *Trade and Market in the Early Empires*, Free Press, New York, 1957. See also *The Great Transformation*, Beacon Press, Boston, 1957.

179. In conversation with Illich. See Teodor Shanin, *Russia as a "Developing Society"*, Macmillan, London, 1985.

180. Elie Halevy, *The Growth of Philosophical Radicalism*, Kelly Reprint, Clifton, N.J., 1972

181. Michel Foucault, *A History of Sexuality*, vol. I, Random House, New York, 1978

182. For an introduction to Goodman's writings, see *Growing Up Absurd: Problems of Youth in the Organized Society* (Vintage Books, New York, 1960); *People or Personnel* (Random House, New York, 1968); and *New Reformation: Notes of a Neolithic Conservative* (Random House, New York, 1970).

183. *Gender*, p. 158. See also Paulo Freire, *Pedagogy of the Oppressed*, Seabury Press, New York, 1970

184. John Holt was a friend who spent time with Illich in Cuernavaca. He was the author of a number of books on education, including *Escape from Childhood* (E.P. Dutton, New York, 1974) and *Teach Your Own* (Dell, New York, 1981), and he founded an association for the families of unschooled children called Growing Without Schooling (2269 Massachusetts Ave., Cambridge, Mass. 02140). Letters from Holt to Illich are included in *A Life Worth Living*, ed. Susannah Sheffer, Ohio State University Press, Columbus, 1990.

185. Gerhart Ladner, *The Idea of Reform*, Gannon, Santa Fe, N.M., 1970

186. One of Goody's principal works is *The Development of the Family and Marriage in Europe*, Cambridge University Press, Cambridge, 1983

187. See note 160

188. Robert Mackey and Carl Mitchum, *Bibliography of the Philosophy of Technology*, published as a special supplement to *Technology and Culture* 14, no. 2 (April 1973) and as a hardbound volume by the University of Chicago Press. Reprint with author index, Ann Arbor, WI: Books on Demand CBI, 1985. Mitchum is a colleague of Illich's at the Pennsylvania State University, where he directs the Science, Technology and Society Program. The book I have listed is only one of his many bibliographic essays on the philosophy of technology.

189. Lynn White, *Medieval Technology and Social Change*, Oxford University Press, New York, 1962

190. Richard Southern, *The Seven Ages of the Theatre*, Hill and Wang, New York, 1963

191. *In the Vineyard of the Text*

192. Walter Ong, S.J., *Orality and Literacy: The Technologization of the Word*, Methuen, London, 1982

193. Ludolf Kuchenbuch is a professor of history at the University of Hagen, Germany.

194. Marshall McLuhan, *The Gutenberg Galaxy: The Making of Typographic Man*, University of Toronto Press, 1962

195. Vicente Huidobro, *Tout à coup*, Editions au Sans Pareil, Paris, 1925. The lines come from poem # 11.

196. Adam Parry, ed., *The Making of Homeric Verse: The Collected Papers of Milman Parry*, The Clarendon Press, Oxford, 1971. Albert Lord, *The Singer of Tales*, Harvard University Press, Cambridge, Mass., 1960.

197. Morris Berman, *Coming To Our Senses: Body and Spirit in the Hidden History of the West*, Simon and Schuster, New York, 1989

198. Thomas Luckmann, *The Invisible Religion*, Macmillan, New York, 1970

199. Christopher Dawson, *The Formation of Christendom*, Sheed and Ward, New York, 1967

200. Gaston Bachelard, *Water and Dreams: An Essay on the Imagination of Matter*, The Dallas Institute of Humanities and Culture, Dallas, 1983

201. In 1992, four years after this interview was recorded, I again discussed with Illich the question he raised in *H_2O and the Waters of Forgetfulness*. A Dutch friend, Reginald Luijf, had read the present book in manuscript and told me that the brief exchange between Illich and me about H_2O had not settled the question that was troubling him. Luijf is also a friend of Illich's and a scholar with a deep interest in the work of Gaston Bachelard. He wanted to know whether Illich was saying that industrialization had actually changed the inner being of water or only disabled our perception of it. When his son Joscha sits down by a fountain, he wondered, is he still able to dream? I put this question to Illich, and he answered that it was something that he wanted to consider, not give a judgement about. However, he said that he was more inclined today to think that "perhaps the waters of the Ganges that are still bathed in every morning at sunrise for the purpose of purification have lost that power." And yet, I responded, when I raised the question of whether baptism might cease to be efficacious because of the change in water, you said a violent no. "The theologian spoke," he answered, "the post-twelfth-century theologian. But by now in 1992 I wonder if God might not have to redeem us by fire because we have done away with water."

202. Thomas Berry, *The Dream of the Earth*, Sierra Club Books, San Francisco, 1988

203. See note 129

204. Popocatépetl and Iztaccíhuatl are great volcanic mountains that command the valley in which Illich lives in Mexico.

205. John 11:25

206. Illich's friend Bob Mendelsohn was a Chicago paediatrician. See

Robert S. Mendelsohn, *Confessions of a Medical Heretic*, Contemporary Books, Chicago, 1979

207. Ludwik Fleck, *Genesis and Development of a Scientific Fact*, eds. Thomas Trenn and R.K. Merton, with a Foreword by Thomas Kuhn, Chicago, 1979, and Thomas Kuhn, *The Structure of Scientific Revolutions*, University of Chicago Press, 1962

208. David Cayley, *The Age of Ecology*, James Lorimer, Toronto, 1991, pp. 115–125

209. Ernst Ulrich von Weizsäcker is the former chancellor of the University of Kassel, in Germany, and now the director of the Institute for Climate and Environment, in Wuppertal.

210. See note 117

211. Mircea Eliade, *The Sacred and the Profane: The Nature of Religion*, Harper and Row, New York, 1961

212. Carolyn Merchant, *The Death of Nature: Women, Ecology and the Scientific Revolution*, Harper and Row, San Francisco, 1980

213. Harvey Cox, *The Secular City*, Macmillan, New York, 1966

214. Hypertext refers to the internal integration of information systems. From any word one can proceed directly to another linked word or concept. This makes possible an unprecedented kind of "reading," which reduces text to data.

215. Elizabeth Kübler-Ross, *On Death and Dying*, Macmillan, New York, 1969

216. Johan Huizinga, *The Waning of the Middle Ages*, E. Arnold and Co., London, 1924

217. Will Herberg is a sociologist and Martin Marty a theologian. Illich came into contact with them in the 1950s through Joseph Fitzpatrick at Fordham University, and they influenced his thinking about the social function of religion. See particularly Herberg, *Protestant, Catholic, Jew: An Essay in American Religious Sociology*, Doubleday, Garden City, N.Y., 1955

218. Eudo C. Mason, *Rilke*, Oliver and Boyd, London, 1963, p. 19

219. Jacques Derrida, "Structure, Sign and Play in the Discourse of the Human Sciences," in *The Structuralist Controversy*, Johns Hopkins University Press, Baltimore, 1970

220. See *Gaia: A Way of Knowing*, ed. William Irwin Thompson (The Lindisfarne Press, Great Barrington, Mass., 1987); James Lovelock, *The Ages of Gaia* (W.W. Norton, New York, 1988); and David Cayley, *The Age of Ecology* (James Lorimer, Toronto, 1991), pp. 163–182

221. Hans Jonas, *The Imperative of Responsibility*, University of Chicago Press, 1984

222. Illich's friend Nils Christie is a Norwegian criminologist. See *Limits to Pain* (Norwegian University Press, Oslo, 1981) and *Beyond Loneliness and Institutions* (Norwegian University Press, Oslo, 1989).

223. This incident is mentioned in Nils Christie's forthcoming book, *Crime Control as Industry: A New Gulag?* He cites *Corrections Digest*, Nov. 27, 1991.